Forensic Science

An Illustrated Dictionary

JOHN C. BRENNER

CRC PRESS

Boca Raton   London   New York   Washington, D.C.

Library of Congress Cataloging-in-Publication Data

Brenner, John C.
   Forensic science : an illustrated dictionary / by John C. Brenner.
        p.   cm.
   Rev. ed. of: Forensic science glossary. c2000.
   Includes bibliographical references.
   ISBN 0-8493-1457-7 (alk. paper)
   1. Forensic sciences--Dictionaries. I. Brenner, John C. Forensic
   science glossary. II. Title.
HV8073B677 2003
363.25'03—dc22   2003055804
                                                                                       CIP

Visit the CRC Press Web site at www.crcpress.com

© 2004 by CRC Press LLC

No claim to original U.S. Government works
International Standard Book Number 0-8493-1457-7
Library of Congress Card Number 2003055804
Printed in the United States of America 1 2 3 4 5 6 7 8 9 0
Printed on acid-free paper

Preface

Forensic Science — An Illustrated Dictionary introduces terms commonly used in the field of forensic science to members of the law enforcement community, students taking courses in forensic science or criminal justice, and prosecutors and defense attorneys involved in criminal court cases. Knowing the meanings of these forensic terms becomes crucial in understanding and communicating with forensic scientists. The results of the forensic scientist's findings from the analysis of evidence are conveyed in a laboratory report, which to a nonscientist contains unfamiliar and unusual forensic terms. Knowing the definitions of those laboratory terms will aid in the interpretation and understanding of the laboratory report findings.

The field of forensics is a very diverse, exciting, and sometimes confusing science. *Forensic Science — An Illustrated Dictionary* is designed to explain difficult forensic terms. The definitions, along with the use of illustrations associated with certain forensic terms, will give the nonscientist a better understanding of those terms. The use of forensic laboratories has become an integral part of most criminal investigations. The investigators and the attorneys need to understand these forensic terms when either talking to the forensic scientist or reading the scientist's forensic laboratory reports.

In recent years Hollywood has produced several television shows about crime fighters. Although the story lines may be glamorized, the forensic science portions of these programs use many of the terms found and illustrated in this text.

This second edition has greatly expanded the number of forensic science terms from the previous book, the *Forensic Science Glossary*. The field of forensics has grown tremendously since the last edition. With the introduction of advanced procedures and methods of analysis, many new terms and words have emerged. *Forensic Science — An Illustrated Dictionary* has added many of these new forensic words used in criminal court cases, forensic entomology and forensic psychiatry, forensic interviewing of children, as well as crime scene reconstruction, to mention a few. Though this book is limited to forensic science, *Forensic Science — An Illustrated Dictionary* will become a tremendous and valuable reference book to a new court reporter typing his/her first homicide trial, a new assistant district attorney preparing for his/her first rape/murder trial, or even a high school or college student who has an interest in the field of forensic science. Using this book to either look up forensic terms or study the illustrations will give the layperson a better understanding of how exciting, unique, and complicated the field of forensic science can be.

The Author

John C. Brenner, while serving full time in the U.S. Navy, earned a B.S. in Health Care Administration from the University of Southern Illinois. Upon completion of his naval career he began his education in the field of forensic science, receiving an M.S. in Forensic Science from the University of New Haven Connecticut. He is a member of the Northeastern Association of Forensic Scientists (NEAFS). Mr. Brenner has spent 20 years as a forensic scientist with the New York State Police, having been trained in toxicology, serology, and DNA analysis. While providing testimony for more than 160 criminal court cases including homicides, rapes, blood assaults, burglaries, and DWIs, the author developed the idea for his first book, *Forensic Science Glossary*. Developing *Forensic Science — An Illustrated Dictionary* is one way of giving something back to the forensic community for the knowledge and experience he has gained working in the field of forensics.

Acknowledgments

Being a Christian man I know that my talents and ideas come from God. I want to thank Him for giving me the idea for this book and for the great interest I have in the field of forensic science.

Although only one name appears on the cover as the author, many people contributed to making this book a reality. Members of the New York State Police, such as Inspector Gerald Zeosky, who allowed me to take several pictures of laboratory instruments at the Forensic Investigation Center, Sr. Investigators Terrence Mullen and Tom Martin from the firearms section, T/Sgt. Craig Grazier, T/Sgt. James Campbell, and T/Sgt. Dennis Lyons, as well as Investigators John Egan and Drew McDonald from the Troop G Forensic Investigation Unit (FIU) all provided pictures and information for this book.

Michael Sikirica, M.D. and Susan LaCombe provided excellent autopsy pictures, and Dawn Flansburgh looked over the entire manuscript, checking the spelling and grammar.

With the encouragement of Becky McEldowney, CRC Press senior editor of life science, and her staff I was able to put together a much more expanded version of the *Forensic Science Glossary*, now including additional disciplines in the field of forensic science.

Table of Contents

A

A Single-letter designation of the purine base adenine.

AAFS American Academy of Forensic Sciences. The oversight body for certification of criminalists.

Abandonment A parent or caregiver leaving a child without adequate supervision or provision for the child's needs for an excessive period. State laws vary in defining adequacy of supervision and the length of time a child may be left alone or in the care of another before abandonment is determined to have occurred. The age of the child is an important factor.

ABFO (American Board of Forensic Odontology) scales An L-shaped piece of plastic used in photography that is marked with circles, black-and-white bars, and 18% gray bars to assist in distortion compensation and provide exposure determination. For measurement, the plastic piece is marked in millimeters.

Abrasion A skin injury caused by scraping off of superficial skin due to friction against a rough surface.

Absorbance The measure of concentration of material present; the negative log (base 10) of transmittance [$-\log 1/T$] of product of extinction coefficient, path length, and concentration, written as $A = Ebc$.

Absorption The incorporation of liquids or gases into the body. Absorption is also the process by which liquid hazardous materials are soaked up by sand, sawdust, or other material to limit the spread of contamination. A mechanical phenomenon wherein one substance penetrates into the inner structure of another, as in absorbent cotton or a sponge. An optical phenomenon wherein atoms or molecules block or attenuate the transmission of a beam of electromagnetic radiation.

Absorption band A region of the absorption spectrum in which the absorbance passes through a maximum point.

Absorption elution An improved, direct way of showing the presence of agglutinogens. In this method, antigenic material is first allowed to come in contact with antisera. The homologous antibody is specifically absorbed by a given agglutinogen.

Absorption inhibition A classical, indirect way of demonstrating the presence of an agglutinogen. This method involves the addition of a tittered antiserum to the bloodstain.

Absorption spectrum A plot, or other representation of absorbance, or any function of absorbance, against wavelength, or any function of wavelength.

Absorptivity (a) Absorbance divided by the product of the sample pathlength (b) and the concentration of the absorbing substance (c); $a = A/bc$.

Abuse excuse   A legal tactic by which a person charged with a crime claims that past victimization justified his or her retaliation.

Abused child   Any person under the age of 18 years, in the charge of a caregiver, who is physically or emotionally harmed by the caregiver's act or omission; also known as *maltreated child* .

Accelerant   Any material used to initiate or promote the spread of a fire. The most common accelerants are flammable or combustible fluids. Whether a substance is an accelerant depends not on its chemical structure, but on its use. An accelerant may be a solid, liquid, or in some instances, a gas.

Acceleration marks   Marks that are just the opposite of skid marks. The tires are being rotated by the axle and when done fast enough, the outside of the tire, the tread, takes time to catch up to the rest of the tire, which is being held by the coefficient of friction between the tires and the road surface. Therefore, the acceleration marks are heavy at the beginning and lighten up as the tire tread catches up.

Acclimate   To become accustomed to a different climate or environment.

Accommodation of sexual maltreatment   Process by which a child attempts to cope with sexual maltreatment. The child may dissociate from her or his body, pretend that nothing has happened, and fail to disclose the maltreatment, deny the maltreatment, delay disclosing the maltreatment, or recant a disclosure.

Accomplice   A person who knowingly and voluntarily unites with the principal offender in a criminal act through aiding, abetting, advising, or encouraging the offender.

Accountability   The quality of subordinate workers being responsible for their own work and answerable to a superior.

Accreditation   (1) A formal process by which a laboratory is evaluated, with respect to established criteria, for its competence to perform a specified kind of measurement; (2) the decision based upon such a process; (3) formal recognition that a testing laboratory is competent to carry out specific tests or specific types of tests. [(3) – ISO Guide 2 1986 (E/F/R)].

Accuracy   Closeness of the agreement between the result of a measurement and a true value of the measured quantity.

Acetaldehyde (CH$_3$CHO)   A colorless liquid having a pungent and fruity odor; highly flammable and toxic, used chiefly to manufacture acetic acid. The first product of ethanol metabolism. Also known as *ethanol*.

Acetate   A salt or ester of acetic acid. A manufactured fiber in which the fiber-forming substance is called *cellulose acetate* . Where not less than 92% of the hydroxyl groups are acetylated, the term triacetate may be used as a generic description of the fiber.

Acetone   The simplest ketone. A solvent for gunpowder. A highly flammable, water-soluble solvent.

Acid phosphatase   An enzyme found in high concentration in seminal fluid. Any nonspecific phosphatase requiring an acid medium for optimum activity.

Acid phosphatase test One of the most published and most widely employed techniques for semen identification. This enzyme can be found in the male prostate gland and is sometimes abbreviated as *AP*. Acid phosphatase in human seminal fluid originates from the prostate gland (often referred to as *prostatic acid phosphatase*).

Acoustic coupler A device used to attach a modem to the telephone system by placing the telephone handset on a set of rubber cups.

Acquisition The process of taking photographs or images of a piece of evidence using IBIS equipment. These acquired images are used to generate signatures, or mathematical representations of images.

Acquittal A verdict after a trial that a defendant in a criminal case has not been proven guilty beyond a reasonable doubt of the crime charged.

Acrylamide monomer Produced by the reduction of acrylonitrile by either liquid ammonia or by calcium bisulfite.

Acrylic fiber Generic name for a manufactured fiber in which the fiber-forming substance is any long-chain synthetic polymer composed of at least 85% by weight of acrylonitrile units.

Actinic rays Light rays of short wavelengths occurring in the violet and ultraviolet parts of the spectrum, which produce chemical changes, as in photography.

Action (legal) Lawsuit brought by one or more individuals seeking redress for or prevention of a wrong or protection of a right.

Action, revolver A firearm, usually a handgun, with a cylinder having several chambers so arranged as to rotate around an axis and be discharged successively by the same firing mechanism.

Action, semiautomatic A repeating firearm requiring a separate pull of the trigger for each shot fired, and which uses the energy of discharge to perform a portion of the operating or firing cycle (usually the loading portion).

Activation The heating of the adsorbent layer on a plate to dry out the moisture and maximize its attraction and retention power.

Active alert Dog's trained indication includes a more active behavior, such as digging, barking, or scratching.

Active decay That phase of corpse decomposition that follows bloat, is characterized by much maggot activity, and terminates with a rapid decrease in body weight.

Activity node An individual's past and present homes, current and previous work sites, and residences of partners, friends, and family members.

Activity space Those places regularly visited by a person in which the majority of their activities are carried out. It comprises an individual's activity sites and the routes used to travel between them, and is contained within the awareness space.

Actuator (**1**) Part of the firing mechanism in certain automatic firearms that slides forward and back in preparing each cartridge to be fired. Also called *trigger actuator*. (**2**) A manually or mechanically operated component that transmits a certain action or energy to other components that are dependent upon movement of the actuator in order to function.

Actus reus   Proof that a criminal act has occurred.

Acute   Severe, usually crucial, often dangerous in which relatively rapid changes are occurring. Acute exposure runs a comparatively short course.

Acute effect   A pathologic process caused by a single substantial exposure.

Acute exposure   A single encounter to toxic concentrations of a hazardous material or multiple encounters over a short period of time (usually 24 hours).

Acute stress disorder   Condition that is characterized by symptoms similar to those of post-traumatic stress disorder but that can be diagnosed within 4 weeks after an extremely traumatic event.

Acute tolerance   The development of tolerance within the course of a single exposure to a drug.

ADA (adenosine deaminase)   An enzyme found in the serum of blood.

Adaptation   The tendency of certain receptors to become less responsive or cease to respond to repeated or continued stimuli.

Adapter back   An auxiliary back for a camera that permits different size film than it was originally constructed to use.

Adapter ring   Allows one to make two different-sized pieces of equipment compatible; lens and filter using a Series-7 holder, for example.

Addiction   Implies a very severe form of dependence, one involving an overwhelming compulsion for the use of a particular drug.

Adenine (A)   A nucleic acid consisting of a chemically linked sequence of subunits. Each subunit contains a nitrogenous base, a pentose sugar, and a phosphate group. One of the four building blocks of DNA. In the DNA molecule adenine forms a chemical bond with thymine.

Adenosine triphosphate (ATP)   A nucleoside triphosphate that upon hydrolysis results in energy availability for processes such as muscle contraction and synthesis of macromolecules, including protein and carbohydrates.

Adhesive lifter   Any of a variety of adhesive coated materials or tapes used to lift fingerprints or footwear impressions. They are primarily used to lift powdered impressions from nonporous surfaces.

Adiabatic flame temperature   Theoretically, the highest temperature at which a fuel can burn. It is derived mathematically. Because certain combustion products tend to disassociate at high temperatures, the true maximum burning temperature, even under ideal conditions, is usually slightly lower.

Adipocere   A peculiar waxy substance consisting of salts and fatty acids and formed from the decomposition of corpse tissues, especially in moist habitats; also called *grave-wax*.

Adjudicated   Settled in a court of law.

Adjudicated father   Man determined by the court to be the father, usually through a court action and genetic testing.

Adjudication   Giving or pronouncing a judgment or decree; also the judgment given. Decision made by a court or administrative agency with respect to a case.

Administrative documentation   Records such as case-related conversations, evidence receipts, description of evidence packaging and seals, and other pertinent information.

Administrative review   An evaluation of the case report and supporting documentation for consistency with laboratory policies, editorial correctness, and compliance with the submission request.

Admissible   Evidence that can be legally and properly introduced in a civil or criminal trial.

Adoption   Legal proceeding in which an adult takes, as his or her lawful child, an individual (usually a minor) who is not the adoptive parent's natural offspring. The adopted child may lose all legal connection to the previous parent, and the adoptive parent undertakes the responsibility of providing for the child until he or she becomes an adult.

Adsorbent   The stationary phase for adsorption thin-layer chromatography. A solid or liquid that adsorbs other substances, e.g., charcoal, silica, metals, water, and mercury.

Adsorption   (1) The action of a body, such as charcoal, in condensing and holding a gas or soluble substance upon its surface. (2) The adherence of atoms, ions, or molecules of a gas or liquid to the surface of another substance. (3) Finely divided or microporous materials having a large active surface area are strong adsorbents. (4) The attraction between the surface atoms of a solid and an external molecule by intermolecular forces.

Adulterant   Material used to increase the mass of a controlled substance. Adulterants produce physiological effects and give the illusion that more controlled substance is present than its actual content.

Advanced Chemiluminescent Enhancement System™ (ACES™)   Used for the nonradioactive quantitation of small amounts of human DNA.

Adversary system   The trial methods used in the United States and some other countries, based on the belief that truth can best be determined by giving opposing parties full opportunity to present and establish their evidence, and to test by cross-examination the evidence presented by their adversaries, under established rules of procedure before an impartial judge and/or jury.

Aedeagus   The reproductive organ of a male insect.

Aerial perspective   Effect of depth produced by haze in a photograph. Distant objects are recorded with lighter zones and with colors distorted toward blue, giving a three-dimensional impression.

Affidavit   A sworn statement by a witness. For the expert witness, an affidavit can be analogous to a small article or paper. The expert signs it in the presence of a notary, and the attorney then uses it to indicate the expert's findings and conclusions. Because an affidavit cannot be cross-examined, it has less legal significance than a deposition.

Affirmative defense   Without denying the charge, defendant raises extenuating or mitigating circumstance such as insanity, self-defense, or entrapment to avoid civil or criminal responsibility. In trial, a position by the defendant that places the burden on the defendant to prove his or her claim. Insanity or self-defense is an example of an affirmative defense.

Affirmed   In the practice of appellate courts, the word means that the decree or order at issue is declared valid and will stand as rendered in the lower court.

AFIS   Automated Fingerprint Identification System that enables computers to make rapid and accurate comparisons between fingerprints and the vast number of fingerprints in police records.

AFTE   Association of Firearms and Toolmark Examiners.

Agar   A polysaccharide extracted from seaweed. A gelatinous product extracted from certain red algae used chiefly as a gelling agent in culture media.

Agarose   The neutral gelling fraction of agar commonly used in gel electro-phoresis.

Agglutination   The clumping together of living cells as a result of a reaction between the cells and an appropriate immune serum.

Agglutinin   A chemical product of the process of immunization arising in blood serum and causing the red corpuscles, with which it is brought into contact, to coalesce into floccules.

Agglutinogen   An antigen that stimulates production of a specific antibody (agglutinin) when introduced into a host animal body. Outdated term for *red-cell antigen* .

Agnosia   Impairment or loss, associated with brain injury, of the ability to recognize or comprehend the meaning of stimuli, including familiar objects and symbols.

Air scent search   Search of a designated area by a canine trained to indicate the location of particular scents; includes searches for narcotics, land mines, agricultural products, missing persons, and dead persons.

Air sole   An outsole or midsole incorporating an air pocket or cushion.

Airways   Any parts of the respiratory tract through which air passes during breathing.

AK   Abbreviation for the enzyme adenylate kinase; these red cell isoenzymes are fairly stable in dried bloodstains.

Albumin   One of a group of heat-coagulable, water-soluble proteins occurring in egg-white, blood serum, milk, and many animal and vegetable tissues.

Alcohol   An organic compound having a hydroxyl (-OH) group attached. The lower molecular weight alcohols, methanol (CH_3OH), ethanol (C_2H_5OH), and propanol (C_3H_7OH), are water soluble.

Alcohol dehydrogenase (ADH)   The main enzyme that catalyzes the conver-sion of ethanol to acetaldehyde.

Aldehyde dehydrogenase (ALDH)   The enzyme that converts acetaldehyde to acetate.

Alert   A trained behavioral indication given by a dog in response to locating the source of decomposition scent.

Algorithm   A set of well-defined rules for the solution of a problem in a finite number of steps.

Alignment defect   Characters that write improperly in the following respects: a twisted letter, horizontal malalignment, vertical malalignment, or a character "off-its-feet." These defects can be corrected by special adjustments to the typebar and typeblock of a typebar machine.

Aliphatic   One of the main groups of hydrocarbons characterized by the straight- or branched-chain arrangement of constituent atoms. Aliphatic hydrocarbons belong to one of three subgroups: **(1)** alkanes or paraffins, all of which are saturated and comparatively unreactive; **(2)** the alkenes or alkadiens that are unsaturated (containing double [C=C] bonds) and are more reactive; **(3)** alkynes, such as acetylene (that contain a triple [C≡C] bonds).

Aliquot   A measured amount of liquid taken from the main portion.

Alkali   A basic substance (pH greater than 7) that has the capacity to neutralize an acid and form a salt.

Alkaline phosphatase   A phosphatase active in alkaline media.

Alkaloid   One of a group of nitrogenous organic bases, especially one of vegetable origin, having a powerful toxic effect on animals and man, such as nicotine, cocaine, strychnine, or morphine.

Alkanes   An aliphatic hydrocarbon having the chemical formula $C_6H_{2n}+2$. Also known as *paraffin*.

Alkyd resin   A class of adhesive resins made from unsaturated acids and glycerol; used as a bonding agent in paint and lacquers.

Allegation (legal)   The statement in a pleading of what a party expects to prove. For example, an indictment contains allegations of crime against the defendant. Charge or complaint to be proven true or false at a hearing or trial. In a child maltreatment case, an allegation is made in the form of a petition or complaint containing statements about specific acts of the respondent or defendant that the petitioner or complainant anticipates proving at trial.

Allele   One of a series of alternative form of a gene (or VNTR) at a specific locus in a genome. In DNA analysis the term *allele* is commonly extended to include DNA fragments of variable length and sequence that may have no known transcriptional product but are detected in a polymorphic system.

Allele frequency   A measure of the commonness of an allele in a population; the proportion of all alleles of that gene in the population that is of this specific type.

Allelic marker   Allele form of a gene used to identify chromosomal segments suspected of association with a certain phenotype. For example, allelic markers may be used with a family pedigree in which a phenotype is common to identify chromosomal segments that contain the gene responsible for the phenotype.

Allograph   A writing or signature made by one person for another; or a style (block capital, print script, or cursive form) of one of the 26 graphemes of the English alphabet or of the ligatures and other symbols that accompany it.

FIGURE A.1 An alternate light source manufactured by SPEX®.

Allometry The growth of part of the body in relation to the growth of the whole. The adjective form is *allometric*.

Allotypes Genetically determined polymorphic variants. The term was first introduced to describe the different antigenic forms of rabbit gamma globulins. It was later extended to include polymorphic variants of plasma proteins in general (e.g., haptoglobins, Gc groups) but now includes red cell and white cell polymorphisms.

Alloy A solid form of the liquid mixture of two or more metals, or of one or more metals with certain nonmetallic elements, as in brass, bronze, or carbon steel.

Altered document A document that contains a change, either as an addition or a deletion.

Alternate light source Equipment used to produce visible and invisible light at various wavelengths to enhance or visualize potential items of evidence (fluids, fingerprints, clothing fibers, etc.) (Figure A.1).

Alu A family of repeat DNA sequences, cleaved by the restriction enzyme Alu I, dispersed throughout the genomes of many animal species. The family consists of about 50,000 copies, at 300 bp each, per human genome.

Alveolar ducts The smallest of the lungs' airways that connect terminal bronchioles and alveolar sacs. Sometimes called *bronchioles*.

Alveoli (*singular*, alveolus) Microscopic air sacs in which gas exchange between the blood and the lungs occurs.

Amadeo Rossi and Co. A firearms manufacturer.

Ambient Pre-existing or of the normal environment.

FIGURE A.2 Various types of ammunition that can be found in firearm examinations.

Ambusher   An offender who attacks a victim once he or she has been enticed to a location, such as a residence or workplace, controlled by the offender.

Ametabolous   An insect life cycle lacking distinct life stages; without metamorphosis, or "development without change." The immature forms are similar to the adults, differing only in that they are smaller and not yet sexually mature.

Amicus curiae   Friend of the court; a person who petitions the court for permission to provide information to the court on a matter of law that is in doubt, or one who is not a party to a lawsuit but who is allowed to introduce evidence, argument, or authority to protect one's interest.

Amino acid   The building blocks of proteins coded by triplets of bases in DNA blueprint. Any one of a class of organic compounds containing the amino (NH_2) group and the carboxyl (COOH) group.

Amitriptyline   A tricyclic antidepressant drug, found to impair skilled performance and to be additive with ethanol in its adverse effects.

Ammonia   A colorless gaseous alkaline compound that is very soluble in water, has a characteristic pungent odor, is lighter than air, and is formed as a result of the decomposition of most nitrogenous organic material, such as tissue from dead bodies.

Ammoniacal   Pertaining to ammonia or its properties.

Ammunition   (**1**) One or more loaded cartridges consisting of a primed case, propellant, and with one or more projectiles. Also referred to as *fixed* or *live ammunition* . (**2**) Compressed gas cylinder used in air guns as a means of propelling projectiles (Figure A.2).

Amnesia   Partial or total loss of memory for past experiences.

Amnestic syndrome   Inability to remember events more than a few minutes after they have occurred, coupled with the ability to recall the recent and remote past.

Amobarbital   A barbiturate derivative used as a sedative or hypnotic; available in ampules for intravenous or intramuscular injection for the control of seizures.

Amorph   **(1)** A gene that apparently has no end product, e.g., a specific antigenic determinant. Sometimes referred to as a silent gene. **(2)** A mutation that obliterates gene function; a null mutation.

Amosite   A monoclinic amphibole form of asbestos having long fibers and a high iron content; used in insulation.

Amphetamine   A drug that is representative of a class of structurally related compounds known as phenethylamines. Basis of a group of hallucinogenic, habit-forming drugs that affect the central nervous system (CNS). The sale and use restricted to physicians; trade name Benzedrine.®

Ample letter   That which encompasses more than the standard inner space in a given letter. Characterized by fulsomeness and expanded ovals and loops.

Amplification   The production of additional copies of a chromosomal sequence, found as intrachromosomal or extrachromosomal DNA.

Amplification blank   A control that consists of only amplification reagents without the addition of sample DNA. This control is used to detect DNA contamination of the amplification reagents and material. Also known as a *kit reagent blank*.

Amplified fragment length polymorphism (AMP/FLP)   Polymerase chain-reaction amplified restriction fragment lengths consisting of a variable number of tandem repeats.

Amplify   To increase the strength or amplitude of extracted DNA material.

Amylase   An enzyme found in plant and animal tissue that promotes the conversion of starch and glycogen into maltose.

Amyloidosis   A metabolic disorder marked by extracellular deposition of amyloid (an abnormal protein) in the tissues; this usually leads to loss of function and organ enlargement.

Analgesic   Any drugs, such as salicylates, morphine, or opiates used primarily for the relief of pain.

Analysis   The determination of the composition of a substance.

Analyte or **Target analyte**   Substance to be identified or measured.

Analytical   The branch of chemistry dealing with techniques that yield any type of information.

Analytical balance   Instrument used to measure out or weight different types of dry chemicals. The measurement for weighing the substance is designated as grams (Figure A.3).

Analytical gel   A gel that consists of all the digested DNA evidence and control DNA samples for a particular forensic case.

FIGURE A.3 Analytical balances used for measuring reagents, dry chemicals, and for measuring the accuracy of manual pipettes (the amount of fluid dispensed).

Analytical run (series)   A set of measurements carried out successively by one analyst using the same measuring system, at the same location, under the same conditions, and during the same short period of time.

Analytical sensitivity   The ability of a method or instrument to discriminate between samples having different concentrations or containing different amounts of the analyte. The slope of the analytical calibration function.

Analytical specificity   Ability of a measurement procedure to determine solely the measurable quantity (desired substance) it purports to measure and not others.

Analytical wavelength   Any wavelength at which an absorbance measurement is made for the purpose of the determination of a constituent of a sample.

Anaphylaxis   An allergic hypersensitivity reaction of the body to a foreign protein or drug.

Anarthria   Loss of the ability to form words accurately, caused by brain lesion or damage to peripheral nerves that carry impulses to the articulatory muscles.

Anatomic   Relating to the shape of the body or parts of the body. As it relates to the foot, the natural shape of the foot.

Anatomically detailed dolls (ADD)   Dolls that show various explicit anatomical details of some body parts, such as genitals, breasts, and/or open mouth and rectal orifices. Their use in child abuse investigations is controversial.

Anchor point   A fixed, designated point used to orient the boundaries of a search.

Anemia   Any condition in which the number of red blood cells, the amount of hemoglobin, and the volume of packed red blood cells per 100 mL of blood are less than normal. It may result from increased destruction of red cells, excessive blood loss, or decreased production of red cells.

   Aplastic Anemia caused by aplasia of bone marrow or its destruction by chemical agents or physical factors.

   Autoimmune hemolytic Acquired disorder characterized by premature erythrocyte destruction owing to abnormalities in the individual's own immune system.

   Hemolytic Anemia caused by hemolysis of red blood cells resulting in reduction of normal red cell lifespan.

   Iron-deficiency Anemia resulting from a demand on stored iron greater than can be met.

   Megaloblastic Anemia in which megaloblasts are found in the blood; usually due to a deficiency of folic acid or vitamin B_{12}.

   Microangiopathic hemolytic A hemolytic process associated with thrombotic thrombocytic purpura (TTP), prosthetic heart valve, and burns. It is visualized in the peripheral blood smear by fragmentation of the red cells and other bizarre morphology.

   Pernicious A type of megaloblastic anemia due to a deficiency of vitamin B_{12}, directly linked to absence of intrinsic factor (IF).

   Sickle-cell Hereditary, chronic anemia in which abnormal sickle-or crescent-shaped erythrocytes are present. It is due to the presence of hemoglobin S in the red blood cells.

Angle of impact   The internal angle at which blood strikes a target surface relative to the horizontal plane of that surface. Thus, a straight-on impact would have an impact angle of 90°.

Angle of incidence   The angle of incidence as used here conforms to that used in optics to describe reflection and refraction of light rays. The angle is measured with respect to the normal to the surface, rather than to the surface itself. The normal is an imaginary line perpendicular (90°) to the plane of the surface. Thus, a straight-on impact (along the normal) is said to have an angle of incidence of zero.

Anidex   A manufactured fiber in which the fiber-forming substance is any long-chain synthetic polymer composed of at least 50% by weight of one or more esters of a monohydric alcohol and acrylic acid.

Aniline ink   A fast-drying printing ink that is a solution of a coal tar dye in an organic solvent or a solution of a pigment in an organic solvent or water.

Animation   A computer program that allows the reconstructionist to develop a videotape of an accident sequence to be used as an exhibit to his/her opinion of the accident scenario.

Anisotropic   Having different properties in different directions, i.e., when a fibrous substance conducts heat more rapidly along its fibers than across them. Exhibiting double refraction, as a lens or mineral. An object that has properties that differ according to the direction of measurement when viewed in polarized light.

Ankle   The joint formed at the lower end of the two leg bones, where the fibula and tibia meet the talus bone of the foot.

Anneal   The formation of double strands from two complementary single strands of DNA and RNA. In the second step of each PCR cycle, primers bind or anneal to the 3' end of the target sequence.

Annealing   The pairing of complementary single strands of DNA to form a double helix.

Annulus   Ringlike space between the tip of a primer and the case, propellant primer compound, and the projectile.

Anode   In an electrolytic cell, the electrode at which oxidation occurs; the positive terminal of an electrolytic cell.

Anonymous loci   Specific sites on a chromosome where the gene functions have not been identified.

Anosmia   Loss of capacity to smell odors.

Anoxia   Deficiency in or lack or oxygen. It may occur in newborns during the transition from the maternal supply or oxygenated cord blood to independent breathing. Brain cells are particularly vulnerable to continued anoxia.

Anthophyllite   A natural magnesium-iron silicate; a variety of asbestos occurring as lamellae, radiations, fibers, or massive in metamorphic rocks. Also known as *bidalotite*.

Anthropologist   An individual who studies the origin, behavior, and the physical, social, and cultural development of humans.

Anthropometry   Method of identification, devised by Alphonse Bertillon in the late 19th century, consisting of a set of body measurements thought to form a unique profile. The system has been obsolete for a century, but is an important precursor of fingerprint identification.

Anthropophagi   An organism that consumes human flesh.

Anti-aliasing   A technique or system to reduce or eliminate *jaggies*, the jagged visual effect caused by the pixels in diagonal lines of low-resolution displays.

Antibody   A protein produced for body defense in response to an antigen. An antibody is a substance that appears in the plasma or body fluids as a result of stimulation by an antigen and will react specifically with that antigen in some observable way.

Anticoagulant   A substance such as EDTA that prevents coagulation or clotting of the blood.

Antidepressant   A drug, such as imipramine and tranylcypromine, that relieves depression by increasing central sympathetic activity.

Antigen   A foreign substance, usually a protein, capable of stimulating an antibody response for body defense. Any substance that, when introduced parenterally into an individual lacking the substance, stimulates the production of an antibody that, when mixed with the antibody, reacts with it in some observable way.

Antigenic determinant   The particular site on an antigen molecule that combines with the corresponding antibody.

Antigenicity   Potency as an antigen.

Antihuman globulin (Coombs reagent)   An antibody produced in an animal, usually a rabbit, in response to the injection of human globulin.

Antilock braking system (ABS)   This is a braking system designed to brake the vehicle in the most effective manner, without locking up the tires and causing the tires to go into a skid. This system is used differently than standard brakes when braking in an emergency situation. The brake pedal is stepped on and held in place while the electronic system takes over and modulates or applies the brakes until the wheels want to lock up, and then releases and brakes again.

Antimony   Metallic element with the chemical symbol Sb and atomic number 51. This element is commonly alloyed with lead to harden the bullet. It is also present as antimony sulfide in the primer mix.

Antiparallel   A term used to describe the opposite orientations of the two strands of a DNA double helix; the 5' end of one strand aligns with the 3' end of the other strand.

Antisera   Injecting human serum into various animals, such as the horse, goat, sheep, rabbit, duck, hen, or guinea pig, can produce antihuman sera.

Antiserum   Any immune serum that contains antibodies active chiefly in destroying a specific infecting virus or bacterium.

Antisocial personality disorder   A personality disorder characterized by repeated rule breaking, chronic manipulativeness, impulsive and irresponsible behavior, callous attitudes toward others, and a lack of guilt or remorse for wrongdoing.

Anvil marks   Microscopic marks impressed on the forward face of the rim of a rimfire cartridge case as it is forced against the breech end of the barrel by the firing pin. These marks are characteristic of the breech under the firing pin and have been used to identify a firearm.

Aortic stenosis   Thickening and hardening of the cusps of the aortic valve leading to a reduction in flow from the left ventricle (Figure A.4).

AP   Abbreviation for armor-piercing ammunition.

Aperture   Adjustable opening, also referred to as *f-stop*, that controls the amount of light that is focused on the film.

Aperture preference   Term used to describe the automatic exposure system used on some cameras, in which a specific aperture is selected but the shutter speed adjusts automatically to expose the film to the correct amount of light.

Aplasia   Failure of an organ or tissue to develop normally.

Apogee   The maximum altitude a projectile will reach when shot in the air. Used here to define the maximum height a motorcycle driver or rider will reach when impacting an object, usually a vehicle.

Appeal (legal)   A request by the losing party in a lawsuit that the judgment be reviewed by a higher court. Request to a higher court to change the decision of a trial court. Usually appeals are made and decided on

FIGURE A.4 Aortic stenosis. (Courtesy of forensic medical examiner Michael Sikirica, M.D.)

questions of law only; issues of fact are left to the trial judge's or jury's discretion.

Appeals court   Court that hears an appeal after a trial court has made a judgment. The appeal is usually based on the contention that the trial judge misinterpreted the law or misused judicial authority when rendering a decision.

Approved test provider   A proficiency test provider who has complied with the test manufacturing guidelines established by a proficiency review committee.

Aqueous solution   A solution with water used as a solvent.

Aramid   A manufactured fiber in which the fiber-forming substance is any long-chain synthetic polyamide in which at least 85% of the amide linkage is attached directly to two aromatic rings.

Arch area   The area of the sole of the shoe immediately below the longitudinal arch of the foot.

Arch support   A device made of leather or synthetic material that can be shaped to a person's longitudinal arch and inserted or built into a shoe to give support to that person's natural arch.

Archaeologist   An individual that engages in the systematic recovery and study of material evidence of past human life and cultures, such as tools, buildings, pottery, and graves.

Archive   Collection of documents and records purposefully stored for a defined period of time.

Arcnet   An older networking topology using RG2 coax achieving 2Mb/s.

Area of origin, fire-related   General area where a fire started. This term is used when a fire originates in a large area or when the exact point of origin cannot be determined.

FIGURE A.5A Debris placed in a corner of a room to enhance the fire's intensity.

Aromatic An organic compound having as part of its structure a benzene ring. The term *aromatic* as used in the fragrance industry describes essential oils not necessarily in the chemical sense.

Arraignment In a criminal case, the proceeding in which an accused person is brought before a judge to hear the charges filed against him or her and to enter a plea of guilty or not guilty. Sometimes called *preliminary hearing* or *initial appearance* .

Arrest Process of taking a person into custody. Peace officers must have probable cause to arrest individuals.

Arsenic **(1)** A chemical element (As). **(2)** A medicinal and poisonous element; a brittle steel-gray hexagonal mineral, the native form of the element.

Arson The criminal act of intentionally setting fire to a building or other property (Figure A.5A, B, and C).

FIGURE A.5B The fire following a trail of debris that was placed on the floor.

Arson trail   The use of various types of materials, such as cloth rags, newspapers, or wood, that have some type of flammable liquid poured on the material by which the fire can travel along. This trail can leave a distinct mark on the floor of a fire scene (Figure A.6A, B, and C).

Arterial spurting   Characteristic bloodstain patterns on a target surface resulting from blood exiting under pressure from a breached artery. These patterns are characterized by their specific appearance and shape.

Arthropod   Any of the invertebrate animals with jointed appendages, an exoskeleton consisting of chitin and protein, a segmented body to which jointed appendages are articulated in pairs and an open circulatory system that includes the insects, crustaceans, and arachnids.

Artificial decomposition scent   Chemicals produced commercially for scent training that reproduce compounds that occur during decomposition (putrescine and cadaverine).

FIGURE A.5C A fire scene with burn pattern.

Artificial light   Any light other than daylight.

Artificial light film   Color film balanced for use in tungsten artificial light, usually of 3200°K. Packs are usually marked *tungsten* or *Type B* .

ASA   American Standard Association, formerly a standardized rating number for film based on its sensitivity to light.

Asbestos   A white or light-gray mineral, obtained chiefly from actinolite and amphibole, occurring in long slender needles or fibrous masses that may be woven or shaped into acid-resisting, nonconducting, and fireproof articles.

Ascites   Accumulation of watery fluid and cells in the abdominal cavity (Figure A.7).

ASCLD   American Society of Crime Laboratory Directors.

Asepsis   The state of being free from pathogenic microorganisms.

Asphyxia   (**1**) A condition in which the exchange of oxygen and carbon dioxide in the lungs is absent or impaired. (**2**) Lack of oxygen or excess of carbon dioxide in the body. Asphyxia may lead to unconsciousness, seizures, damage to various sensory systems, and death (Figure A.8).

Assault   Threat to inflict injury with an apparent ability to do so. Also, any intentional display of force that would give the victim reason to fear or expect immediate bodily harm.

Assault rifle   Automatic weapon designed to be fired by one man. Ammunition is fed from a magazine.

Assigned value   Best available estimate of the true value.

Assisted writing   The result of a guided hand, produced by the cooperation of the two minds and two hands of two persons.

Asthma   A chronic condition in which constriction (spasm) of the bronchial tubes occurs in response to irritation, allergy, or other stimuli.

FIGURE A.6A Burn pattern remaining on the floor after a fire.

Atavism   The view that crime is due to a genetic throwback to a more primitive and aggressive form of human being.

Atherosclerosis   Deposition of plaques of cholesterol esters in blood vessels, resulting in narrowing of the vessel lumen and restricting blood flow (Figure A.9).

Atom   The smallest unit of an element that still retains the chemical characteristics of that element. An atom is made up of protons and neutrons in a nucleus surrounded by electrons. A molecule of water (H_2O) consists of two atoms of hydrogen and one atom of oxygen.

Atomic absorption (AA)   A method of qualitative and quantitative element analysis where the element to be analyzed is dissociated from its chemical bonds after which the atoms of this element will absorb radiation of energy specific for that element. The amount of energy absorbed is proportional to the concentration of that element in the specimen. Atomic absorption

FIGURE A.6B Material used to make a fire trail, and debris piled in the corner of a room to ensure an intense fire.

has applications in many fields of science. Its main application in forensic science is to analyze cotton swabs for some of the elements in primer residue.

Atomic emission spectroscopy   Technique based on the emission of light by excited, vaporized, and atomized elements. Excitation can arise from any of a number of energy sources. The instruments are usually polychromatic devices. The method is most useful for quantitative analysis; qualitative use is also popular.

Atomic mass spectroscopy   Technique based on detection of vaporized and atomized elements and their ionized isotopes. The detection and display of the spectra are based on the mass-to-charge ratios of the ions. The method is specific for qualitative analysis and also valuable for quantitative analysis.

FIGURE A.6C Paper arranged in a pattern for the fire to follow, and a can of gasoline used as the accelerant.

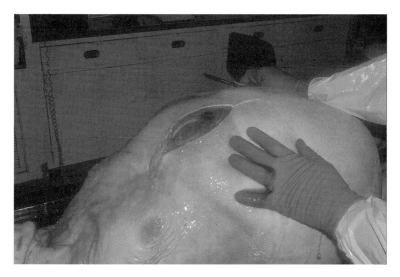

FIGURE A.7 Ascitic fluid accumulation in the abdomen of an elderly woman with a large ovarian tumor. (Courtesy of forensic medical examiner Michael Sikirica, M.D.)

Atomic weight The average weight (or mass) of all the isotopes of an element, as determined from the proportions in which they are present in a given element, compared with the mass of the 12 isotopes of carbon (taken as precisely 12,000), which is the official international standard; measured in daltons.

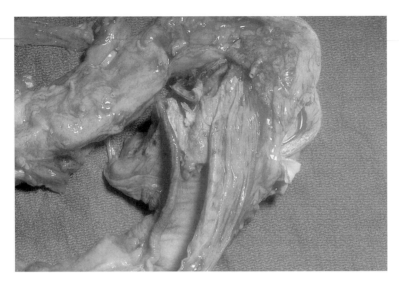

FIGURE A.8 Asphyxia due to aspiration of a large bolus of meat into the trachea occurring in an elderly man with poor swallow reflex. (Courtesy of forensic medical examiner Michael Sikirica, M.D.)

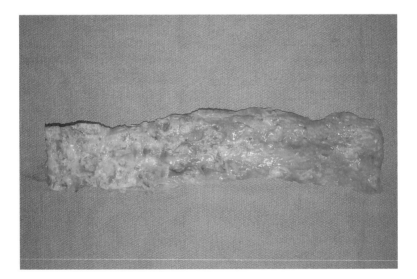

FIGURE A.9 Atherosclerosis of aorta with roughened calcified plaque limiting flow. (Courtesy of forensic medical examiner Michael Sikirica, M.D.)

Atomize   To break into discrete atoms, usually by the application of extreme heat, as in atomic absorption. To break a liquid into tiny droplets, as occurs in fuel-injected engines or in the production of aerosol sprays.

Atrophy   A loss of function due to age, disuse, or disease.

Attenuated total reflection (ATR)   Reflection that occurs when an absorbing coupling mechanism acts in the process of total internal reflection to make the reflectance less than unity.

Attenuation   An adjustment of the signal amplifier response that results in the reduction of the electronic signal.

Attest   To bear witness to; to affirm as true or genuine.

Attorney-at-law   (1) An advocate, counsel, or official agent employed in preparing, managing, and trying cases in the courts. (2) An officer in a court of justice, who is employed by a party in a case to manage it for him.

Attribution theory   A theory in social psychology that deals with the explanations people make for the cases of their behavior and the behavior of others.

Atypical antibody   An antibody that occurs as an irregular feature of the serum, e.g., anti-D.

Audio   The sound portion of a television signal.

Audio dubbing   Addition of sound to previously recorded tape.

Audit   An independent review conducted to compare the various aspects of the laboratory's performance with a standard for the performance.

Autism   Mental introversion in which thinking is governed by personal needs and the world is perceived in terms of wishes rather than reality; extreme preoccupation with one's own thoughts and fantasies.

Autistic disorder   Severe and chronic disturbance in children that affects communication and behavior; also known as *early infantile autism*, *childhood autism*, or *Kanner's syndrome*. Symptoms include withdrawal from contact with others, limited social response, language disturbances, ritualistic behavior and insistence on sameness, abnormalities in response to the sensory environment, self-stimulatory behavior, self-injurious behavior, inappropriate affect, limited intellectual functioning, and repetitive body movement.

Auto iris   Automatically regulates the amount of light entering the camera.

Auto white balance   Electronically adjusts camera color levels.

Autoantibody   An antibody that reacts with the red cells of the individual in whose serum it is found. It usually reacts upon the red cells of most other individuals as well.

Autoclave   An airtight vessel for heating and sometimes agitating its contents under high steam pressure; used for industrial processing, sterilizing, and cooking with moist or dry heat at high temperatures (Figure A.10).

Autoerotic fatality   Death occurring during solo sexual activity. Such deaths are accidental and most often involve hanging.

AUTOEXEC.BAT   A text file generally found in the root directory of a bootable floppy disk or hard disk on a computer running MS/PC-DOS or OS/2 that establishes the second level of the operating environment as the computer boots up.

Autofocus   Automatically sets the focus (distance) from scene to camera.

Autoignition temperature   The lowest temperature at which a gas or vapor–air mixture will ignite from its own heat source or a contacted heated surface without a spark or flame.

FIGURE A.10 An enclosed chamber for the sterilization under pressure of laboratory glassware, instruments, plastic tubes, etc.

Autolysis   The destruction of cells after death due to lack of ability to metabolize oxygen needed by enzymes for cell activity.

Automatic   **(Photography)** Self-thinking, or in the case of a mechanical device, preprogrammed and self-regulating. **(Firearms)** A firearm capable of ejecting a cartridge casing following discharge and reloading the next cartridge from the magazine.

Automatic action   A firearm design that feeds cartridges, fires, and ejects cartridge cases as long as the trigger is fully depressed and there are cartridges available in the feed system.

Automatic camera   A camera with a built-in exposure meter that automatically adjusts the lens opening, shutter speed, or both for proper exposure.

Autopsy   A physical examination of the corpse through dissection to determine cause of death (also *necropsy* and *postmortem*) (Figure A.11).

Autorad   An x-ray film of the hybridization between the radioactive probe and the complementary exposed strand of DNA.

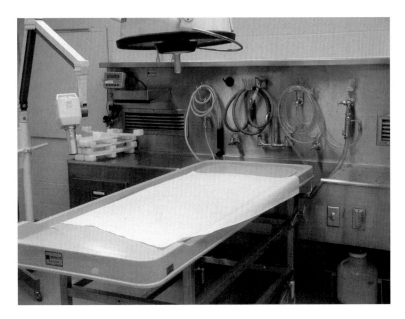

FIGURE A.11 Examination table used when performing an autopsy.

Autoradiogram (autoradiography)   A technique for detecting radioactivity in a specimen by producing an image on a photographic film or plate. A DNA probe tagged with a radioactive isotope such as ^{32}P (radioactive phosphorus) is exposed to a piece of x-ray film where the probe hybridizes to complementary sequences on the blot in contact with the film (Figure A.12).

Auto-safety   A locking device on some firearms designed to return to the *ON* or *SAFE* position when the firearm is opened.

AutoSearcher   A CODIS program that automatically searches all DNA profiles in a user-specified index against all profiles in one or more other user-specified indexes.

Autosome   Nonsex chromosome. There are 22 autosomes in the human genome.

Auxiliary lens   A lens element added to a regular lens to shorten or increase the focal length.

Awareness space   Locations and areas that a person is aware of and possesses at least a minimum level of knowledge about. It contains, but is larger than, the activity space.

Axial illumination   Narrow nonangular illumination surrounding the optical axis of a transmitted light microscope, produced by a low numerical aperture setting of the condenser. It improves contrast and allows more accurate and precise determination of refractive indices by immersion methods and causes a decrease in resolving power.

Axillary   Attached to a joint.

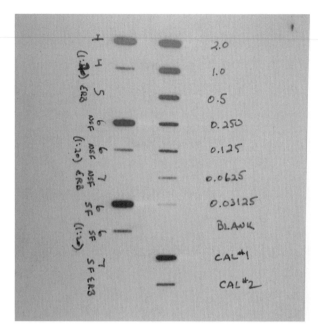

FIGURE A.12 The results of the quantitation of DNA on photographic film using the slot blot method.

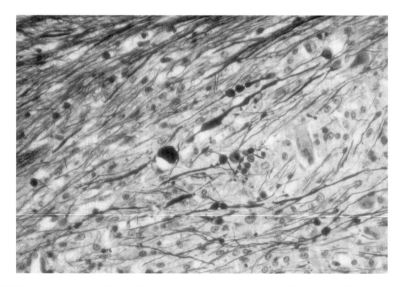

FIGURE A.13 Axons stained with a silver stain showing beading and ballooning due to diffuse axonal injury following a motor vehicle accident. (Courtesy of forensic medical examiner Michael Sikirica, M.D.)

Axon   The part of a nerve cell that conducts nervous impulses away from the nerve cell body to the remainder of the cell (i.e., dendrites); large number of fibrils enveloped by a segmented myelin sheath (Figure A.13).

Azeotrope   A mixture of two or more compounds that have a constant boiling point. The composition of the vapor above the azeotropic mixture has the same relative concentration of the compounds as does the boiling liquid. Azeotropic mixtures cannot be separated by fractional distillation.

Azlon   Any textile fiber derived from protein, such as casein.

Azo dye   A result of the Griess test where nitrites from gunpowder residues are converted to an orange-red dye.

B

B (bulb) **(1)** Setting on the shutter ring indicating that the shutter will stay open as long as the shutter release button is depressed. **(2)** Professional 1-in. reel-to-reel format videotape.

Back up or Backup Either the act of creating a duplicate copy of working programs and data or the actual copy of programs and data, used for disaster recovery. Ideally, such copies are stored off site.

Background The part of the scene that appears behind the principal subject of the picture.

Background discrimination The ability of a measuring instrument, circuit, or other device to distinguish signals from background noise.

Background radiation Radiation from a source other than the test sample specifically being analyzed.

Backlighting Light shining on the subject from the direction opposite the camera; distinguished from frontlighting and sidelighting.

Backscatter The light reflected back to the camera in underwater photography caused by flash reflection of particles suspended in the water.

Backspatter Blood that is directed back toward its source of energy. Backspatter is often associated with gunshot wounds of entrance.

Bail Money or other security (such as a *bail bond*) given to secure a person's release from custody, which is at risk should he or she subsequently fail to appear before the court. *Bail* and *bond* are often used interchangeably.

Bail bond The obligation, signed by the accused to secure his or her presence at trial, which he or she may lose by not properly appearing for trial. Also referred to as *bond*.

Bailiff A court attendant who keeps order in the courtroom and has custody of the jury.

Ball The part of the foot just behind the large toe, formed by the intersection of the first metatarsal phalangeal joint.

Ball ammunition Military small arms ammunition with full-metal-jacket bullets; also known as *hard ball*.

Ball-point pen A writing instrument having as its marking tip a small, freely rotating ball bearing that rolls the ink onto the paper. Many of these pens use highly viscous, nonaqueous ink, but in recent years construction of some pens has been adapted to use water-based inks.

Ballistics The study of a projectile in motion, following the projectile travel from primer ignition to barrel exit, to target entry and until motion is stopped. Often confused with *firearms identification*.

Ballistics, exterior The study of the motion of the projectile after it leaves the barrel of the firearm.

Ballistics, interior   The study of the motion of the projectile within the firearm from the moment of ignition until it leaves the barrel.

Ballistics, terminal   The study of the projectile's impact on the target.

Band   A radioactive signal on an autorad usually caused by a fragment of human or bacterial DNA that combines with a radiolabeled DNA probe.

Band-shifting   The phenomenon where DNA fragments in one lane of an electrophoresis gel migrate across the gel more rapidly than identical fragments in a second lane.

Banyan vines   A network operating system produced by Banyan Systems. Vines has a minor following because of its name services.

Bar   Historically, the partition separating the general public from the space occupied by the judges, lawyers and other participants in a trial. More commonly, the term means the whole body of lawyers. The "case at bar" is the case currently being considered.

Barbiturate   A derivative of barbituric acid that produces depression of the central nervous system and consequent sedation.

Barium   Alkaline earth metal with chemical symbol Ba, atomic number 56. Present as barium nitrate in the primer.

Barium nitrate   A common oxidizer of the primer compound used in gun cartridges.

Barr bodies   A condensed, inactivated X-chromosome inside the nuclear membrane in interphase somatic cells of women.

Barrel   That part of a firearm through which a projectile travels under the impetus of powder gases, compressed air, or other like means; may be rifled or smooth.

Barrier filter   A filter used in fluorescence microscopy that suppresses unnecessary excitation light that has not been absorbed by the fiber and selectively transmits only the fluorescence.

Base drawing   The scale drawing made of the accident scene that shows all the landmarks and detail to set the scene. It generally does not contain any measurements or any points of impact (POI) or points of rest (POR).

Base sequence   The order of bases in a DNA molecule, example ATCGGACT.

Baseline   The ruled or imaginary line upon which the writing rests.

Baselining   Adjusting the baselines of detected dye colors to the same level for a better comparison of relative signal intensity.

Base pair (bp)   A chemical bonding partnership composed of adenine (A) double bonding with thymine (T) and cytosine (C) triple bonding with guanine (G) coming together to form a DNA double-helix molecule.

Bases   Chemical units (adenine, thymine, guanine, and cytosine) whose order in DNA molecules governs the genetic code.

Batch or Analytical batch   Group of one or more specimens or samples that are analyzed under conditions approaching repeatability. Usually it should contain calibrators and quality-control specimens or samples in addition to the samples to be analyzed.

Battered child syndrome   Medical condition, occurring in infants and young children, in which there is evidence of repeated injury inflicted by others to the nervous system, skin, or skeletal system. Frequently, the child's medical history, as given by the caregiver, does not adequately explain the injuries. Many courts recognize this syndrome as an accepted medical diagnosis.

Battered woman syndrome   A collection of symptoms that are manifest in women who have suffered prolonged and extensive abuse from their spouses.

Battery   A beating, or wrongful physical violence. The actual threat to use force is an *assault*; the use of it is a *battery*, which usually included an assault.

Battery pack   Rechargeable, portable power source.

Bayonet mount   A casting on the rear of a lens corresponding to an appropriate fitting on the camera body.

BB   Air-rifle projectile of 0.177-in. diameter or a shotgun pellet of 0.18-in. diameter.

BBB shot   Shotgun pellet of 0.19-in. diameter.

BBS (Bulletin board system)   A system for people to call into with their home computers and modems to exchange messages, software, or pictures. These systems usually are free to their users.

Becké line   The bright halo near the boundary of a fiber that moves with respect to that boundary as the microscope is focused through the best focal point.

Becké line method   A method for determining the refractive index of a fiber relative to its mountant by noting the direction in which the Becké line moves when the focus is changed. The Becké line will always move toward the higher refractive index medium (fiber or mountant) when focus is raised and will move toward the lower refractive index medium when focus is lowered. This is a traditional means for matching a particle with an immersion liquid.

Beer's law   The absorbance of a homogeneous sample containing an absorbing substance is directly proportional to the concentration of the absorbing substance.

Behavior chain   The complete behavior including all of its steps, e.g., in wilderness work, a dog searches for the subject, finds the subject, returns to the handler and lets him know he has found the subject, leads the handler back to the subject, and is rewarded.

Behavioral medicine   Multidisciplinary field that integrates behavioral science approaches with biomedical knowledge and techniques.

Behavioral science   The scientific study and analysis of human behavior. This term is often used to describe the investigative study of criminal behavior.

Bench trial   A trial in which the judge, rather than the jury, makes the decision.

Bench warrant   An order issued by a judge for the arrest of a person.

Benzene   A hexagonal organic molecule having a carbon atom at each point of the hexagon, and a hydrogen atom attached to each carbon atom. Molecules that contain a benzene ring, are known as *aromatic*.

Benzidine   A grayish-yellow, white or reddish gray crystalline powder. It is used in organic synthesis and the manufacture of dyes, especially of Congo red. Also used for the detection of bloodstains and as a stiffening agent in rubber compounding.

Benzoylecognine   A cocaine metabolite.

Beretta   A handgun manufacturer.

FIGURE B.1 External bevel due to gunshot wound with passage of the bullet outward.

Bertillonage   A method of classifying human beings by a set of detailed body measurements, invented by Alphonse Bertillon, a clerk in the French Sûreté in 1883, but rendered obsolete by fingerprinting.

BETA   Sony-format $1/_2$-in. videotape.

Beveling (external or internal)   Defects that occur when a projectile passes through a flat bone. The perforation in the bone is typically larger and more cone shaped as the bullet passes from the entrance through the bone to the exit (Figure B.1).

Beyond a reasonable doubt   The standard in a criminal case requiring that the jury be satisfied to a moral certainty that every element of a crime has been proven by the prosecution. This standard of proof does not require that the state establish absolute certainty by eliminating all doubt, but it does require that the evidence be so conclusive that all reasonable doubts are removed from the mind of the ordinary person.

Bias   Difference between the expectation of the test result and an accepted reference value. A systematic error inherent in a method or caused by some artifact or idiosyncrasy of the measurement system. Temperature effects and extraction inefficiencies are examples of errors inherent in the method. Blanks, contamination, mechanical losses, and calibration errors are examples of artifact errors. Bias can be either positive or negative, and several kinds of error can exist concurrently. Therefore, net bias is all that can be evaluated.

Big Floyd   The FBI supercomputer that contains software allowing it to search criminal records and draw conclusions from the available information in the hunt for those responsible for an individual crime.

Bill of Particulars   A statement used to inform the defense of the specific occurrences intended to be investigated in trial and to limit the course of evidence to the particular scope of the inquiry. An amplification of the pleading.

Bin or Binning   A conservative method of calculating population frequency by combining groups of fragment sizes into defined groups instead of making calculations from a single fragment size.

Bind over   To hold a person for trial on bond (bail) or in jail. If the judicial official conducting a preliminary hearing finds probable cause to believe the accused committed a crime, he or she will "bind over" the accused, normally by setting bail for his or her appearance at trial.

Bindle paper   Clean paper folded to use to contain trace evidence, sometimes included as part of the packaging for collecting trace evidence. Most of the time, white paper is used and has the consistency of butcher paper, the paper used in deli markets.

Biohazard bag   A container for materials that have been exposed to blood or other biological fluids, and have the potential to be contaminated with various diseases such as hepatitis, AIDS, or other viruses. The bag is a heavy plastic red color with the biohazard symbol printed on the outside.

Biological fluids   Fluids that have human or animal origin, most commonly encountered at crime scenes (e.g., blood, mucus, perspiration, saliva, semen, vaginal fluid, and urine).

Biological sample bag (Biobag)   A collection of biological stains such as saliva, seminal stains, bloodstains, and vaginal secretions, acquired from physical evidence from submitting agencies, sealed in a plastic bag. The items contained in the biobag can be swabs (vaginal, oral, anal, dried secretions), fingernail scrapings, control bloodstains or small cuttings from the physical evidence.

Biological theory of crime   An explanation for the causes of criminal behavior that uses heredity and constitutional characteristics of the lawbreaker.

Biological weapon   Biological agents used to threaten human life (e.g., anthrax, smallpox, or any infectious disease).

Biomechanics   The science that concerns itself with the structure and mechanical movements of parts of the body, such as the foot.

Biopsy   A small piece of tissue excised for the purpose of analysis.

Bipod   A two-legged rest or stand, as for a rifle or machine gun.

Bipolar questions   Queries that present two alternatives. They are a useful compromise between open-ended and "yes–no" questions when an interviewer wants to find out what the interviewee believes about a specific issue.

Birefringence   The splitting of a light beam into two components, which travel at different velocities, by a material. The numerical difference in refractive indices for a fiber, given by the formula for birefringence ãnã – nZã. Birefringence can be calculated by determining the retardation (r) and thickness (T) at a particular point in a fiber and by using the formula $B = r$ (nm)/$1000T$ (_m).

Bite mark   A circular or oval (doughnut) (ring-shaped) patterned injury consisting of two opposing (facing) symmetrical, U-shaped arches separated at their bases by open spaces. Following the periphery of the arches are a

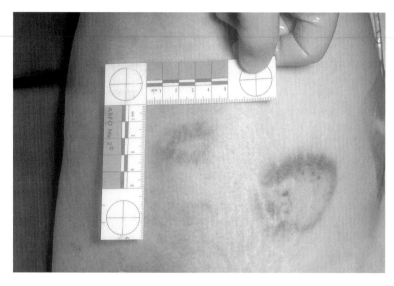

FIGURE B.2 Human bite marks in a victim of homicide. A scale is used to measure the size of the bite mark. (Courtesy of forensic medical examiner Michael Sikirica, M.D.)

series of individual abrasions, contusions or lacerations reflecting the size, shape, arrangement, and distribution of the class characteristics of the contacting surfaces of the human dentition (Figure B.2).

Bitmap A mosaic of dots or pixels defining an image, including dot matrix imprints. The smoothness of the image contour depends upon the fineness of resolution and the number of dots or pixels per inch.

Black powder The earliest form of propellant. It is a mechanical mixture of potassium nitrate or sodium nitrate, charcoal, and sulfur.

Blank **(1)** The measured value obtained when a specified component of a sample is not present during the measurement. In such a case, the measured value (or signal) for the component is believed to be due to artifacts and should be deducted from a measured value to give a net value due solely to the component contained in the sample. The blank measurement must be made so that the correction process is valid. **(2)** Biological specimen with no detectable drugs added, routinely analyzed to ensure that no false–positive results are obtained.

Blasting cap A small explosive charge triggered by lighting a safety fuse or applying an electric current, used to detonate high explosives.

Blind area search Training routine where handler does not know where scent source is located.

Blind external proficiency test A test that is presented to a forensic laboratory through a second agency and appears to the analysts to involve routine evidence. A proficiency test sample for which the analyst is unaware of the test nature of the sample at the time of analysis.

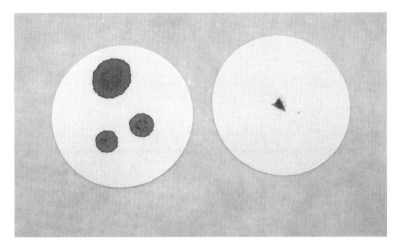

FIGURE B.3 Bloodstains left on filter paper after placing the wet filter paper on the evidence. The chemical screening reagent for blood would be added to the bloodstains that are on the filter paper.

Bloat That transient phase in corpse decomposition that follows the fresh phase and is characterized by excessive swelling, produced by gases trapped internally.

Blobbing The accumulation of ink on the exterior of the point assembly of a ball-point pen, that drops intermittently to the surface being written upon.

Blood group An immunologically distinct, genetically determined class of human erythrocyte antigens, identified as A, B, AB, and O. A classification of red blood cell surface antigens, ABO is the best known of the blood group systems.

Blood type A way of saying which blood group antigens are present on the person's red cells.

Bloodborne pathogen Infectious, disease-causing microorganism that may be found or transported in biological fluids.

Bloodstain Liquid blood that has dried once it has come in contact with a surface (Figure B.3).

Blowback An operating principle of automatic and semiautomatic firearms. The fired cartridge blows back against the breechblock, forcing it to the rear, and extracting and ejecting the expended cartridge casing. Blowback also describes the blowing back of blood and other tissue onto a firearm or a shooter from a near contact or contact shot (Figure B.4).

Blunt ending The effect produced on commencement and terminal strokes of letters, both upper and lowercase, by the application of the writing instrument to the paper prior to the beginning of any horizontal movement; an action that usually omits any beard, hitch, knob, or tick.

Blur Indistinct image caused by movement or inaccurate focusing.

Boat A dish-shaped figure consisting of a concave stroke and a straight line, sometimes forming the base of letters.

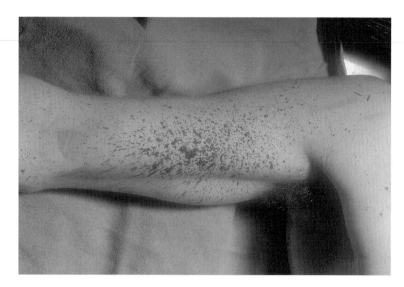

FIGURE B.4 A pattern of blood left on an individual's arm resulting from blowback from a person being shot by a firearm. (Courtesy of forensic medical examiner Michael Sikirica, M.D.)

Body   That portion of a letter, the central part, that remains when the upper and lower projections, the terminal and initial strokes, and the diacritics are omitted.

Body bag   A heavy waterproof bag usually closed with a zipper and used to transport a corpse.

Body dump site   The location where an offender disposes of the murder victim's body.

Body language   Nonverbal communications associated with posture, facial expressions, and mannerisms.

Boiling point   The temperature at which the vapor pressure of a liquid equals the atmospheric pressure and the liquid becomes vapor.

Bolt action   A firearm in which the breech closure is in line with the bore at all times. It is manually reciprocated to load, unload, and cock and is locked in placed by breech-bolt lugs and engaging abutments usually in the receiver.

Booking   The process of photographing, fingerprinting, and recording identifying data of a suspect following arrest.

Borderline personality disorder   A personality disorder characterized by impulsivity and instability in moods, behavior, self-image, and interpersonal relationships.

Bore   The interior of a barrel forward of the chamber.

Bore brush   A brush usually having brass, nylon, or plastic bristles, which is used to clean deposits from the bore of a firearm (Figure B.5).

Bore diameter   **(1)** In a rifled barrel, it is the minor diameter of a barrel, which is the diameter of a circle formed by the tops of the lands. **(2)** In a shotgun,

FIGURE B.5 Various sizes of bore brushes.

it is the interior dimensions of the barrel forward of the chamber but before the choke.

Bounce lighting **(1)** A light source reflected off of another surface and then onto the subject. **(2)** Flash or tungsten light bounced off the ceiling or walls in order to give the effect of natural or available light.

Boundaries The perimeter of border surrounding potential physical evidence related to the crime scene.

Boustrophedon Writing in which alternate lines are written in opposite directions and even have the posture as well as the direction of reversed letters.

Bovine albumin Any one of a class of protein substances found in the blood of a bovine animal. Also known as *bovine albumin serum (BSA)*.

Bow A vertical curved stroke, as in capitals "D" and "C."

bp An abbreviation for *base pair*; distance along DNA is measured in bp.

Brady material Can be generally defined as any evidence that may be favorable to the defendant and that shows or tends to show that the defendant is not responsible for the commission of the crime for which they were arrested, or mitigate the circumstances under which the crime was committed.

Bradycardia Slow heart rate, usually fewer than 60 beats per minute.

Braille A system of representing letters, numerals, etc., by raised dots that a visually impaired person can read by touch.

Brain stem Part of the brain from the medulla to the midbrain, excluding the cerebellum. The brain stem is the main control center of breathing, blood pressure, swallowing, and consciousness. It connects the cerebral hemispheres with the spinal cord.

Brantingham and Brantingham crime site selection model A m o d e l o f crime geometry within the environmental criminology perspective developed at Simon Fraser University. It suggests that crimes are most likely to occur in those areas where an offender's awareness space intersects with perceived suitable targets.

"Brass" A slang term sometimes used for fired cartridge cases.

Brawner rule States that a defendant is not responsible for criminal conduct when, as a result of a mental disease or defect, he or she lacks substantial capacity either to appreciate the criminality (wrongfulness) of the conduct or to conform his or her conduct to the requirements of the law. Also known as the *ALI* rule.

Break-over angles The angle between the point of contact of the front or rear tire of the vehicle and the lowest point of the vehicle. This angle is important for the vehicle to get up and down driveways, culverts, etc.

Breech The part of a firearm at the rear of the bore into which the cartridge of propellant is inserted.

Breech block The locking and cartridge head-supporting mechanism of a firearm that does not operate in line with the axis of the bore.

Breech blot The locking and cartridge head-supporting mechanism of a firearm that operates in line with the axis of the bore.

Breech face That part of the breech block or breech bolt that is against the head of the cartridge case or shotshell during firing.

Breech-face markings Negative impression of the breech face of the firearm found on the head of the cartridge case after firing.

Brentamine fast salt blue B A chemical used for the detection of the enzyme acid phosphatase, which is found in high concentrations in seminal fluid. This chemical reagent is a preliminary screening test for the presence acid phosphatase in seminal fluid or on seminal-stained evidence.

Brentamine reaction A chemical used for the detection of acid phosphatase, this enzyme is found in high concentrations in seminal fluid. This chemical reagent is a preliminary screening test for the presence of prostatic acid phosphatase in seminal fluid or on seminal-stained evidence. This reaction relies on the liberation of naphthol from sodium-naphthly phosphate by the enzyme, acid phosphatase, and the concomitant formation of a purple azo dye by the coupling of naphthol with buffered Brentamine Fast Blue B (Figure B.6).

Bridge A device attached to a network cable to connect two like topologies.

Brief A written statement prepared by one side in a lawsuit to explain to the court its view of the facts of a case and the applicable law.

Broach Rifling tool consisting of a series of circular cutting tools mounted on a long rod. The rifling is cut in on pass of the broach through the gun barrel.

Broad sense heritability (H_2) The proportion of total phenotypic variance at the population level that is contributed by genetic variance. Heritability in the broad sense is $h_2 = V_G/V_T$.

Bronchi (*singular,* bronchus) Large divisions of the trachea that convey air to and from the lungs.

FIGURE B.6 A chemical reaction test for the presence of seminal fluid on the filter paper. A positive reaction will result in a purple color.

Bronchiole   A small-diameter airway branching from a bronchus.

Bronchitis   Inflammation of the mucous membrane of the bronchial tubes, usually associated with a persistent cough and sputum production.

Bronchospasm   Contraction of the smooth muscle of the bronchi, causing narrowing of the bronchi. This narrowing increases the resistance of air flow into the lungs and may cause a shortness of breath typically associated with wheezing.

Browning Arms Co.   A firearms manufacturer.

Brutalization   The proposition that the use of capital punishment actually increases the crime rate by sending a message that it is acceptable to kill those who have wronged us.

BTU (British Thermal Unit)   The amount of heat energy required to raise the temperature of one pound of water by $1°F$. One BTU equals 252 calories.

Buccal cells   Cells derived from the inner cheek lining. These cells are present in the saliva or can be gently scraped from the inner cheek surface.

Buckshot   Lead pellet ranging in size from 0.20-in. to 0.36-in. diameter.

Buffer   **(Computer science)** An area of memory in which information is stored while the computer is on. **(Chemistry)** A solution that tends to resist changes in pH as acid or base is added.

FIGURE B.7 (A) Projectile with land and groove impressions. (B) Expended projectile with rifling impressions.

Buffy coat   The whitish layer of cells (white blood cells plus platelets) overlaying the red cell pellet after centrifugation of whole blood.

Bulb   A shutter speed setting used to hold the shutter open for extended periods with the use of a shutter release cord or continuous pressure on the shutter release button.

Bulimia nervosa   Eating disorder characterized by repeated episodes of binge eating followed by inappropriate compensatory behaviors such as self-induced vomiting, misuse of laxatives, diuretics, enemas, or other medications; fasting; and excessive exercise. The episodes usually occur at least twice a week for three months, in individuals whose self-evaluation is influenced by body shape and weight.

Bullet-bearing surface   That part of the outer surface of a bullet that comes into direct contact with the interior surface of the barrel (Figure B.7A and B).

Bullet creep   The movement of a bullet out of the cartridge case due to the recoil of the firearm and the inertia of the bullet. Also called *bullet starting*. Also known as *popping*.

Bullet, frangible   A projectile designed to disintegrate upon impact on a hard surface in order to minimize ricochet or spatter.

Bullet jacket   Usually a metallic cover over the core.

Bullet, lead   A standard lead bullet having a harder metal jacket over the nose formed from a lead alloy, also known as *metal-point bullet*. This non-spherical projectile is for use in a rifled barrel (Figure B.8A and B).

Bullet recovery system   Any method that will allow the undamaged recovery of a fired bullet. Water tanks and cotton boxes are most commonly in use (Figure B.9).

Bullet wipe   A dark ring-shaped mark made up of lead, carbon oil, and dirt brushed from a bullet as it enters the skin, and found around the entry wound. The discolored area on the immediate periphery of a bullet hole,

FIGURE B.8 (A) Pistol cartidge with copper-jacketed projectile. (B) Rifled cartridge with metal point bullet.

caused by bullet lubricant, lead, smoke, bore debris, or possibly, jacket material. Sometimes called *burnishing* or *leaded edge*.

Bumper fracture Fractures that typically occur due to the impact of a vehicle on the calves of a decedent with fractures of the tibia or fibula. They may be unilateral or lateral (Figure B.10).

Burden of proof In the law of evidence, the duty of a party to prove a fact in dispute affirmatively. The obligation of a party to convince the trier to fact as to the truth of a claim by establishing by evidence a required degree of belief concerning a fact. In civil cases, proof must be by a preponderance of the evidence. In criminal cases, all crime elements must be proved by the government beyond a reasonable doubt. In some equity issues and more recent decisions of the Supreme Court the standard of proof is clear and convincing evidence.

Buried source Phase of training where a dog is taught to indicate the location of a scent coming from a buried source.

Burn Wound resulting from the application of too much heat. Burns are classified by the degree of damage caused: first-degree scorching or painful redness of the skin, second-degree formation of blisters, and third-degree destruction of outer layer of the skin (Figure B.11). **(Photography)** An

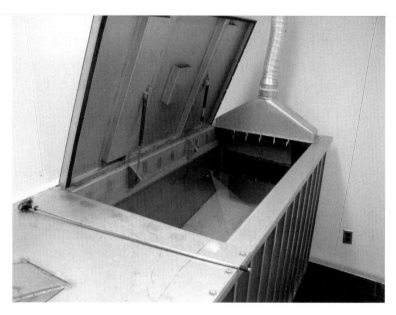

FIGURE B.9 A metal tank filled with water allowing the firearm examiner to recover bullets from the test firing of handguns.

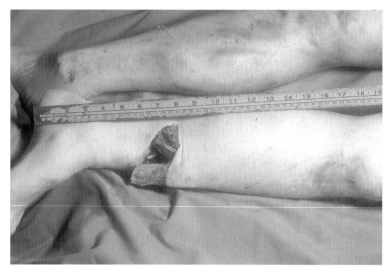

FIGURE B.10 Measuring the height of a bumper fracture above the heel. (Courtesy of forensic medical examiner Michael Sikirica, M.D.)

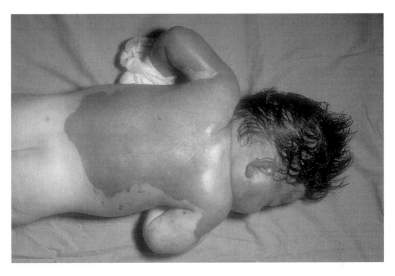

FIGURE B.11 Immersion type burns in an infant who was dipped into hot water. (Courtesy of forensic medical examiner Michael Sikirica, M.D.)

afterimage produced on a TV screen caused by excessive light falling on the recording camera's tube.

Burn pattern   The visible path of fire on a surface or surfaces.

Burning   Normal combustion in which the oxidant is molecular oxygen.

Burning rate   The rate at which combustion proceeds across a fuel.

Burr holes   Small holes made in the skull in order to place an intracranial pressure monitor, access the brain so as to evacuate blood clots, or reduce spinal fluid pressure (Figure B.12).

Burr striations   (**1**) A roughness or rough edge, especially one left on metal in casting or cutting. (**2**) A tool or device that raises a burr.

Burring   A division of a written line into two or more, more or less equal portions, by a nonlinked area generally running parallel to the direction of line generation, but moving away from the radius of a curving stroke, sometimes referred to as *splitting*.

Butabarbital   A short- to intermediate-acting barbiturate derivative.

Butalbital   An occasionally encountered short-acting barbiturate closely related to Talbutal and less closely to Amobarbital and Secobarbital. Intoxication can result in lethargy, confusion, disorientation, and ataxia.

Butane   A fuel gas having the formula C_4H_{10}. One of the constituents found in LP gas.

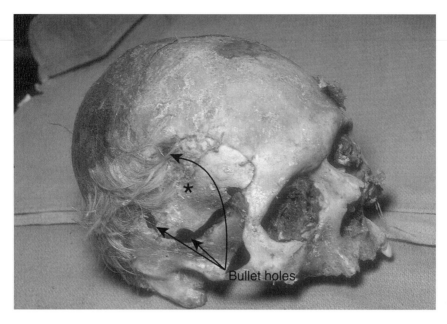

FIGURE B.12 Burr holes on a skeletonized skull used by a neurosurgeon to begin a craniotomy procedure for evacuation of an acute blood clot. * indicates where the craniotomy took place. (Courtesy of forensic medical examiner Michael Sikirica, M.D.)

Butt In handguns, the bottom part of the grip or grip frame. In long guns, it is the rear of shoulder end of the stock.

Byte A basic unit of data storage that contains a single character.

C

Cable release A flexible, enclosed wire used to release the shutter mechanism.

Cabletron A company that provides data communications equipment such as hubs, concentrators, bridges, and routers.

Cadaver dog Canines specially trained to find human decomposition scent and alert their handlers to its location.

Cadaverine Malodorous chemical compound produced during decomposition.

Caliber **(Firearms)** The approximate diameter of the circle formed by the tops of the lands of a rifled barrel. **(Ammunition)** A numerical term, without the decimal point, included in a cartridge name to indicate a rough approximation of the bullet diameter.

Calibrant Substance used to calibrate, or to establish the analytical response of, a measurement system.

Calibrate To determine, by measurement or comparison with a standard, the correct value of each scale reading on a meter or other device, or the correct value for each setting of a control knob.

Calibration **(1)** Set of operations that establishes, under specified conditions, the relationship between values indicated by a measuring instrument or measuring system, or values represented by a material measure, and the corresponding known values of a measurement. **(2)** Determining the response of some analytical method to known amounts of a pure analyte.

Calibration curve Relationship between the signal response of the instrument and various concentrations of analyte in a suitable solvent or matrix.

Calibrator Pure analyte in a suitable solvent or matrix, used to prepare the calibration curve.

Calorie The amount of energy required to raise the temperature of 1 g of water by 1°C.

Camera A photographic apparatus used to expose sensitized film or plates to reflected light images formed by a lens. Also, an electronic device to change film or live action into video signals.

Camera angle The photographer's point of view of a subject or scene as viewed through the lens or viewfinder.

Candidate match A possible match between two or more DNA profiles discovered by CODIS software. Qualified DNA analysts must verify candidate matches.

Canine cadaver search The investigation of a particular area deemed by forensic investigators to contain human remains according to a strategy designed for that particular context.

Cannabidiol A constituent of cannabis, which, upon isomerization to a tetrahydrocannabinol, has some of the physiologic activity of marijuana.

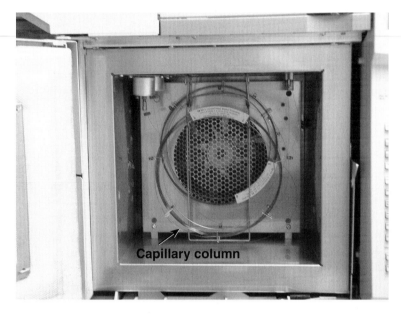

FIGURE C.1 A narrow-bore glass tube that is found inside a gas chromatography instrument. This is where the separation of the chemical compounds takes place.

Cannabinol   ($C_{21}H_{26}O_2$) A physiologically inactive phenol formed by spontaneous dehydrogenation of tetrahydrocannabinol from cannabis.

Cannabis   A genus of tall annual herbs in the family *Cannabaccae* having erect
stems, with 3 to 7 elongated leaflets and pistillate flowers in spikes along
the stem. Commonly known as *marijuana* or sometimes referred to on
the street as *grass* or *pot*.

Cannelure   A circumferential groove generally of a knurled or plain appearance
in a bullet or the head of a rimless cartridge case.

Canvass   To ascertain information by systematically interviewing all people in
a certain vicinity or area (in Britain, called *intensive inquiry*).

Capillary   (Gas chromatography) A narrow-bore glass tube. Gas chromatography employs glass tube capillary columns having an inside diameter of
approximately 0.2 to 0.5 mL and a length of 3 to 300 m. The walls of a
capillary column are coated with an adsorbent or adsorbent medium (a
liquid phase in which the sample dissolves) (Figure C.1). **(DNA analysis)**
The glass tube capillary columns have a polymer gel moving through the
column that allows the small fragments of DNA to separate (Figure
C.2).

Capital crime   A crime punishable by death.

Carbine   A rifle of short length and lightweight originally designed for mounted
troops.

Carbon   The element upon which all organic molecules are based.

Carbon copy   A copy of a typewritten document made by means of carbon
paper. An exact replica; duplicate.

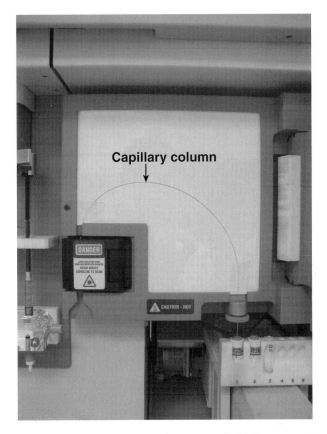

FIGURE C.2 Capillary electrophoresis is used to separate DNA fragments; a liquid polymer flows through the capillary along with different sized DNA fragments.

Carbon dioxide   A molecule consisting of one atom of carbon and two atoms of oxygen, which is a major combustion product of the burning of organic materials. Carbon dioxide (CO_2) is the result of complete combustion of carbon.

Carbon ink (India ink)   One of the oldest forms of writing ink; commonly referred to as India ink even though the ink was first used in China. In its simplest form carbon ink consists of amorphous carbon shaped into a solid cake with glue. It is converted into a liquid for writing by grinding the cake and suspending the particles in a water-glue medium. Occasionally, a pigmented dye is added to improve the color.

Carbon monoxide (CO)   A colorless, odorless, very toxic gas, formed by burning carbon or organic fuels. A gaseous molecule having the formula CO, which is the product of incomplete combustion of organic materials. Carbon monoxide has an affinity for hemoglobin that is approximately 200 times stronger than that of oxygen. It is highly poisonous.

Career criminals   The select group of criminals responsible for an unduly large amount of crime in a particular area.

FIGURE C.3 Firearm cartridge in which the primer compound is contained in a centrally positioned primer cap.

Caregiver   Person responsible for another's health and welfare, such as a parent or guardian, another person within the home, or a person in a relative's home, foster care home, or residential institution. A caregiver is responsible for meeting an individual's basic physical and psychological needs and for providing protection and supervision.

Carrion   Decaying animal flesh.

Cartridge   (Photography) A lightproof container that is loaded with film in the dark and can be handled and placed in the camera in the light. **(Firearms)** A single unit of ammunition consisting of the case, primer, and propellant with or without one or more projectiles. Also applies to a shot shell.

Cartridge case head   The base of the cartridge case which contains the primer.

Cartridge, centerfire   Any cartridge that has its primer central to the axis in the head of the case (Figure C.3).

Cartridge, rimfire   A flange-headed cartridge containing the priming mixture inside the rim cavity.

Case (IBIS)   A folder that is the basic unit of the Integrated Ballistics Information System, into which information about evidence is placed. These folders are known as cases and are labeled carefully for IBIS to keep the information they contain organized and easily accessible.

Case file   The collection of documents comprising information concerning a particular investigation. (This collection may be kept in case jackets, file folders, ring binders, boxes, file drawers, file cabinets, or rooms. Subfiles often used within case files to segregate and group interviews, media coverage, laboratory requests and reports, evidence documentation, photographs, videotapes, audiotapes, and other documents.)

FIGURE C.4 A metal case that is lightproof. It is used for the development of the auto-radiograph.

Case law   Law created as a by-product of court decisions made in resolving unique disputes, as distinguished from statutory and constitutional law.

Case records   All notes, reports, custody records, charts, analytical data, and any correspondence generated in the laboratory pertaining to a particular case.

Case screening   The process by which investigative cases are removed (based on solvability factors) from the work load, making resources available for those holding greater promise of solution.

Cassette   A film cartridge or magazine. A lightproof holder used in autoradiography for exposing x-ray film to radioactive blots (Figure C.4).

Casting   **(Footwear)** The filling of a three-dimensional footwear impression with material that takes on and retains the characteristics that were left in that impression by the footwear. Also, a method of making a mold by first making a three-dimensional model of a shoe and then making a cast from that model (Figure C.5A and B). **(Human remains)** Term also used to refer to the initial search for a scent.

FIGURE C.5A A three-dimensional cast mold impression from a workboot. Three-dimensional impressions that retain sufficient detail can be identified with a specific item of footwear.

FIGURE C.5B Cast mold impressions from different styles of shoes and sneakers. These three-dimensional impressions are found predominantly on exterior surfaces such as sand, soil, or snow.

Cast-mold Three-dimensional representation of a footwear impression left at a crime scene. Cast-molds can be made from dental stone or plaster of paris, which are gypsum-plaster products. Cast-molds can also be used for teeth and tire impressions (Figure C.6).

FIGURE C.6 Three-dimensional impressions that retain sufficient detail can be identified with a specific item of footwear.

Cast-off pattern Blood that has been projected onto a surface from other than an impact site. This pattern is produced when blood is thrown from a bloody object in motion.

Casual shoe A shoe designed for easy, informal wear, normally having a leather upper and either a leather or a soft synthetic shoe.

Catalyst A substance that increases the rate of chemical reaction without undergoing a permanent change in its structure.

Catecholamines Substances of a specific chemical nature (pyrocatechols with an alkylamine side chain). Catecholamines of biochemical interest are those produced by the nervous system (e.g., epinephrine [adrenaline] or dopamine) to increase heart rate and blood pressure, or medicines with the same general chemical structure and effect.

Cathode The electrode at which reduction takes place in an electrochemical cell.

Cation A positively charged atom, or group of atoms, or a radical that moves to the negative pole (cathode) during electrolysis.

Caucasian A member of the white-skinned division of the human race so called from a skull found in the Caucasus, which was taken as establishing the type.

Caucasoid Have or pertaining to the so-called "white race," characterized by skin color ranging from very white to dark brown; a member of the ethnic group; a Caucasian.

Cause determination Developing an explanation of the circumstances and conditions that bring together a fuel, an ignition source, and an oxidizer to produce a fire.

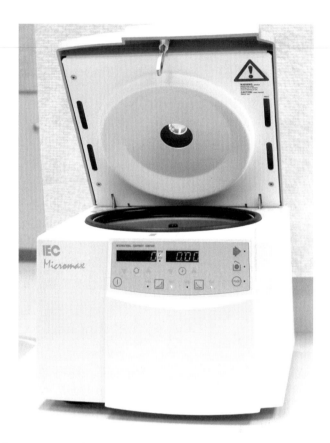

FIGURE C.7 A rotary machine with accessory containers, tubes, and rotors for the separation by controlled centrifugal force of substances having different densities.

Cause of death   Disease or injury that initiates the lethal train of events leading
         to death, for example, coronary heart disease or a gunshot wound of the heart.
Caustic   Having the ability to strongly irritate, burn, corrode, or destroy living
         tissue.
Caveat   A warning; a note of caution.
CDM   Criterion Die and Machine Company, a firearms manufacturer.
CD-ROM   A compact disc (CD, like those used for music) that stores computer
         data.
Central processing unit (CPU)   The part of a computer system that does the
         actual "thinking" or information processing of the computer.
Centrifuge   A rotating device for separating liquids of different specific gravities
         or for separating suspended colloidal particles, such as clay particles in
         an aqueous suspension, according to particle-size fractions by centrifugal
         force (Figure C.7).
Cephalothorax   The anterior body region in some arthropods consisting of the
         fused head and thorax.

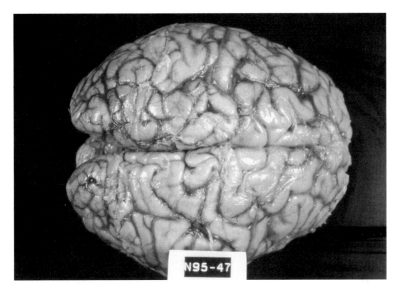

FIGURE C.8 Cerebellum. The massive dorsally located organ of the central nervous system forming that part of the brain below and behind the cerebrum. (Courtesy of forensic medical examiner Michael Sikirica, M.D.)

Cerebellum The large brain mass located at the posterior base of the brain, responsible for balance and coordination of movement (Figure C.8).

Cerebral contusion Bruising of brain tissue, marked by swelling and hemorrhage and resulting in loss of consciousness.

Cerebral edema Swelling of the brain caused by excessive buildup of fluid in the tissue. Also, there is high-altitude cerebral edema, which is seen in mountain climbers, hikers, or skiers who ascend too rapidly to high altitudes (Figure C.9).

Cerebral infarctions Death of tissue in the cerebrum due to lack of blood flow to the area.

Cerebrum The largest portion of the brain; includes the cerebral hemispheres (cerebral cortex and basal ganglia) (Figure C.10).

Certification Procedure by which a certifying body formally recognizes that a body, person or product complies with given specifications. The recognition of a particular level of professional qualifications.

Certified reference material (CRM) A reference material, one or more of whose property values have been certified by a technical procedure, accompanied by or traceable to a certificate or other documentation that has been issued by a certifying body.

Certiorari To be informed of; an action or writ issued by a superior court requiring an inferior court to produce a certified record of a particular cased tried by the latter. The purpose of said action is to enable the higher court to inspect the proceedings to determine whether or not there were any irregularities. Most commonly used by the Supreme Court of the United States as a discretionary device to chose the cases it wishes to hear.

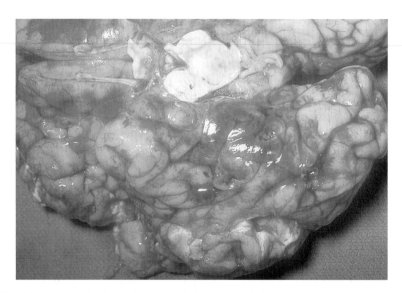

FIGURE C.9 Cerebral edema. Swelling of the brain with flattening of the cerebral convolutions in a case of hyposic or ischemic brain injury. (Courtesy of forensic medical examiner Michael Sikirica, M.D.)

FIGURE C.10 Cerebrum of an adult. (Courtesy of forensic medical examiner Michael Sikirica, M.D.)

Chain of custody (COC) **(1)** Procedures and documents that account for the integrity of a specimen or sample by tracking its handling and storage from its point of collection to its final disposition. **(2)** A process used to maintain and document the chronological history of the evidence.

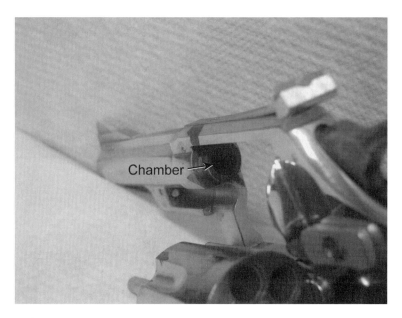

Chamber

FIGURE C.11 Cylinder chambers.

(**3**) Handling samples in a way that supports legal testimony to prove that the sample integrity and identification of the sample have not been violated, as well as the documentation describing these procedures.

Chain reaction A self-propagating chemical reaction in which activation on one molecule leads successfully to activation of many others. One type of chain reaction is called *combustion reaction* .

Challenge for cause Objection to the seating of a particular juror for a stated reason (usually bias or prejudice for or against one of the parties in the lawsuit); the judge has discretion to deny the challenge. Occurs when individuals are interviewed during any jury selection. If the judge agrees that there is a justification for the attorney's claim of bias, a juror may be excused for cause.

Chamber (**Firearms**) The rear part of the barrel bore that has been formed to accept a specific cartridge. Revolver cylinders are multi-chambered (Figure C.11). (**Drug chemistry**) A glass chamber or metal box in which thin-layer chromatography development is carried out for the detection of various drugs (Figure C.12).

Chamber marks Individual microscopic marks placed upon a cartridge case by the chamber wall as a result of any or all of the following: (**1**) chambering, (**2**) expansion during firing, and (**3**) extraction.

Chambers A judge's private office. A hearing in chambers takes place in the judge's office outside of the presence of the jury and the public.

Changing bag Bag made of opaque material that allows film to be loaded into cassettes or tanks outside a darkroom.

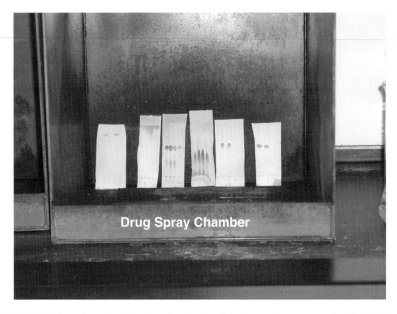

FIGURE C.12 Spraying chamber for developing thin-layer chromatograph (TLC) plates in drug chemistry.

Character (**Bioscience**) Some attribute of an individual within a species for which various heritable differences can be defined. (**Handwriting**) Any typed or handwritten mark, sign, or insignia, abbreviation, punctuation mark, letter, or numeral, whether legible, blurred, or indistinct.

Charred document A document that has become blackened and brittle through burning or through exposure to excessive heat.

Chelex® A chelating resin that has a high affinity for polyvalent metal ions. It is composed of stytrene divinylbenzene copolymers containing paired iminodiacetate ions, which act as chelating groups.

Chemical color tests Chemical reactions producing colors when compounds or classes of compounds are brought into contact with various chemical reagents.

Chemical change Rearrangement of the atoms, ions, or radicals of one or more substances, resulting in the formation of new substances, often having entirely different properties. Also known as a *chemical reaction* .

Chemical enhancement The use of chemicals that react with specific types of evidence (e.g., blood, semen, lead, fingerprints) in order to aid in the detection or documentation of evidence that may be difficult to see.

Chemical etching A form of texturing a mold utilizing an acid bath that erodes selective portion of the metal, leaving a resulting texture or pattern.

Chemical formula The collection of atomic symbols and numbers that indicates the chemical composition of a pure substance.

Chemical ionization   A type of mass spectrometry in which a molecule reacts under relatively low energy with a reagent gas rather than fragmenting extensively.

Chemical-protective clothing   Clothing specifically designed to protect the skin and eyes from direct chemical contact. Descriptions of chemical-protective apparel include nonencapsulating and encapsulating (referred to as liquid-splash protective clothing and vapor-protective clothing, respectively).

Chemical threat   Compounds that may pose bodily harm if touched, ingested, inhaled, or ignited. These compounds may be encountered at a clandestine laboratory, or through a homemade bomb or tankard leakage (e.g., ether, alcohol, nitroglycerin, ammonium sulfate, red phosphorus, cleaning supplies, gasoline, or unlabeled chemicals).

Chemiluminescence   Nonradioactive method for DNA analysis using VNTR probes that are tagged with alkaline phosphatase, which reacts with a detection reagent to generate light. The light produces an image on an x-ray film.

Chemistry   A basic science concerned with (**1**) the structure and behavior of atoms (elements); (**2**) the composition and properties of compounds; (**3**) the reactions that occur between substances and the resultant energy exchange; and (**4**) the laws that unite these phenomena into a comprehensive system.

Child abuse   Act of commission by a parent or caregiver that is not accidental and that harms or threatens to harm a child's physical or mental health or welfare.

Child neglect   Failure of a parent or other person legally responsible for a child's welfare to provide for the child's basic needs and a proper level of care with respect to food, clothing, shelter, hygiene, medical attention, or supervision. Child neglect is an act of omission.

Child pornography   Pictures or other visual media portraying a child involved in sexual activity.

Child prostitution   Form of sexual exploitation in which a child is solicited for sexual conduct or contact.

Chimera   An organism whose cells derive from two or more distinct zygote lineages, e.g., the vascular anastomoses that may occur between twins (a twin of genetic type O may have a bone marrow implantation from its twin of group A; throughout life, therefore, he has a major red cell population of group O and a minor population of red cells of group A).

Chi-square (χ^2)   A statistical test to determine how closely an observed set of data values corresponds to the values expected, under a specific hypothesis.

Chitin   A nitrogenous polysaccharide formed primarily of units of N-acetyl glucosamine occurring in the cuticle of arthropods.

Chlordiazepoxide hydrochloride   Crystals, toxic in high concentration, that are one type of central nervous system depressant.

Chloroform   An early use of chloroform was that of an anesthetic in some types of surgeries. Chloroform undergoes considerable biotransformation in man, with the formation of carbon dioxide and hydrochloric acid.

Choke/shotgun   The constriction of the barrel of a shotgun to reduce the spread of shot as it leaves the gun to increase its effective range.

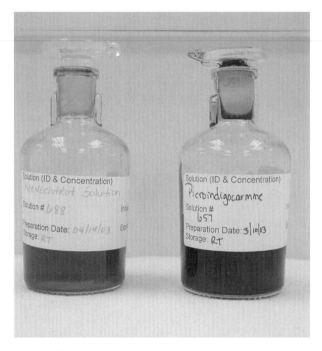

FIGURE C.13 Chemical regents used for the staining of spermatozoa or sperm cells.

Chop shop   A location, often an automobile repair shop or salvage yard, where a stolen car is stripped of its parts (radio, doors, trunk lid, engine, etc.); the remains are cut up and sold for scrap metal.

Choropleth map   A thematic map that uses colors or shading to depict variations in area-based data.

Christmas tree stain   Two chemicals used together to stain sperm cells; *Kernechtrot solution* will stain the head of the sperm cell a two-tone reddish pink color and the *picroindigocarmine solution* will stain the tail of the sperm cell a bluish green color (Figure C.13).

Chromatin   A darkly staining substance located in the nucleus of the cell that contains the genetic material composed of deoxyribonucleic acid (DNA) attached to a protein structure.

Chromatogram   The complete array of distinctively colored bands produced by chromatography. A series of peaks and valleys printed or written on a paper chart where each peak represents a component or mixture of two or more unresolved components in a mixture separated by gas or liquid chromatography (Figure C.14).

Chromatography   A method for the separation and analysis of small quantities of substances by passing a solution through a column of finely divided powder that selectively adsorbs the constituents in one or more sharply defined, often colored, bands. This method for separation can be done using thin-layer silica plates (Figure C.15).

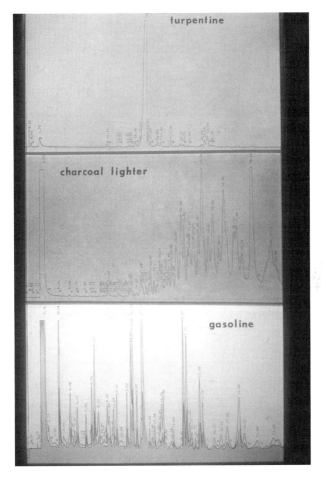

FIGURE C.14 Gas chromatograms of turpentine, charcol lighter fluid, and gasoline. A special high-resolution column known as a capillary column was used. The mixture of hydrocarbon is separated into its compoinents, with the peaks representing at least one different component.

Chromogen   Any organic coloring matter or substance capable of yielding a dye.

Chromosome   A nuclear structure in eukaryotes that carries a portion of the genome. The human has 46 chromosomes per nucleus, 22 homologous pairs of autosomes, and 2 sex chromosomes.

Chromosome theory of inheritance   The unifying theory stating that inheritance patterns may be generally explained by assuming that genes are located in specific sites on chromosomes.

Chronic   Persistent, prolonged, repeated.

Chronic condition   Disability or illness that persists for a long time or for a person's entire life; also known as *chronic illness* .

Chronic effect   A pathologic process caused by repeated exposures over a period of long duration.

FIGURE C.15 The separation of drugs that have been spotted on thin-layer silica plates. Special chemical sprays that produce a color reaction are applied to the plates. This method of separation is performed inside a spraying chamber.

Chronic exposure   Repeated encounters with a hazardous substance over a period of long duration.

Chronic tolerance   The gradual decrease in degree of effect produced at the same blood concentration in the course of repeated exposure to that drug.

Chronograph   An instrument for recording graphically the moment or duration of an event, measuring intervals of time.

Chrysotile   A fibrous form of serpentine that constitutes one type of asbestos.

Cicero   A typographic unit of measurement used predominantly in Europe. It consists of 12 Didot points, each measuring 0.01483 in. Thus, a Cicero is 0.1776 in. or 4.511 mm.

CIL (Canadian Industries Ltd.)   Imperial/Canuck. A firearms and ammunition manufacturer.

Circle of confusion   An optical term describing the size of an image point formed by a lens.

Circumstantial evidence   That evidence that only suggests an association with a past occurrence. Any evidence in a case for which an inference is needed to relate it to the crime. Not observed by an eyewitness. Most physical evidence, with the exception of blood alcohol determination and drug identification, is circumstantial. DNA evidence is circumstantial. Fact from which another fact can be reasonably inferred. For example, proof that a parent kept a broken appliance cord may connect the parent to the infliction of unique marks on a child's body.

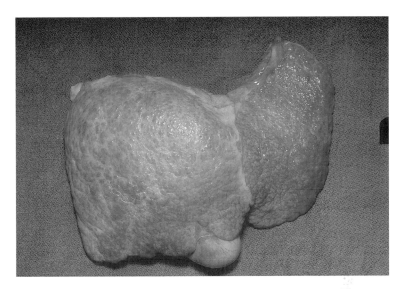

FIGURE C.16 Cirrhosis of the liver in a long-term alcoholic.

Cirrhosis Fibrosis of the liver, can be caused from long-term alcoholism; also
    may be caused by viral infections or metabolic disease (Figure C.16).

Civil Of or pertaining to the state or its citizenry. Relates to an individual's
    private rights and remedies sought through civil action, in contrast to
    criminal proceedings.

Civil commitment The legal proceeding by which a person who is mentally ill
    and imminently dangerous is involuntarily committed to a psychiatric
    hospital.

Class A group of items that share common properties.

Class characteristic Not all characteristics encountered in document examina-
    tion are peculiar to a single person or thing, and one that is common to
    a group may be described as a class characteristic. Traits that define a
    group of items collectively.

Clicker Small, hand-held device that makes a clicking noise; used as a condi-
    tioned reinforcement to signal to a dog that it did the desired behavior
    and a reward is coming.

Clingers Aquatic insect representatives that have behavioral and morphological
    adaptations for attachment to surfaces in stream riffles and wave-swept
    rocky zones of lakes (e.g., *Ephemeroptera* , *Heptageniidae* , *Trichoptera* ,
    Hydropsychidae).

Clip A separate cartridge container used to rapidly reload the magazine of a
    firearm. Sometimes improperly used to describe removable magazine.
    Also called *stripper*.

Clitoris Erectile tissue in females analogous to a male penis, located above the
    urethra and covered by the clitoral hood.

Clogged (dirty) typeface   Over prolonged use, the typeface becomes filled with lint, dirt, and ink, particularly in letters with closed loops, such as o, e, p, and g. If this condition is allowed to continue without cleaning, the printed impression will actually print with the clogged areas shaded or solid black.

Clone   Describes a large number of cells or molecules identical with a single ancestral cell or molecule.

Close grid search   Pattern where a dog works within 5 to 15 ft ahead of the handler quartering the wind; the handler can observe the dog.

Close surveillance   The subject is kept under constant surveillance, the aim of which is not to lose the subject even at the risk of being discovered (also called *tight surveillance*).

Close-up   A photograph taken close to the subject or evidence, often requiring an auxiliary lens. *Macro* and *micro* are degrees of close-up.

Closing argument   Attorney's final statement to the court summing up the case and the points proven as well as those points not proven by opposing counsel; also known as *final argument* .

Clot   A blood clot is formed by a complex mechanism involving plasma protein fibrinogens, platelets, and other clotting factors. It is observed as a network of fibrous material (fibrin and red blood cells). Subsequently, the blood clot begins to retract, causing a separation of the remaining liquid portion that is now referred to as *serum* .

Cloth ribbon   A type of ribbon used in some models of typewriters.

Cluster   The smallest unit of disk data storage.

CMOS   Complementary metal-oxide semiconductor; a type of low-power memory that stores information about the configuration of IBM clone AT. A battery operates it, so it is not erased when the machine is turned off. When the battery goes dead, so does the computer's ability to communicate with various components.

Coagulation   The process of stopping blood flow from a wound. This involves the harmonious relationship of the blood-clotting factors, the blood vessels, and the fibrin-forming and fibrin-lysing system.

Coagulopathy   A disease affecting the blood-clotting process.

Cocaine   A colorless to white crystalline powder. Used as a local anesthetic (medicine or dentistry), usually as the hydrochloride. Also known by street names, such as *coke* , *snow*, or *freebase* .

Codeine   A narcotic alkaloid that is used in medicine and cough syrups; highly toxic and habit-forming narcotic.

CODIS (Combined DNA Index System)   CODIS refers to the entire system of DNA indexes (convicted offender index, close biological relatives index, population file, forensic index, unidentified persons index, missing persons index, and victim index) maintained at the national, state, and local levels.

CODIS comparisons   Comparisons of one DNA record to another for the purpose of establishing an association between two specimens.

Coefficient of form A numerical term indicating the general profile of a projectile.

Coefficient of inbreeding (F) The proportion of homozygous loci in an individual, or the probability that both alleles at corresponding loci were inherited from the same ancestor.

Coefficient of relationship (r) The proportion of genes that any two individuals have in common. It is the proportion of the genomes inherited from a common ancestor, or the probability that two individuals have inherited a specific gene or DNA fragment from a common ancestor.

Coefficient of variation (CV) or Relative standard deviation Measure used to compare the dispersion of variation in groups of measurements. It is the ratio of the standard deviation (SD) to the mean (X), multiplied by 100 to convert it to a percentage of the average. $CV = SD\ X \times 100$.

Cognition Processes involved in thinking, including perceiving, recognizing, conceiving, judging, and reasoning.

Cognitive Related to the process used for remembering, reasoning, understanding, thinking, or using judgment.

Cognitive avoidance Strategy that focuses on trying to forget a situation by distracting oneself to keep from thinking about a situation, or blaming someone else for one's predicament.

Cognitive interview Guided memory search, using techniques designed to enhance a witness's memory of an event by facilitating complete and accurate reporting.

Cold match A cold match occurs when CODIS matches two DNA profiles with no prior indication that the profiles are related. One profile may be in the offender index and the other in the forensic index, or both profiles may be in the forensic index. Cold matches must be confirmed by qualified DNA analysts.

Collaborative studies or Interlaboratory test comparisons Organization, performance, and evaluation of tests on the same or similar items or materials by two or more different laboratories in accordance with predetermined conditions. The main purpose is validation of analytical methods or establishment of reference methods.

Collagen A fibrous insoluble protein found in the connective tissue, including skin, bone, ligaments, and cartilage; represents about 30% of the total body protein.

Collateral material Articles not directly associated with a sex offender's crimes but that provide evidence or information regarding sexual preferences, interests, or activities. These can be erotic, educational, introspective, or intelligence material.

Collected standards A sample of writing made during the normal course of business or social activity, not necessarily related to the matter in dispute.

Collision-primary The impact between a vehicle and another vehicle or a vehicle and a fixed object.

Collision-secondary The impact between the occupant and some interior component of the vehicle.

Collision-tertiary The impact between the occupant and the restraint system.

Collodion Cellulose nitrate deposited from a solution of 60% ether and 40% alcohol; used for making fibers and film in membranes.

Color The sensation produced in the eye by a particular wavelength or group of wavelengths of visible light.

Color balance The ability of a film to reproduce the colors of a scene. Color films are balanced in manufacture for exposure to light of a certain color quality daylight, tungsten, etc. Color balance also refers to the reproduction of colors in color prints, which can be altered during the printing process.

Color balancing filter Filters used to balance color film with the color temperature of the light source and to prevent the formation of colorcasts. An 85B filter is used with tungsten film in daylight, an 80A filter with daylight film in tungsten light.

Color compensating (CC) filters Comparatively weak color filters used to correct for small differences between the color temperature of the illumination and that for which the film was manufactured.

Color conversion filters Fairly strong color filters used for exposing film in light of a type markedly different from that for which the film was made.

Color negative film Film that records the colors of the subject in complementary hues that are subsequently reversed again in the printing paper to give the correct colors.

Color reversing film Film that produces a direct positive by effectively reversing the negative image during processing. Transparency (slide) film is of this type.

Colt Firearms A firearms manufacturer.

Coma State of profound unconsciousness from which the patient cannot be aroused.

Combination gun A multiple-barreled firearm designed to handle different sizes or types of ammunition.

Combustible liquid Any liquid that has a flash point at or above 100°F (37.7°C) and below 200°F (93.3°C).

Combustion An exothermic chain reaction between oxidation and reducing agents, or between oxygen and fuel.

Common law Body of law based on judicial decisions (precedents or customs and usages); generally derived from justice, reason, and common sense rather than legislative enactments.

Comparison The act of setting two or more items side by side to weigh their identifying qualities. It implies not only a visual but also a mental act in which the elements of one item are related to the counterparts of the other.

Comparison microscope Essentially two microscopes connected to an optical bridge that allows the viewer to observe two objects simultaneously with the same degree of magnification. This instrument can have a monocular or binocular eyepiece (Figure C.17).

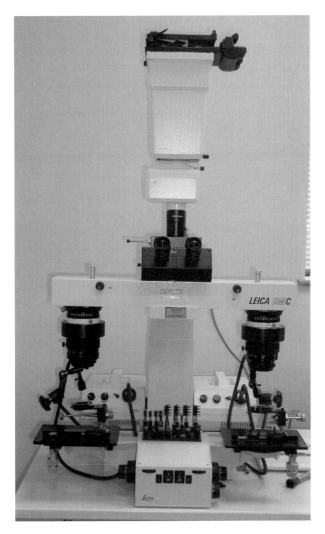

FIGURE C.17 A firearms examiner's (ballistics) comparison microscope. It has an optical bridge, separate objectives, dual focusing stages, specimen holders, and two illuminators, the angles and intensities of which are independently adjustable.

Comparison samples A generic term used to describe physical material/evidence discovered at crime scenes that may be compared with samples from persons, tools, and physical locations. Comparison samples may be from either an **unknown/questioned** or a **known** source.

Samples whose source is **unknown/questioned** are of three basic types:

1. Recovered crime scene samples whose source is in question (e.g., evidence left by suspect and/or victims).

2. Questioned evidence that may have been transferred to an offender during the commission of the crime and taken away by him or her. Such questioned evidence can be compared with evidence of a known source and can thereby be associated/linked to a person/vehicle/tool of a crime.
3. Evidence of an unknown/questioned source recovered from several crime scenes may also be used to associate multiple offenses that were committed by the same person and with the same tool or weapon.

Samples whose source is **known** are of three types:

1. A **standard/reference** sample is material of a verifiable/documented source which, when compared with evidence of an unknown source, shows an association or linkage between an offender, crime scene, or victim.
2. A **control/blank** sample is material of a known source that presumably was uncontaminated during the commission of the crime.
3. An **elimination** sample is one known source taken from a person who had lawful access to the scene, to be used for comparison with evidence of the same type.

Compensator   Any variety of optical devices that can be placed in the light path of a polarizing microscope to introduce fixed or variable retardation comparable with that exhibited by the fiber. The retardation and signs of elongation of the fiber may then be determined. Compensators may employ a fixed mineral plate of constant or varying thickness or a mineral plate that may be rotated to alter the thickness presented to the optical path (and retardation introduced) by a set amount.

Competence to plead guilty   The ability of a defendant to understand the possible consequences of pleading guilty to criminal charges instead of going to trial and to make a rational choice between the alternatives.

Competency   In the law of evidence, possession of characteristics that qualify a witness to observe, recall, and testify under oath; personal qualifications of the witness to give testimony, which differs from the witness's ability to tell the truth.

Competency test   The evaluation of a person's ability to perform work in any functional area prior to the performance of independent casework.

Complainant   (1) The party who complains or sues; one who applies to the court for legal redress, also called the *plaintiff*. (2) Legal document that initiates the criminal court process; written statement by the investigating officer(s), outlining the facts in a particular criminal violation and charging the suspect with the crime. The complaint must include facts to support a finding that probable cause exists to believe a crime has been committed and the defendant suspect committed it, and it must outline the element of the crime. Although the officer is called the complainant, ordinarily the district or county attorney's office will prepare the complaint, using the officer's written report, and have the officer sign it.

Complete digestion   The action of a restriction enzyme in completely cutting the DNA at a specific site.

Compound   A chemical combination of two or more elements, or two or more different atoms arranged in the same proportions and in the same structure throughout the substance. A compound is different from a mixture in that the components of a mixture are not chemically bonded together.

Compression molded   A molding method, in which a molding compound is placed into an open mold cavity, after which the mold is closed as heat and pressure are applied, causing the molding compound to melt and conform to the size and shape characteristics of the mold cavity.

Concentration   The amount of a substance in a stated unit of a mixture or solution. Common methods of stating concentration are percent by weight, percent by volume, or weight per unit volume. Amount of a drug in a unit volume of biological fluid, expressed as weight/volume. Urine concentrations are usually expressed either as nanograms per milliliter (ng/ml), micrograms per milliliter (μg/ml), or milligram per liter (mg/l). Example: there are 28,000,000 micrograms in an ounce, and 1000 nanograms in a microgram.

Concentrator   A device used to attach workstations and servers to a 10 Base-T network.

Concentric fractures   Patterns of cracks in glass pierced by a missile like a bullet, which runs between the radial fractures and which originate on the side of the glass from which the impact came.

Conclusion   A scientific conclusion results from relating observed facts by logical, common sense reasoning in accordance with established rules or laws.

Concur (legal)   To agree with the judgment of another. When one court concurs with another, it agrees with or follows the precedent set by that court's decision.

Concurrent sentence   Sentences for more than one violation that are to be served at the same time rather than one after the other. Three 5-year terms served concurrently add up to no more than 5 years imprisonment; three 5-year terms served consecutively impose a 15-year sentence.

Concussion   Sudden shock to or jarring of the brain, which may or may not cause a loss of consciousness.

Conductivity   The ability of a material to transfer energy from one place to another. Thermal conductivity describes a substance's ability to transmit heat. Electrical conductivity describes a substance's ability to transmit electrical current. Conductivity is the opposite of *resistivity* .

Confession   An oral or written statement acknowledging guilt.

Confidence interval   Range of values that contains the true value at a given level of probability. A statistical measure of confidence is a calculated value. A 95% confidence interval equates to the expectation that the value in question will lie within the range stated 95% of the time and outside the range 5%. A certain allele in a population may have a calculated frequency of 1 in 500 people with confidence limits of 1 in 400 to 1 in

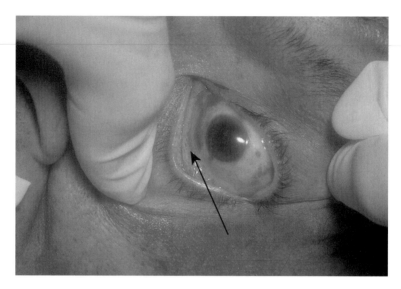

FIGURE C.18 Conjunctiva. (Courtesy of forensic medical examiner Michael Sikirica, M.D.)

600 at the 99% confidence interval. This level of probability is called the *confidence level* .

Confidence level or Confidence coefficient   Measure of probability, as associated with a confidence interval, expressing the probability of the truth of a statement that the interval will include the parameter value.

Confidence limits   The extreme values or end values in a confidence interval. Limits attached to a confidence interval. The 95% confidence limits, for example, when measuring a 10-kb allele on a gel in a certain laboratory may be 9.9 to 10.1 kb.

CONFIG.SYS   A text file generally found in the root directory of a bootable floppy disk or hard disk on a computer running MS/PC-DOS or OS/2 that establishes the first level of the operating environment as the computer is booting up.

Confirmatory test   Second test by an alternative chemical method for unambiguous identification of a drug or metabolite. In serology, a chemical reaction that confirms the presence of a blood stain as human or nonhuman in origin.

Conjoined letters   Two letters that have been written in the common manner such that the terminal stroke of the first is the initial stroke of the second.

Conjunctiva (*plural* conjunctivae)   The delicate mucous membrane that covers the exposed surface of the eyeball and lines the eyelids (Figure C.18).

Connecting stroke   An expression commonly used to refer to the fusion of the terminal stroke of one lowercase cursive letter and the initial stroke of another, having no identifiable or describable entity of its own.

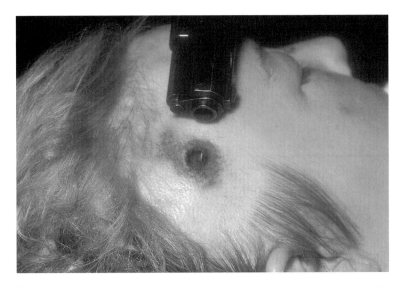

FIGURE C.19 Contact wound in a suicide with a .380 caliber handgun. (Courtesy of forensic medical examiner Michael Sikirica, M.D.)

Connection subtypes

> **Supported** — The body of the letter rests against or retraces the stem.
> **Looped** — The initial stroke forms a loop with the stem of the letter.
> **Unsupported** — The body of the letter does not follow or retrace the stem.

Consensus value   Value produced by a group of experts or referee laboratories using the best possible methods. It is an estimate of the true value.

Consent search   Exception to the requirement for a search warrant; written or oral permission is required from a person with authority to give it.

Consequence Management   Measures to protect public health and safety; restore essential government; and provide emergency relief to governments, businesses, and individuals from the consequences of terrorism. FEMA is the lead agency as stated in a Presidential Decision Directive (PDD).

Conservative estimate   An estimate designed to deliberately overestimate the occurrence of any particular profile in the population. Depending on the circumstances of the case, this may or may not "favor the defendant."

Conspiracy   A combination of two or more persons who purpose is to commit an unlawful or criminal act, or to commit a lawful act by criminal means.

Contact wound   A wound that results when a small weapon is fired in contact with the skin. May be divided into tight or loose contact wounds based on the amount of pressure used against the skin (Figure C.19).

Contempt of court   (**1**) Willful disobedience of a judge's command or of an official court order. Either an act or an omission tending to obstruct or interfere with the orderly administration of justice in the court. (**2**) To impair the dignity of the court or to impair respect for its authority.

FIGURE C.20 Small balloons filled with drugs recovered from the stomach of a body packer after rupture of one balloon. (Courtesy of forensic medical examiner Michael Sikirica, M.D.)

Continuance (legal)   Court order that postpones legal action, such as a court hearing, until a later time.

Contraband   In forensic toxicology and drug testing facilities, this refers to suspected controlled substances (Figure C.20).

Contraction   A form of word abbreviation wherein one or more letters are omitted.

Contrast   The difference in intensities of light falling on various parts of a subject. The density range of a negative, print, or slide; the brightness range of a subject or the scene lighting.

Contrast filter   A colored filter used to make a colored subject stand out either lighter or darker (for black-and-white film).

Control chart   Plot of test results with respect to time or sequence of measurements, with limits drawn within which results are expected to lie when the analytical scheme is in a state of statistical control.

Control limits   The limits shown on a control chart beyond which it is highly improbable that a point could lie while the system remains in a state of statistical control.

Control zones   Areas at a hazardous materials incident whose boundaries are based on safety and the degree of hazard; generally includes the hot zone, decontamination zone, and support zone.

Controlled substances (discipline)   The identification of controlled drug substances either in pure, legal, or illicit dosage forms.

Controlling   Establishing standards of performance, measuring current performance in relation to established standards, and taking corrective action as required.

Controls   Samples of predetermined concentration (known or unknown to the analyst) treated as unknowns in an assay. Controls are included as part of quality control for each test run. Specimens or samples used to determine the validity of the calibration, i.e., the linearity and stability of a quantitative test or determination over time. Controls are prepared from the reference material (separately from the calibrators, i.e., weighed or measured separately), purchased, or obtained from a pool of previously analyzed specimens or samples. Where possible, controls should be matrix-matched to specimens or samples and calibrators. Reference controls are those samples from a known individual or from a known source.

Contusion   A bruise that is either superficial or internal. An injury caused by blunt object impact without laceration with surface discoloration due to subsurface hemorrhaging. An injury to subsurface tissue caused by a blow from a blunt instrument that does not break the skin.

Contusion ring   Bruising at the edges of a gunshot wound caused by penetration of the skin by a bullet.

Convection   Transfer of heat by the movement of molecules in a gas or liquid, with the less dense fluid rising. The majority of heat transfer in a fire is by convection.

Convicted offender file   The CODIS computer file (or index) that contains DNA identification records resulting from the DNA profiling of convicted offenders.

Convicted offender laboratory   The forensic DNA laboratory responsible for a DNA profile developed from a sample provided by a known convicted offender.

Convicted offender sample   A biological sample containing DNA that is collected from a convicted offender for the purpose of DNA profiling. These DNA profiles are used to establish an index of DNA identification records that can then be searched for matches against the DNA derived from a crime scene DNA profile.

Convicted offenders   Persons who have been convicted of crimes in federal, state, or local courts where the applicable law permits establishment of a DNA record for the convicted person.

Conviction   A judgment of guilt against a criminal defendant.

Conviction match   A conviction match occurs when CODIS matches a DNA profile developed from crime scene evidence to a DNA profile from a convicted offender, but the crime from which the evidence was collected, has already been solved. The convicted offender's DNA profile matching against the evidence used to convict him or her usually causes a conviction match. For *inter*state matches, a conviction match usually indicates that the perpetrator has been convicted of a different crime in another state. This is not a cold hit, because the information is most likely captured in the state's criminal history record system.

Convoy   A countermeasure to detect a surveillance; a convoy, usually a person, is employed to determine whether or not a subject is under surveillance.

Convulsion   Involuntary muscle contraction and relaxation.

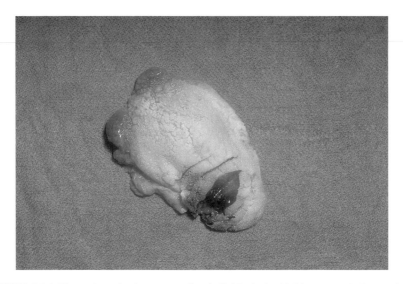

FIGURE C.21 Hemorrhage in the tongue of an individual who bit his tongue during a seizure or convulsion. (Courtesy of forensic medical examiner Michael Sikirica, M.D.)

Convulsive disorder   Clinical syndrome, the central feature of which is recurrent muscular seizures. Also, recurrent disturbances of consciousness, with or without muscular components and accompanied by changes in the electrical potential of the brain (Figure C.21).

Copper-clad steel   A composite structure of copper and steel used for the manufacture of certain bullet jackets. Metallic element with the chemical symbol Cu and atomic number 29 that commonly comprises "cartridge brass" that is typically 70% copper and 30% zinc (Zn).

Copy pencil   A pencil whose marking substance consists of a mixture of graphite and aniline dye. When the pencil stroke is moistened the dye develops into a strong purple or in some cases, a blue color. The developed stroke is more difficult to erase than ordinary pencil writing. Some refer to this kind of writing instrument as an *indelible pencil* .

Cord cell   Fetal cells obtained from the umbilical cord at birth. They may be contaminated with Wharton's jelly.

Core   A fiber or fibers running lengthwise through the center of a cordage.

Cornea   The transparent membrane that covers the colored part of the eye.

Coronary artery   Either of two arteries arising in the aortic sinuses that supply the heart tissue with blood.

Coroner   An officer responsible for determining manner and cause of death. A court official in medieval England whose duties included investigating sudden and unexpected deaths and deaths from injury; in the United States, an elected official with death investigation duties.

Corpse   A dead human body sometimes referred to as *remains* or *the deceased* .

Corpus delicti   The proof that a crime has been committed — consisting of two components: (**1**) that each element of the crime be satisfied and (**2**) that someone is responsible for inflicting the injury or loss sustained. "Body of the crime." For the state to introduce a confession or convict the accused, it must prove a *corpus delicti* , i.e., the occurrence of specific injury or loss and a criminal act as the source of the loss.

Correction filter Filters used to alter colors to suit the color response of the film.

Correlation The process of comparing the signatures of acquired images. The IBIS correlation engine compares images by examining how similar the two signatures are.

Correlation coefficient A statistical measure of the extent to which variations in one variable are related to variations in another.

Corridor Arbitrary parallel paths to be traversed in searching an area, perpendicular to the search baseline and backline, and starting at the anchor point.

Corroborating evidence Supplementary evidence that tends to strengthen or confirm the initial evidence.

Corrosion The degradation of metals or alloys due to reaction with the environment. The corrosive action on the metals or alloys is accelerated by acids, bases, or heat.

Corrosive Having the ability to destroy the texture or substance of a tissue.

Cortex The middle layer of human hair containing the particles of pigment that gives the hair its individual color. The main structural component of hair consisting of elongated and fusiform (spindle-shaped) cells. The cortex may contain pigment grains, air spaces called *corticalfusi* , and structures called *ovoid bodies* . Also refers to the outer layer of an organ such as the brain or kidney.

Coupled exposure meter Exposure meter built into the camera and linked with the aperture or shutter speed controls, or both.

Coupled rangefinder A rangefinder connected to the focusing mechanism of the lens, which is focused while measuring the distance to the subject or object.

Court-appointed special advocate (CASA) Individual (usually a volunteer) who serves to ensure that the needs and best interests of a child in judicial proceedings are fully protected.

Court Martial Military tribunal that has jurisdiction of offenses against laws of the service in which the offender is engaged. Military status is not sufficient. The crime must be service-connected.

> **General** Presided over by a law officer, has not less than five members, tries defendants on all military offenses, and can prescribe any permitted sanction.
>
> **Special** Presided over by three members, may try noncapital offenses, but limited in authority as to sanctions that can be prescribed.
>
> **Summary** Presided over by a single commissioned officer, and limited in respect to the personnel over whom it can operate and sanctions it may prescribe. The accused may refuse trial by summary court martial, but the charges can then be referred to a higher level.

Court order   Directive, issued by the court that has the authority of the court and is enforceable as law; written command or directive given by the judge.

Crack   Concentrated form of cocaine, which is used in vapor form. It is smoked or inhaled through *crack pipes*. It is a highly addictive drug that causes psychotic behavior, which is often violent. Almost pure form of the drug cocaine hydrochloride, obtained from a shrub native to Bolivia and Peru. It can cause increased alertness and energy, runny nose, and decreased appetite when snorted, injected, or smoked.

Cracker   A person who enters a computer system illegally to commit a crime such as sabotage or theft of information.

Creep   Movement of the bullet out of the cartridge case while in the cylinder or chamber.

Crepe rubber   A natural, unvulcanized rubber used for soles and heels. Most crepe rubber made today is synthetic crepe rubber.

Crime location   A geographic location associated with a given crime. There may be several different locations connected to a single crime; for example, in a homicide there may be the victim's encounter, an attack, the murder, and a body dump site.

Crime scene (discipline)   The identification, documentation, collection, and/or interpretation of material at a location external to a laboratory facility. Scene reconstruction is also part of this discipline.

Crime scene documentation   May include notes or examination documentation, photographs, video, sketches, and other documents (including electronic versions) that are used to record and support the actions or conclusions of an examiner.

Crime scene reconstruction   The process of determining the nature of events that occurred at a scene from an evaluation of physical evidence and other relevant information. Analysis and reconstruction of a crime scene that logically links a detailed series of scientific *explanations* to provide an understanding of the sequence of events. Each explanation is developed, linked, and evaluated by applying *scientific method* to available data. This process involves proposing, testing, and evaluating explanatory connections among the physical evidence related to the events. The purpose of the analysis is to find the *best explanation* of related events.

Crime scene security and integrity   The actions necessary to control access to a scene; establish and maintain a record of custody and control for a scene and all items collected from a scene; and protect against loss, cross contamination, or deleterious change of evidence or potential evidence within a scene.

Crime scope (CS-16)®   A complete system for fluorescence examination; rugged and compact instrument that may be used in the laboratory or at a crime scene (Figure C.22).

Criminal court   Court that has jurisdiction over cases alleging violations of criminal law. Some judicial districts do not distinguish between the types

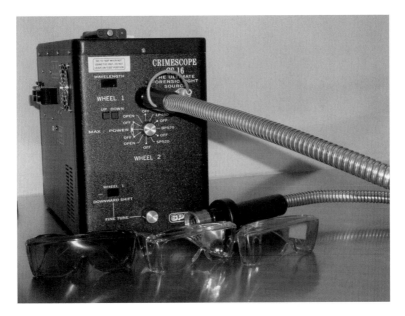

FIGURE C.22 An alternate light source made by SPEX® uses different wavelengths of light. With special color glasses one can observe various types of stains found on evidence.

of cases a particular judge will hear; in other jurisdictions, specific judges are assigned to criminal court.

Criminal geographic targeting (CGT)   A computerized spatial profiling model that determines the most probable area of offender residence through the production of a jeopardy surface or geoprofile from a criminal hunting algorithm. It is the primary methodology used in geographic profiling.

Criminal homicide   The unlawful taking of a human life.

Criminal investigative analysis   Use of investigative techniques including indirect personality assessment, equivocal death analysis, investigative suggestion, trial strategy, characteristics and traits (profile) of an individual.

Criminal justice agency   An agency or institution of the federal, state, or local government, other than the office of the public defender that performs as part of its principal function, activities relating to the apprehension, investigation, prosecution, adjudication, incarceration, supervision, or rehabilitation of criminal offenders.

Criminal justice system interviewer   Interviewer whose goal is to obtain objective, verifiable information from the child, the parents, and the offender that will meet legal standards for admissibility to court.

Criminal profiling   The use of psychological principles as a crime investigation technique to guide police toward suspects who possess certain personal characteristics as revealed by the way a crime was committed.

Criminal prosecution Process that begins with the filing of charges against a person who has allegedly violated criminal law and includes the arraignment and trial of the defendant. Criminal prosecution may result in fines, restitution, imprisonment, or probation. Most criminal defendants are entitled to a jury trial.

Criminalistics The scientific recognition, identification, preservation, and interpretation of physical evidence.

Criminology The scientific study and investigation of crime and criminals.

Criterion or criteria Objective test to evaluate whether the laboratory activity meets the standard. This is often a restatement of the standard in the form of a question that can be answered yes, no, or not applicable (n/a).

Critical reagents Reagents such as commercial supplies and kits that have an expiration date. A substance used because of its chemical or biological activity. These reagents are essential to certain chemical reactions.

Cropping The elimination of part of an original image on a single negative during printing either because of automation or enlargement.

Cross-examination The questioning of a witness produced by the other side.

Cross-reacting substance In immunoassays, refers to substances that react with antiserum produced specifically for other substances.

Cross sensitivity A quantitative measure of the response for an undesired constituent or interferent as compared to that for a constituent of interest.

Cue Signal provided by the trainer that a certain routine or set of behaviors is expected.

Cursive A form of continuous writing, in which letters are connected to one another, and designed according to some commercial system; the most common allograph of a grapheme.

Custody hearing Legal process, usually in family or juvenile court, to determine who has the right of legal or physical custody of a minor. It may involve one parent against the other, a parent against a third party, or a parent against a social services agency seeking protective custody in juvenile court.

Cusum chart In a cusum chart, each result is compared with a reference, usually the assigned or target value. The differences from the reference are then accumulated, respecting the sign, to give a cumulative sum of differences from the standard. The cusum chart has the advantage of identifying small persistent changes in the analytical scheme faster than the Shewhart chart.

Cuticle **(Hair analysis)** The protective outer sheath of the hair, formed by a series of overlapping scales. **(Entomology)** The outer covering of insects and arthropods that is made of chitin.

Cut-off concentration Concentration of a drug in a specimen or sample used to determine whether the specimen or sample is considered positive or negative. In some circumstances it is recommended that the cut-off concentration should be set equal to the limit of detection.

Cutoff level (threshold) Value serving as an administrative breakpoint (or cutoff point) for labeling a screening test result positive or negative.

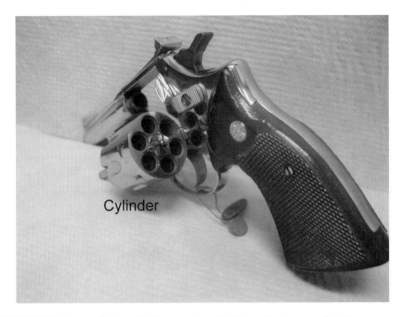

Cylinder

FIGURE C.23 The revolving cylinder contains six firing chambers, each able to accommodate a single cartridge.

Cutouts   Individuals used by criminal enterprise organizations who know nothing about the operation other than the message being passed.

Cyanide (CN)   A highly toxic chemical especially in the form of gas (hydrogen cyanide).

Cyanoacrylate fuming   Important method for the visualization of latent fingerprints; also called *super glue fuming* .

Cyanosis   Bluish discoloration of the skin and mucous membrane due to deficient oxygenation of the blood; usually evident when reduced hemoglobin exceeds 5%. It is present in many heart and respiratory conditions.

Cyber forensics   The extraction of evidence that particular digital data passed over some medium between two points in a network.

Cylinder   Rotating chambered breech of a revolver (Figure C.23).

Cytochrome P450   A detoxifying enzyme found in liver cells.

Cytosine (C)   One of the four nucleotide bases in DNA.

D

DAB DNA Advisory Board. A board on DNA quality assurance methods appointed by the FBI director in accordance with the DNA Identification Act of 1994.

Damages Money awarded by a court to a person injured by the unlawful act or negligence of another person.

Damascus barrel An obsolete barrel-making process. The barrel is formed by twisting or braiding together steel and iron wires or bars. The resulting cable is then wound around a mandrel and forged into a barrel tube. This type of barrel is also called a *laminated barrel* .

Dangerousness Behavior that involves acts of physical violence or aggression by one person against another.

Dark-field microscopy Descriptive of the appearance of the image of the specimen when this technique is used. Various details of the specimen appear as bright features on a dark field or background. Dark-field microscopy can be used to accentuate refraction images.

Daubert test A standard for determining the reliability of scientific expert testimony in court currently adopted by many jurisdictions. Five factors are utilized to assess the scientific theory or technique testing of theory, use of standard and controls, peer review, error rate, and acceptability in the relevant scientific community.

Daylight color film Color film designed to be used with daylight or a light source of equivalent color temperature, including blue flashbulbs and electronic flash. The film is balanced to 5400 EK.

Death The loss of life characterized clinically by combined failure of respiratory, cardiovascular, and nervous system activity.

Decant The process of pouring off the supernatant during separation from a pellet after a mixture has been centrifuged or left to settle.

Deception Conscious distortion of behavior or self-report.

Decipher To determine the meaning of, as hieroglyphics or illegible writing, or to translate from cipher into ordinary characters, or to determine the meaning of anything obscure.

Decision The judgment reached or given by a court of law.

Decision rule The requirement whether a jury must reach a unanimous verdict or whether a majority vote will suffice for a verdict.

Declination The difference between true north as shown on a topographic map and magnetic north as indicated by the magnetic needle on a compass.

Decomposition Postmortem degenerative rotting of the corpse. Chemical breakdown, separating compounds into their component parts; includes breakdown

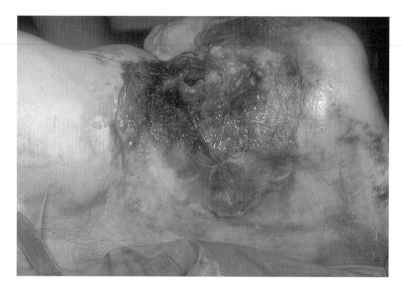

FIGURE D.1 Decubitus formation on the back of an elderly adult; severe due to prolonged immobilization in bed. (Courtesy of forensic medical examiner Michael Sikirica, M.D.)

of proteins by putrefaction, of carbohydrates by fermentation, and of fats by rancidification.

Decontamination (**1**) Removal of hazardous materials from exposed persons and equipment after a hazardous materials incident. (**2**) In the forensic laboratory environment, the cleaning of work benches, scissors, forceps, and other instruments that have come in contact with physical evidence, with 10% bleach and 70% ethanol.

Decubitus May be seen as a bed sore that can produce an ulcer on the body, caused by lying long in one position; this pressure necrosis can be found on elderly patients (Figure D.1).

Default judgment A decision of the court against a defendant because of failure to respond to a plaintiff's action.

Defect Any abnormality or maladjustment in a typewriter that is reflected in its work and leads to its individualization or identification.

Defendant In a civil case, the person being sued. In a criminal case, the person charged with a crime.

Defense wound Stab or incised wounds to the hands, wrists, forearms, and arms that may contain embedded fragments of the weapon (Figure D.2).

Deficiency An inadequacy; lacking in some necessary quality or element. Deficiencies include missing data, incomplete data, or incomplete reports.

Definition Clarity, sharpness, resolution, and brilliance of an image formed by the lens.

Deflagrate To burn with intense heat and light, i.e., gunpowder is said to deflagrate.

Deformable impression An impression that causes the surface to deform, either permanently or temporarily. Permanent deformable impression would

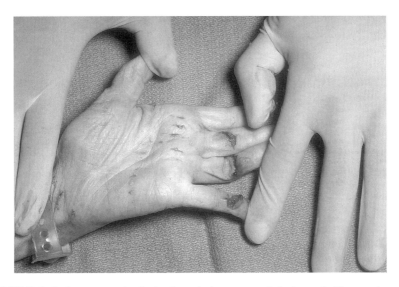

FIGURE D.2 Defense wounds (incised type) that occurred during a knife assault as the deceased attempted to grab a sharp serrated blade. (Courtesy of forensic medical examiner Michael Sikirica, M.D.)

include those impressions in sand, soil, and snow, whereas a temporarily deformed impression would include those on skin, carpeting, etc. Also referred to as a *depressed mark* .

Degradation **(Chemical)** The process of decomposition. When applied to protective clothing, a molecular breakdown of material because of chemical contact; degradation is evidenced by visible signs such as charring, shrinking, or dissolving. Testing clothing material for weight changes, thickness changes, and loss of tensile strength will also reveal degradation (**Bioscience**) In reference to the quality of the DNA in a specimen, degradation is indicated by a smear of DNA fragments on a yield gel. A type of decomposition characteristic of high molecular weight substances such as proteins and polymers. Degradation may result from oxidation, heat, solvents, bacterial action, or in the case of body proteins, from infectious microorganisms.

Degree of wear The extent to which a particular portion of the shoe is worn.

Delirium Extreme mental (and sometimes motor) excitement marked by defective perception, impaired memory, and a rapid succession of confused and unconnected ideas, often with illusions and hallucinations.

Delta A characteristic junction in the looped ridge patterns seen in the fingerprints of approximately 65% of people. The outer, terminal, point of the pattern, nearest the type line divergence.

Delusion Firm belief opposed to reality but maintained in spite of strong evidence to the contrary.

Delustering The treatment of synthetic yarns and fabrics by special pigments or other chemicals in order to reduce their natural luster.

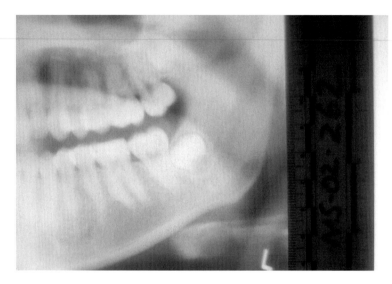

FIGURE D.3 Dental bitewing x-ray is used for identification of unidentified individuals. (Courtesy of forensic medical examiner Michael Sikirica, M.D.)

Delustrant   A substance used to produce dull surfaces on textile fabric; the more common ones are barium sulfate, clays, chalk, titanium dioxide. They are applied in the finishing coat.

Denaturation   **(1)** Describes the conversion of DNA from the double-stranded to the single-stranded state; separation of the strands is most often accomplished by heating. **(2)** A change in the molecular structure of globular proteins that may be induced by bringing a protein solution to its boiling point, or by exposing it to acid or alkalies or to various detergents.

Denier   A unit of rayon or silk yarn size, based on a standard weight of 5 cg per 450 m of silk.

Dense   Dark negative or positive film on paper that is overexposed, overdeveloped, or both.

Density gradient tube   Equipment for measuring the distribution of particles of different density in a soil sample by determining the point at which they are suspended in a glass tube filled with successive layers of liquid of different densities.

Dental records   A standard system for classifying a person's teeth according to distribution, displacement, and their appearance together with any gaps or evidence of remedial work; useful for identifying bodies because of the virtual indestructibility of the teeth (Figure D.3).

Deoxyribonucleic acid (DNA)   The molecule of heredity, a nucleic acid of complex molecular structure forming a principal constituent of the genes; known to play an important role in the genetic action of the chromosomes. DNA is composed of deoxyribonucleic building blocks, each containing a base adenine (A), thymine (T), cytosine (C), or guanine (G); a deoxyribose sugar (S); and a phosphate group (P).

FIGURE D.4 Derringer.

Deposition   Oral or written testimony under oath but outside the courtroom. A written transcript is made of any such oral testimony. Depositions are an important aspect of the discovery process in legal proceedings.

Depressants   Drugs that depress the action of the central nervous system such as phenobarbital, pentobarbital, and alcohol.

Depth of field   The zone between the foreground and background that appears in sharpest focus for a particular lens, distance, and aperture.

Depth of field scale   Scale on a lens barrel showing the near and far limits of depth of field possible when the lens is set at any particular focus and aperture.

Dermis   The layer of the skin just below the epidermis or outer layer. The dermis has a rich supply of blood vessels, nerves, and skin structures.

Derringer   The generic term applied to many variations of pocket-size pistols, either percussion or cartridge, made by manufacturers other than Henry Derringer, up to present time (Figure D.4).

Desiccate   To dry out thoroughly; to remove all moisture.

Designer drugs   Drugs that are produced illicitly by means of chemical technology. They can cause uncontrollable tremors, chills, or sweating and faintness and paranoia when injected or taken in pill form.

Desirable items (ASCLD)   Standards that have the least effect on the work product or the integrity of the evidence, but which nevertheless enhance the professionalism of the laboratory.

Detailing   Dog conducting a close search, frequently on leash and under tight control of the handler.

Detention (legal)   Temporary confinement of a person by a public authority; also known as *placement* .

Developer   A solution used to turn the latent image into a visible image on exposed films or photographic papers.

Diacritical mark or point A sign added to a letter or symbol to give it a particular phonetic value. An accent. Sometimes used to refer to the dots over the "i" and "j."

Diagnosis The use of scientific and skillful methods to establish the cause and nature of a disease process.

Diapause A period during which growth and development is suspended. Both physical and physiological activity is either ceased or greatly diminished. In some insects, this is a response to adverse environmental conditions.

Diatoms Microscopic organisms found in lake and river water that reveal by their presence whether a victim found in these surroundings died by drowning, or were already dead upon entering the water.

Diazepam (valium) The second benzodiazepine derivative to have been approved for human usage has been one of the most frequently prescribed drugs in the United States. It is administered as an antianxiety agent, muscle relaxant, or anticonvulsant.

Dichroism The property of exhibiting different colors, especially two different colors, when viewed in polarized light along different axes.

Didot system A typographic measuring system, used in Europe and based on the Didot point, similar to the U.S.-English pica system.

Diethylamine Water-soluble, colorless liquid with ammonia aroma, used in rubber chemicals and pharmaceuticals, and as a solvent and flotation agent.

Differences Denotes a characteristic or feature that is so strong and reliable that it, in itself, indicates nonidentity. Usually a *difference* will be a different class characteristic, such as the specific design or specific physical size of the design. Normal variations in the impression process, the absence of cuts evident in a questioned impression that appear on the shoe, or the normal advancement of wear with time do not constitute a comparative difference.

Differential extraction A step-wise extraction procedure designed to separate intact sperm heads from lysed sperm and other cell types. The separation generally results in an enrichment of sperm DNA in one cell fraction relative to the other cell fractions. The separate fractions can be analyzed individually.

Diffuser A material used to soften the original light and to disperse it to a degree.

Digraph A group of two successive letters representing a single sound or a complex sound that is not a combination of the sounds ordinarily represented by each in another occurrence, e.g., "ph" in digraph, "ch" in chin.

Dilution The use of water to lower the concentration or amount of a contaminant.

Diminished capacity A variation of the insanity defense that is applicable if the defendant (in the words of the law) lacks the ability to "meaningfully premeditate the crime."

Dinitrotoluene (DNT) An explosive used as a coating on gunpowder to retard the burning rate and to act as a moisture proofing agent.

Diphenylamine   Chemical reagent used in solution with sulfuric acid and acetic acid in the dermal nitrate test. Diphenylamine is also used in smokeless powder as a stabilizer to inhibit decomposition.

Diphthong   The combination of two vowels in succession, the sound of which begins with one and ends with the other, e.g., "oil," "boy," or "out."

Direct attach   A process wherein the lasted upper of a shoe is lowered into the mold cavity after which the mold closes tightly around the shoe upper, after which the midsole or outsole is molded directly onto the upper.

Direct evidence   Proof of facts by witnesses who saw acts done or heard words spoken, as distinguished from circumstantial or indirect evidence. Information offered by witnesses who testify about their own knowledge of the facts. In cases of child maltreatment, for example, it might consist of a neighbor's testimony that he saw the parent strike the child with an appliance cord.

Direct examination   The first questioning of witnesses by the party on whose behalf they are called.

Direct questions   Queries that are phrased in a positive and confident manner, are stated clearly, and address the topic in a forthright manner.

Directed verdict   An instruction by the judge to the jury to return a specific verdict. Usually done when the judge feels that the opposing party fails to present a *prima facie* case. May occur when a necessary defense is not presented.

Direction of flight   The trajectory or flight directionality of a blood drop that can be established by its angle of impact and directionality angle.

Directionality   Relating to or indicating the direction a drop of blood traveled in space from its point of origin. Directionality of a blood drop's flight can usually be established from the geometric shape of the bloodstain.

Directionality angle   The angle between the long axis of a bloodstain and a predetermined line on the plane of the target surface that represents 0°.

Discharge   To cause a firearm to fire.

Discipline   A major area of casework for which a laboratory may seek accreditation.

Disconnector   A device to prevent a semiautomatic firearm from firing full automatic. Some pump action shotguns also have disconnectors.

Discovery   A pretrial procedure by which one party can obtain vital facts and information material to the case to assist in preparation for the trial. The purpose of discovery is to make for a fair trial and to allow each party to know what documents and information the opponent has in its possession.

Discrepancy   Any reported results that differ from the consensus results. Discrepancies may be classified as administrative, systematic, analytical, or interpretive.

Disguised writing   Regardless of the result, a deliberate attempt to alter handwriting in hopes of hiding one's identity.

Dismissal (legal)   Action by the court that removes the court's jurisdiction over a given case.

Dispersion of birefringence   The variation of birefringence with wavelength of light. When dispersion of birefringence is significant in a particular fiber, anomalous interference colors not appearing in the regular color sequence of the Michel–Levy chart may result. Strong dispersion of birefringence may also interfere with the accurate determination of retardation in highly birefringent fibers.

Dispersion staining   A technique for refractive index determination that employs a microscope. Using an annular stop with the substage iris closed, a fiber mounted in a high dispersion medium will show a colored boundary of a wavelength where the fiber and the medium match in refractive index. Using a central stop, the fiber will show colors complementary to those seen with an annular stop.

Displacement   A change in an offender's pattern of behavior as the result of crime prevention efforts, community awareness, or police investigative strategies. There are five types of displacement: spatial (territorial), temporal, target, tactical, and functional (activity).

Disputed document   A term suggesting that there is an argument or controversy over a document, and strictly speaking this is its true meaning. In this text "disputed document" and "questioned document" can be employed interchangeably to signify a document that is under special scrutiny.

Dissociation   Separation or "isolation" of mental processes in such a way that they split off from the main personality or lose their normal thought–affect relationship.

Distal   Indicates farther away from the center of the body.

Distance determination   The process of determining the distance from the firearm, usually the muzzle, to the target based upon pattern of gunpowder or gunshot residues deposited upon that target. Where multiple projectiles, such as shot, have been fired, the spread of those projectiles is also indicative of distance (Figure D.5A and B).

Distillation   A separation process in which a liquid is converted to a vapor and the vapor is then condensed back to a liquid. The usual purpose of distillation is separation of the compounds of a mixture. Steam distillation separates all water-insoluble liquids from solids and water-soluble compounds in a mixture.

Distractors   Challenges to a dog's ability to focus or to the accuracy of decomposition scent training, introduced to prepare the dog for distraction in a real search; usually nonhuman, animal remains.

Diversion   The process of removing some minor criminal, traffic, or juvenile cases from the full judicial process, on the condition that the accused undergo some sort of rehabilitation or make restitution for damages. Diversion may take place before the trial or its equivalent, as when a juvenile accused of a crime may consent to probation without an admission of guilt. If he or she completes probation successfully — e.g., takes a course, makes amends for the crime — then the entire matter may be expunged from the record.

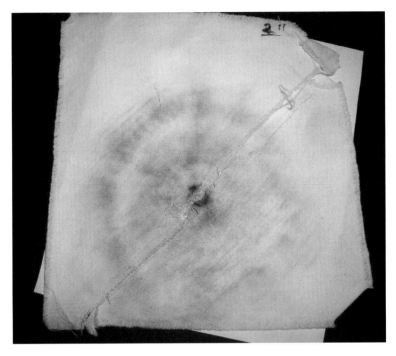

FIGURE D.5A Gunshot at a piece of cloth material at a distance of 2 in. The gunshot powder shows a close pattern of particle residue.

Dizygotic Twins produced from two separate zygotes. Also called *fraternal twins*. On average, one-half of their genomes are shared.

DMAB Stands for paradimethylaminobenzaldehyde.

DNA (deoxyribonucleic acid) A double chain of linked nucleotides (having deoxyribose as their sugar); the fundamental substance of which genes are composed.

DNA databank Database with the collection of convicted offenders' blood or saliva samples, to be used in conjunction with DNA profiles developed in casework samples to solve or link crimes where there are no known suspects.

DNA genetic analyzer An instrument that can separate small fragments of DNA either by using gel electrophoresis or by using capillary electro-phoresis (Figure D.6).

DNA profile A DNA profile consists of a set of DNA identification character-istics, i.e., the particular chemical form at the various DNA locations (loci) that permit the DNA of one person to be distinguishable from that of another person.

DNA record The DNA record includes the DNA profile as well as data required to manage and operate NDIS, i.e., the NDIS agency identifier that serves to identify the submitting agency; the NDIS specimen identification num-ber; information related to the reliability and maintainability of the DNA

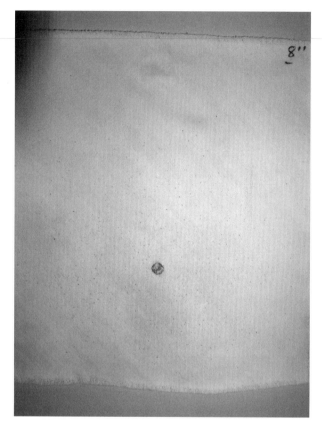

FIGURE D.5B Gunshot at a piece of cloth material at a distance of 8 in. The pattern of the gunshot powder residue is more dispersed.

profiles; and names of the participating laboratories and DNA personnel associated with DNA profiles analyses.

Docket   A list of cases to be heard by a court.

Document   In its fullest meaning, any material that contains marks, symbols, or signs either visible, partially visible, or invisible that may ultimately convey a meaning or message to someone. Pencil or ink writing, typewriting, or printing on paper are the more usual forms of documents.

Document examiner   An individual who scientifically studies the details and elements of documents in order to identify their source or to discover other facts concerning them. Document examiners are often referred to as handwriting identification experts, but today the work has outgrown this latter title and involves other problems than merely the examination of handwriting.

Documentation   Written notes, audio/videotapes, printed forms, sketches or photographs that form a detailed record of the scene, evidence recovered, and actions taken during the search of the crime scene.

Double action   A gun action where the pulling of the trigger to fire a round recocks the gun so that the next round is ready to be fired.

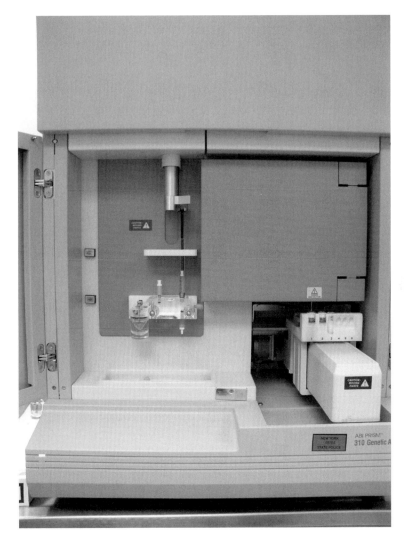

FIGURE D.6 ABI Prism 310 Genetic Analyzer.

Double helix   The structure of DNA first proposed by Watson and Crick, with two interlocking helices joined by hydrogen bonds between paired bases.

Double jeopardy   Putting a person on trial more than once for the same crime; forbidden by the Fifth Amendment to the U.S. Constitution.

Downloading   The transferring of programs and data from a remote computer to your computer, generally by using a modem.

Downwind   A term used to describe the position of the searching dog team relative to the odor source, where the wind is blowing from the source toward the team.

DPX™   A neutral medium used for mounting fibers.

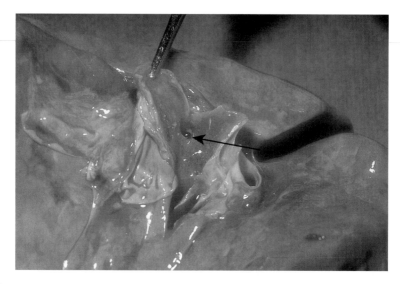

FIGURE D.7 Muddy material aspirated into lungs in a case of drowning in a farm pond. (Courtesy of forensic medical examiner Michael Sikirica, M.D.)

Drag factor   Comes from the tool used to determine the value of the coefficient of friction of the road surface. A portion of a concrete-weighted tire is pulled or dragged along the roadbed by a "fish scale." The investigator reads the scale and divides by the weight of the tire to determine the coefficient of friction. It is called a drag factor because it is determined by dragging the tire.

Drawback effect   The presence of blood in the barrel of a firearm that has been drawn backward due to the effect created by discharged gasses. This is seen frequently in close-range contact gunshot injuries.

Dried remains   The final phase of corpse decomposition that follows advanced decay and is characterized by little faunal activity.

Drip pattern   Blood that drips into blood, resulting in round, satellite blood spatters, 0.1 to 1.0 mm in diameter, around the periphery of the central bloodstain.

Driving edge, fired bullet   The driving edge of a fired bullet with a right twist is the left edge of the groove impression, or the right edge of the land impression. The driving edge of a fired bullet with left twist is the right edge of the groove impression, or the left edge of the land impression.

Drowning, wet   Death from drowning where water fills the lungs (Figure D.7).

Drug   Any natural or synthetic substance that is administered to produce specific physiological or psychological effects.

Drug abuse   The nonmedicinal use of a drug in a manner that is not socially acceptable.

Drug dependence   The primary hazard of the abusive use of drugs is the likelihood for some individuals to develop a "need" or compulsive desire that may occur as a result of a psychological or a physical craving.

Dry drowning Death caused by a body reflex; a spasm of the larynx due to the shock of the victim falling into the water, resulting in the heart stopping.

Due process of law The right of all persons to receive the guarantees and safe-guards of the law and the judicial process. Includes such constitutional requirements as adequate notice, assistance of counsel, and the right to remain silent, to a speedy and public trial, to an impartial jury, and to confront and secure witnesses.

DUI Driving under the influence.

DWI Driving while intoxicated.

DWM Deutsche Waffen und Munitions Fabriken. A German firearms manufacturer.

Dyes Soluble substances that add color to textiles. Dyes are classified into groups that have similar chemical characteristics (e.g., aniline, acid, and azo). They are incorporated into the fiber by chemical reaction, absorption, or dispersion.

Dying declaration A statement made just prior to death with the knowledge of impending death; though hearsay, dying declarations are allowed into evidence in homicide cases in certain jurisdictions (also called *antemortem statement*).

Dyslexia A disturbance of the ability to read.

E

Ecchymosis A form of macula appearing in large, irregularly formed hemorrhagic areas of the skin, originally blue-black and changing to greenish brown or yellow.

Ecdysis Molting. The process whereby an insect sheds its exoskeleton.

Eclampsia An acute disorder of pregnant and puerperal women, associated with convulsions and coma.

Eclosion The process of hatching from the egg or of emerging as an adult.

Ecotage Ecological terrorism; illegal (often violent) efforts by groups to protect the environment.

Edema Accumulation of fluid in body cells or tissues; usually identified as swelling.

EDTA Ethylene diamine tetracetic acid, a preservative that binds the calcium ion in blood and is found in purple stopper vacutainer tubes.

Efface To rub out, to strike or scratch out, or to erase.

Ejaculate The semen released by one ejaculation.

Ejection The act of expelling a cartridge or cartridge case from a firearm.

Ejection pattern The charting of where a particular firearm ejects fired cartridge cases.

Ejector A portion of a firearm's mechanism that ejects or expels cartridges or cartridge cases from a firearm.

Ejector marks Toolmarks produced upon a cartridge or cartridge case on the head, generally at or near the rim, from contact with the ejector.

Electric typewriter A typewriter equipped with an electric motor that assists in operating the typebars and the carriage movements, while the typebars or type element is activated by a series of mechanical linkages.

Electrical burn Characteristic lesions that tend to be on the palms of the hands and tips of the fingers (entry sites) and sole of the feet (exit site). They have a chalky white irregular appearance and will often have raised borders with a central crater. The borders are curved to irregular (Figure E.1).

Electromagnetic radiation The energy (in the form or magnetic and electric fields) given off by a vibrating charge (such as an electron). Every physical object in the universe gives off electromagnetic radiation of one type or another. The phenomenon of sight is due to our eyes being sensitive to a certain type of electromagnetic radiation.

Electron A negatively charged subatomic particle that circles the nucleus of the atom in a cloud. Most chemical reactions involve the making and breaking of bonds held together by the sharing electrons.

Electron capture detector (ECD) A type of gas chromatographic detector that is sensitive to halogenated hydrocarbons and other molecules capable of

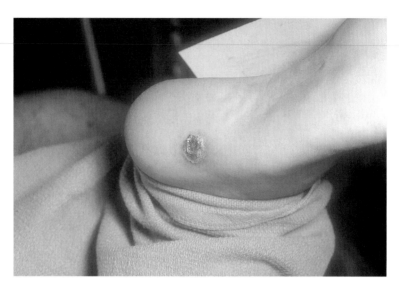

FIGURE E.1 Electrical burn on the sole of a foot occurring on a worker moving an aluminum ladder that contacted overhead power lines. (Courtesy of forensic medical examiner Michael Sikirica, M.D.)

easily gaining an electron. Electron capture is not generally used for hydrocarbon detection.

Electron microscope   A microscope that forms its image by the electrons emitted from the specimen when scanned by a focused beam of electrons.

Electronic flash   Lighting unit utilizing the flash of light produced by discharging a current between two electrodes in a gas-filled tube.

Electronic viewfinder (EVF)   A small TV monitor attached to a video camera for viewing of recorded images.

Electropherogram   Is a chromatographic display with fluorescence intensity indicated as relative fluorescence units (RFU) on the y-axis. After the internal lane size standard has been defined and applied, the electropherogram can be displayed with the base pair size on the x-axis. Four-color image of a sequence, showing peaks that represent the bases (Figure E.2).

Electrophoresis   The process of separating charged molecules, for example, negatively charged DNA fragments, in a porous medium such as agarose, by the application of an electric field. DNA separates according to size with the small fragments moving most rapidly (Figure E.3).

Electrophoretic mobility   A characteristic of living cells in suspension and biological commons (proteins) in solution to travel in an electric field to the positive or negative electrode because of the charge on these substances.

Electrostatic detection apparatus   A device primarily used to detect indented writing on documents that can also be used to detect footwear impressions on paper items.

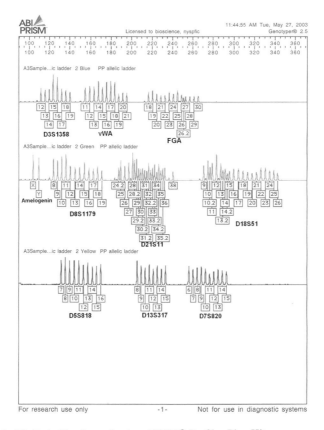

FIGURE E.2 Allelic ladder from the AmpF/STR® Profiler Plus Kit.

Electrostatic lifting device A device consisting of a high-voltage supply used with a special conductive lifting film to electrostatically transfer a dry origin footwear impression from a surface to the film.

Element One of 106 presently known substances that comprise all matter at and above the atomic level. A substance made up of atoms with the same atomic number; common examples are hydrogen, gold, and iron. Also known as *chemical element.*

Elements of a crime Specific factors that define a crime, every element of which the prosecution must prove beyond a reasonable doubt in order to obtain a conviction. The elements that must be proven are (**1**) that a crime has actually occurred, (**2**) that the accused intended the crime to happen, and (**3**) a timely relationship between the first two factors.

Elimination prints Prints of known individuals who customarily inhabit the crime scene area; used to determine whether a latent crime scene print is that of a stranger or of someone who is customarily present.

Elute To remove (adsorbed material) from an adsorbent by means of a solvent. The solvent mixture that acts as the mobile phase in thin-layer chromatography.

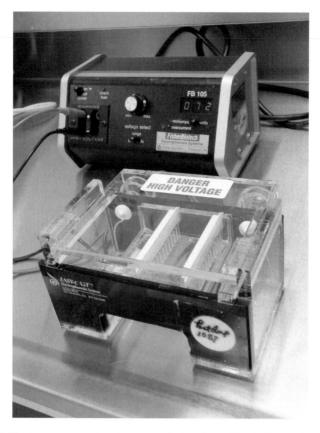

FIGURE E.3 Electrophoresis setup showing gel chamber with plastic combs and a power supply.

Elution The process of removing adsorbed materials from the surface of an adsorbent such as activated charcoal. The solvent in this process is called the *eluant.*

Elytra The leathery, chitinous forewings of a beetle that serve to protect the thin membranous hind wings used for flight.

Embolism Obstruction of a blood vessel by foreign substances or by a blood clot.

Embolization Obstruction of a blood vessel by a transported clot or other mass.

Embolus A mass of undissolved matter present in a blood or lymphatic vessel brought there by the blood or lymph circulation (Figure E.4).

Emission spectroscopy The study of the composition of substances and identification of elements by observation of the wavelength of radiation emitted by the substance as it returns to a normal state after excitation by an external source.

Emotional pretrial publicity Lurid accounts of a crime that stir emotions and make it difficult for prospective jurors to look at the evidence dispassionately.

Emulsion Photographically, a suspension of a salt of silver in gelatin or collodion used to coat film.

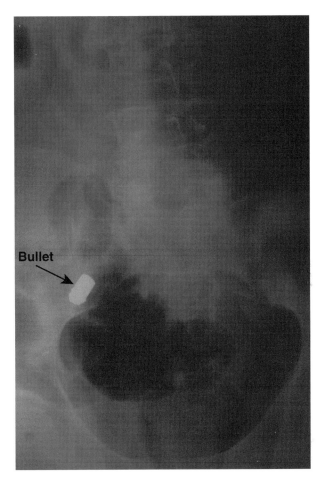

FIGURE E.4 Bullet embolism that occurred when a projectile entered the upper aorta and was carried by blood flow into the iliac artery of the pelvis. (Courtesy of forensic medical examiner Michael Sikirica, M.D.)

Endemic   A disease that occurs continuously in a particular population but has a low mortality rate, such as measles; used in contrast to *epidemic*.

Endocarditis   Inflammation of the lining membrane of the heart. May be due to invasion of microorganisms or an abnormal immunologic reaction.

Enhance   To develop or to bring out from a latent form.

Enlargement   A print made from a smaller negative or slide through magnification.

Enterprise crime   The broad range of crime characterized by criminal networks and illegal relationships, including but not limited to organized drug trafficking, white-collar crime, corruption, economic crime, etc.

Entomotoxicology   The use of arthropods that consume and bioaccumulate drugs and toxins within their bodies, for forensic toxicological analysis in place of human tissues. This method is frequently used when sufficient amounts of human tissue are not available due to decay and skeletonization.

FIGURE E.5 Epidural hematoma (artifact) seen in postmortem examination of some severe burn victims. (Courtesy of forensic medical examiner Michael Sikirica, M.D.)

Entrapment   An act by enforcement agencies that lures an individual into committing a crime not otherwise contemplated, for the purpose of prosecuting him or her. A defense to criminal charges alleging that agents of the government induced a person to commit a crime he or she otherwise would not have committed.

Environmental criminology   An area of criminology focusing on the criminal event rather than just the offender. The primary concern of environmental criminology is the crime setting or place, the where and when, of the criminal act.

Enzyme   A recycling protein molecule that catalyzes a specific chemical reaction. Any of a group of catalytic proteins that are produced by living cells and that mediate and promote the chemical processes of life without themselves being altered or destroyed.

Epidermis   The outermost nonvascular covering of the skin.

Epidural hemorrhage   Bleeding in the space between the dura mater and skull or wall of the vertebral canal around the spinal cord (Figure E.5).

Epistaxis   Hemorrhage from the nose; nosebleed.

Epithelial cells   Large cells with small, round, or oval nuclei, they are derived from the ureters, bladder, and urethra.

Equivocal death analysis (EDA)   A retrospective psychological analysis of the most probable manner of death (accidental, suicidal, or homicidal) in suspicious cases. Also known as *psychological autopsy.*

Erasure (chemical or physical)   The removal of writing, typewriting, or printing from a document. It may be accomplished by either of two means: a chemical eradication in which the writing is removed or bleached by chemical agents, e.g., liquid ink eradicator; or an abrasive erasure in which

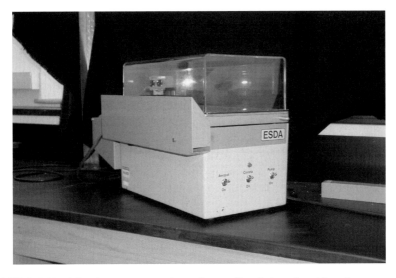

FIGURE E.6 Used by document examiners for reading indented writing from suspected pages.

the writing is effaced by rubbing with a rubber eraser or scratching out with a knife.

Erythrocytes   Red blood cells. A type of blood cell that contains a nucleus in all vertebrates but man and that has hemoglobin in the cytoplasm.

Erythroderma   Intense, widespread reddening of the skin.

Escape theory   Theory of suicide that postulates nine steps — experiencing major disappointment or stress, attributing primary responsibility to self, high self-awareness, emotional distress, distorted thinking, mental narrowing, becoming receptive to suicide, having the opportunity to commit suicide, and committing the act of suicide.

ESDA (electrostatic detection apparatus)   Used to detect indented impressions left from writing on an overlying page (Figure E.6).

Esophagus   The portion of the digestive canal extending from the throat to the stomach. Also referred to as the *gullet*.

Essential items (ASCLD)   Standards that directly affect and have fundamental impact on the work product of the laboratory or the integrity of the evidence.

Estimate value (statistical)   Value of population characteristics obtained from sample data.

Ethernet   A modern networking topology using RG58 or RG8, unshielded, twisted-pair, and fiber-optic cable, achieving 10 Mb/s.

Ethidium bromide   A molecule that binds to DNA and fluoresces under ultraviolet light; used to identify DNA.

Ethylbenzene   A component of gasoline, but also a major breakdown product of pyrolysis released when certain polymers are heated.

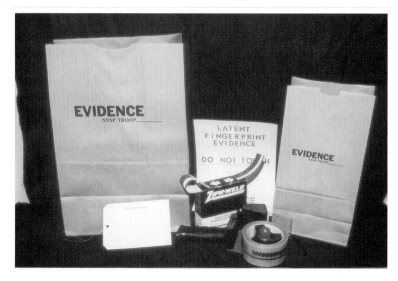

FIGURE E.7 Materials used for the collection of evidence from crime scenes.

Eukaryote A multicellular organism having true membrane-bound nuclei containing chromosomes that undergo mitosis.

Eutectic The lowest melting point of an alloy or solution of two or more substances (usually metals) that is obtainable by varying the percentage of the components. Eutectic melting sometimes occurs when molten aluminum or molten zinc comes in contact with solid steel or copper.

Eutrophic The state of nutrient enrichment as a result of the natural or artificial addition of nutrients to bodies of water, especially lakes, often resulting in high productivity and low transparency.

Evaporation Conversion of a liquid to the vapor state by the addition of latent heat.

Evaporation rate A measure of the quantity of a liquid converted to vapor in a unit of time. Among single component liquids, the rate varies directly with the surface area, the temperature, and the vapor pressure, and inversely with the latent heat of vaporization of the liquid.

Eversion Raising of the outer border of the foot.

Evidence identification (crime scene discipline) The process of assessing material at a scene for the purpose of determining the value or potential value of that material as evidence of a crime.

Evidence identifiers Tapes, labels, containers, and string tags used to identify the evidence, the person collecting the evidence, the date the evidence was gathered, basic criminal offense information, and a brief description of the pertinent evidence (Figure E.7).

Evidence samples   Samples that have been collected by a police agency from the crime scene, an individual or object, such as vehicles, weapons, or furniture that are related to the investigation of the crime.

Evidentiary standards (legal)   Guidelines used in examining evidence to determine whether it has been legally collected and whether it is factual and legally proves or is relevant to the case being heard.

Ex parte **order**   An order issued by a judge (and submitted to the appropriate federal or state judge for approval) authorizing the interception of a written or oral communication.

Examination   The act of making a close and critical study of any evidence samples to discover the facts about them. Various types of examinations are undertaken, including microscopic, visual, photographic, chemical, ultraviolet, and infrared.

Exceptions   Declarations by either side in a civil or criminal case reserving the right to appeal a judge's ruling upon a motion; also, in regulatory cases, objections by either side to points made by the other side or to rulings by the agency or one of its hearing officers.

Excitation fiber   A fiber used in fluorescence microscopy that transmits specific bands or wavelengths of energy capable of inducing visible fluorescence in various substrates.

Exclusion   As in DNA analysis, the comparison of the DNA profile developed from the evidence sample compared to either the DNA profile developed from the victim or from the suspect to see if a particular individual can be excluded. In paternity cases, to see if the putative father is or is not the biological father.

Exclusionary rule   The rule that defines whether evidence is admissible in a trial. In cases where evidence has been illegally obtained, it must be removed from consideration by the fact finders.

Exemplar   A specimen of an identified source acquired for the purpose of comparison with an evidence sample. An example of a person's writing, a standard for use in comparisons, a "collected" or a "request" specimen. Specimens of physical evidence of known origin (used for comparison with similar crime scene evidence).

Exhibit   A document or other article introduced as evidence during a trial or hearing. Item produced during a trial or hearing that is connected with the subject matter before the court and that, upon acceptance by the court, is marked for identification and made a part of the case. Physical evidence offered to the court for inspection may be accepted as an exhibit. An exhibit also may be attached to a document, such as an affidavit, and made a part of that document.

Exigent circumstances   Exception to the requirement for a search warrant when there is no time to get a warrant and failure to search will lead to destruction or concealment of evidence, injury to police or others, or escape of the suspect.

Existing light   That light present at any one time in a given area no matter what the source.

Exoskeleton   A skeleton on the outside of the body whose inner walls serve as a point for the attachment of muscles. All arthropods possess chitinous exoskeletons.

Exothermic reaction   A chemical reaction that involves heat; combustion reaction is a type of exothermic reaction.

Expert testimony   Statements given to the court by witnesses with special skills or knowledge in some art, science, profession, or technical area. Experts educate the court or jury by assisting them in understanding the evidence or in determining an issue of fact. Experts are initially questioned in court about their education or experience to ascertain their qualifications to give professional opinions about the matter in question.

Expert witness   A legal term used to describe a witness who by reason of his or her special technical training or experience is permitted to express an opinion regarding the issue, or a certain aspect of the issue that is involved in a court action. His or her purpose is to interpret technical information in their particular specialty in order to assist the court in administering justice.

Expirated or exhaled blood   Blood that is blown out of the nose, mouth, or a wound as a result of air pressure or air flow that is the propelling force.

Explosion   The sudden conversion of chemical energy into kinetic energy with the release of heat, light, and mechanical shock.

Explosion limit, flammability limit   The highest or lowest concentration of a flammable gas or vapor in air that will explode or burn readily when ignited. This limit is usually expressed as a volume percent of gas or vapor in air.

Explosives   Compounds that are unstable and break down with the sudden release of large amounts of energy.

Explosivity   The characteristic of undergoing very rapid decomposition (or combustion) to release large amounts of energy.

Exposure index   Methods of rating film speed developed by the American Standards Association (ASA), now known as the American National Standards Institute, Inc. (ANSI).

Exposure setting   The lens opening and shutter speed selected to expose the film.

Expunge   To strike out, obliterate, or mark for deletion from the court record.

Exsanguination   Loss of blood from the circulatory system.

Extension cord   An auxiliary wire used to maintain electronic contact between the camera and strobe when the two are separated.

Extension tube   Increases the distance between the lens and the sensitive film in the camera and changes the lens capability.

External Drive   A data storage unit not contained in the main computer housing.

External proficiency testing program   A test program managed or controlled by an independent laboratory system.

Extraction A chemical procedure for removing one type of material from another. Extraction is generally carried out by immersing a solid in a liquid, or by shaking two immiscible liquids together, resulting in the transfer of a dissolved substance from one liquid to the other. Solvent extraction is one of the primary methods of sample preparation in arson debris analysis. In DNA analysis, it is the extraction of DNA material from the nucleus of nucleated cells.

Extractor A mechanism for withdrawing a cartridge or cartridge case from the chamber of a firearm.

Extractor mark Toolmarks produced upon a cartridge or cartridge case from contact with the extractor. These are always found on or just ahead of the rim.

Extradition The process by which one state surrenders to another state a person accused or convicted of a crime in the other state.

Eyepiece The optic found on a camera, microscope, telescope, and so on, used to look through the instrument.

F

Facsimile   An image of printed matter that has been transmitted electronically.

Factual pretrial publicity   Nonsensational but damaging information about the defendant that might cause prospective jurors to believe the defendant committed the crime in question; an account of a defendant's criminal record is factual pretrial publicity.

Fade   A decrease in a video or audio signal intensity.

Fade-in/Fade-out   Gradually changing video from dark to picture or picture to dark.

Fast film   Film that has an emulsion that is very sensitive to light. Such films have high ASA ratings.

Fast lens   Lens with a large aperture, requiring less light.

Fast salt blue B   A chemical reagent used in the identification of seminal fluid, also called *brentamine fast blue* B (*O*-dianisidine tetrazotized).

FAT (file allocation table)   All DOS disks use FATs to keep track of which clusters are assigned to which files. Simply put, the FAT is an address book for locating files on the disk.

Fatigue, material   A material becomes "tired" due to repeated applications of dynamic loads. The material fractures or fails at a strength level significantly less than it would fracture or fail if only static loads were applied.

Feathering   The condition in which the writing/printing fluid spreads laterally in a pattern that usually follows the direction of the surface fibers away from the written or printed line. Characteristic of intaglio printing involving extreme pressures of the plate on the paper; thus, also called *gushing*.

Feces   Animal solid waste material discharged from the rectum through the anus. End product of digestion after absorption of nutrients and reabsorption of water. It consists of undigested food residues, mucosal cells, bacteria, and bile pigments.

Felony   A crime of a graver nature than a misdemeanor, usually punishable by imprisonment in a penitentiary for more than a year and substantial fines.

Femur   The thighbone, which can be measured and used as a guide to the height of the person to whom it belonged.

Fence   A person in the business of buying stolen goods, usually for resale; to buy or sell stolen goods.

Fiber-tip pen (porous-tip pen)   A modern writing instrument in which the marking element or point consists of a porous material through which the ink can flow. These pens are commonly known as *fiber-tip* or *felt-tip pens* or may be referred to as *soft-tip pens*.

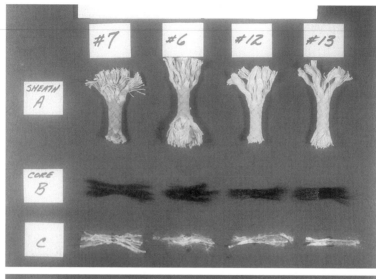
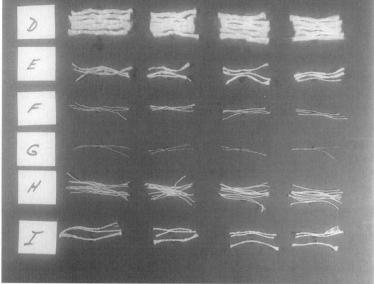

FIGURE F.1 Separation of different types of rope into smaller fibers.

Fibers   A common class of microscopic evidence. They are classified as animal,
vegetable, mineral, or natural, manufactured, or synthetic. Some types of
ropes are composed of numerous of fibers woven together to form the
rope (Figure F.1).

Field of vision   The area a person is able to see through the viewfinder, scope,
or lens.

Filial generation   Successive generation of progeny in a controlled series of crosses, starting with two specific parents (the P generation) and selfing or intercrossing the progeny of each new (F1, F2, …) generation.

Fill-in   Secondary illumination to keep shadow areas from photographing too dark; also known as the *fill light.*

Film   A sheet or strip of celluloid coated with light-sensitive emulsion for exposure in a camera.

Film plane   That portion of the camera body that holds the sensitized film in place during the exposure process. It is also that position of the camera where the image is focused.

Film speed   A means of representing numerically the response of a photographic emulsion to light.

Finder   A viewer through which the picture to be taken may be seen and centered.

Finding   Formal conclusion by a judge or regulatory agency on issues of fact; also, a conclusion by a jury regarding a fact.

Fingerprint pattern type   Formed by a series of lines, corresponding to ridges (hills) and grooves (valleys) on the skin of the fingertip. There are eight basic types of fingerprint patterns (Figure F.2A to D).

> **Plain arch** — The simplest pattern. The ridges enter on one side, rise to form a wave in the center, and exit smoothly on the opposite side.
>
> **Tented arch** — Variation of the plain arch. Ridges at the center are thrust upward in a more abrupt manner similar to the appearance of a tent pole.
>
> **Radial loop** — A pattern in which one or more ridges enter on the side toward the thumb (the side on which the radius bone of the forearm lies), recurve, and then exit on the same side.
>
> **Ulnar loop** — A pattern in which one or more ridges enter on the side toward the little finger (the side on which the ulna bone of the forearm lies), recurve, and then exit toward the same side.
>
> **Plain whorl** — A pattern in which one or more ridges form a complete revolution around the center. Whorls generally have two or more deltas.
>
> **Central pocket loop** — A variation of the plain whorl pattern. Some ridges tend to form a loop pattern that recurves and surrounds a whorl at the center.
>
> **Double loop (Twinned loop)** — Another type of whorl. In it two separate loop formations are present and may surround each other.
>
> **Accidental** — A relatively rare pattern having three or more deltas or all the characteristics of two or more different pattern types (excluding the plain arch). This category is used to accommodate those patterns that do not conform to any of the patterns previously described.

Fingerprint powder   A powder (silver, gray, black, red, or fluorescent) dusted on a latent print with a brush to enhance or bring out the ridge details of a print (Figure F.3).

Finished sketch   A precise rendering of a crime scene with clean, straight lines and typeset or typewritten lettering; usually prepared after leaving the

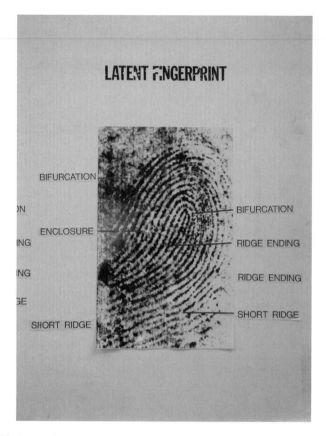

FIGURE F.2A Latent fingerprint.

crime scene with information obtained from the original rough sketch, notes, and photographs taken at the crime scene.

Fire   The light and heat manifested by the rapid oxidation of combustible materials. A flame may be manifested but is not required.

Fire load   Amount of material that can burn. The average fire load of a building is usually stated in British thermal units (BTUs) per square foot to enable the comparison of the propensity of one building to that of another.

Fire pattern   Marks left by fire, smoke, and soot on structures and devices. Several characteristic patterns help identify the relationship and orientation of the fire to the structure horizontal patterns, plumes, V-shape patterns, and saddle burns.

Fire point   The temperature, generally a few degrees above the flash point, at which burning is self-sustaining after removal of an ignition source.

Fire tetrahedron   Fuel, heat, oxygen, and a chemical chain reaction.

Fire triangle   Fuel, heat, and oxygen.

Firearm   An assembly of a barrel and action from which a projectile is propelled by products of combustion.

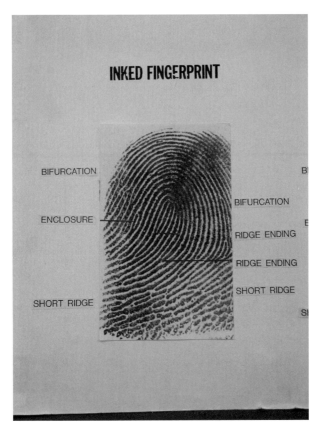

FIGURE F.2B Inked fingerprint.

Firearm identification   A discipline of forensic science that has as its primary
concern determining whether a bullet, cartridge case, or other ammunition
component was fired by a particular firearm.

Firing pin   That part of a firearm mechanism that strikes the primer of a cartridge
to initiate ignition. Sometimes called the *hammer nose* or *striker.*

Firing pin drag marks   The toolmarks produced when a projecting firing pin
comes into contact with a cartridge case or shotshell during the extraction,
ejection cycle (Figure F.4).

Firing pin impression   The indentation in the primer of a centerfire cartridge
case or in the rim of a rimfire cartridge case caused when it is struck by
the firing pin (Figure F.5).

First responder   The initial responding law enforcement officer or other public
safety official or service provider arriving at the scene prior to the arrival
of the investigator in charge.

Fish-eye lens   Wide-angle lens with angle of view that may reach 180°. Depth
of field is practically infinite.

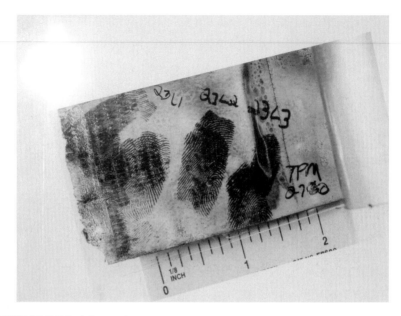

FIGURE F.2C Inked fingerprint on transparent tape.

FIGURE F.2D Fingerprint workstation.

Fixatives A spray or powder applied cautiously to a footwear impression prior to casting, to prevent it from loss of detail when the casting materials are applied to it.

FIGURE F.3 Different types of fingerprint dust powder and brushes.

FIGURE F.4 Microscopic examination of a firing pin drag mark.

Fixed surveillance   Surveillance conducted from a stationary position, such as a parked van, or room facing the subject's residence or workplace, or by posing as a street vendor or utility worker. The aim is to allow the surveillant to remain inconspicuously in one locale (also called *stakeout, plant*).

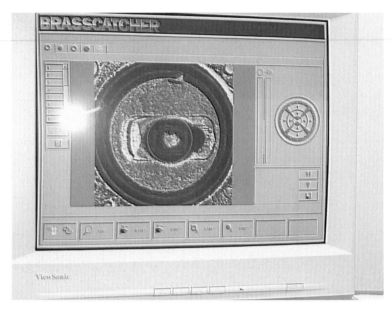

FIGURE F.5 The use of the IBIS for identifying a firing pin impression.

Flame A rapid gas phase combustion process characterized by self-propagation.

Flame ionization detector (FID) A nearly universal gas chromatograph detector. It responds to almost all organic compounds. An FID does not respond to nitrogen, hydrogen, helium, oxygen, carbon monoxide, or water. This detects ionized compounds as they reach the end of the chromatographic column by burning them in an air/hydrogen flame. As the compounds pass through the flame, the conductivity of the flame changes, generating a signal. This is the most commonly used detector in arson debris analysis (Figure F.6).

Flammable Able to ignite and burn.

Flammable liquid A combustible liquid that has a flash point below 80°F according to the U.S. Coast Guard and a temperature of 100°F according to the National Fire Protection Agency (NFPA). Liquids having a vapor pressure of over 40 psi at 100°F are classified as flammable gases. Flammable liquids are a special group of combustible liquids.

Flammable (explosive) range The range of gas or vapor concentration (percentage by volume in air) that will burn or explode if an ignition source is present. Limiting concentrations are commonly called the *lower explosive limit* and *upper explosive limit*. Below the lower explosive limit, the mixture is too lean to burn; above the upper explosive limit, the mixture is too rich to burn.

Flammable vapor A vapor/air mixture of any concentration within the flammable range of that vapor.

Flash A general term for any auxiliary, sudden, brilliant light. A unit holding flashbulbs is referred to as a *flash*.

FIGURE F.6 Two-flame ionization detector (FID) inside a gas chromatograph instrument.

Flash fire   A fire that spreads with unusual speed, as one that races over flammable liquids or through combustible gases.

Flash hole   Vent leading from the primer pocket to the body of the cartridge case.

Flash point   The temperature at which a pool of liquid will generate sufficient vapor to form an ignitable vapor/air mixture. The temperature at which a liquid will produce its lower explosive limit in air. Flash point describes one of several very specific laboratory tests. Frequently, materials can be made to burn below their flash point if increased surface area or mechanical activity raises the concentration of vapor in air above the lower explosive limit.

Flash sensor   Electronic unit actuated by light flash.

Flashback   The movement of a flame to a fuel source; typically occurs via the vapor of a highly volatile liquid or by a flammable gas escaping from a cylinder.

Flight path   The path of the blood drop as it moves through space from the impact site to the target.

Flood   Light source providing a wide, diffused beam of light.

Floppy disk   A small, flat magnetic storage device that can easily be transported or stored.

Flow-back   An increase in the density of an ink line caused by the run of excess ink along the finish of a stroke, occurring when the pen is lifted from the paper.

Flow pattern   A change in the shape and direction of a wet bloodstain due to the influence of gravity or movement of an object.

Fluctuation Alternating changes of direction, position, or conditions, i.e., alternating acceleration and deceleration of writing speed, or alternating expansion and contraction of the writing pattern.

Fluency (Questioned documents) Freedom, and other like terms, referring to a generally higher grade of line quality that is smooth, consistent, and without any evidence of tremor or erratic changes in direction or pen pressure. **(Human remains recovery)** The ability of a dog to produce the trained behavior quickly and accurately.

Fluorescence Property possessed by various substances that glow when exposed to light of a short wavelength. The phenomenon in which some substances absorb light and re-emit part of it as light of a longer wavelength. Fluorescence ceases when incident or exciting illumination ceases.

Fluorescence microscope A variation of the compound laboratory light microscope that is arranged to admit ultraviolet, violet, and sometimes blue radiations to a specimen that then fluoresces.

Fluorosis Accumulation of excessive fluoride in the body, characterized by increased bone density and mineral deposits in tendons, ligaments, and muscles.

Flying finish The diminishing taper of a terminal stroke when the motion of the instrument does not stop at the completion of a word; minute barb sometimes growing out of it.

Flying start The growing taper of an initial stroke, or the delicate initial hook, that appears where the motion of the instrument precedes actual writing.

Focal concerns theory A theory that relates the criminal activities of lower-class gangs to their need to achieve those ends that are most culturally valued through the simplest possible means.

Focal length The distance in millimeters (mm) from the center of the lens to the point where the image comes into critical view.

Focal plane shutter A shutter that operates immediately in front of the focal plane. Usually contains a fixed or variable-sized slit in a curtain of cloth or metal that travels across the film to make the exposure.

Focus Point at which converging rays of light from a lens meet.

Focusing The adjustment of the lens-to-film distance to produce a sharp image of the subject.

Font (= fount) A complete set or collection of letters, figures, symbols, punctuation marks, and special characters that are of the same design and size, for a particular typeface.

Footwear Any apparel that is worn on the foot, such as a shoe, boot, etc.

Footwear database Computerized compilation of shoe sole designs for the purpose of associating a crime scene impression with a manufacturer or to link a crime scene impression from one scene to others (Figure F.7).

Forced hand A person's signature or writing executed while the hand was under the physical compulsion or control of another person.

Forcing cone Tapered beginning of the lands at the origin of the rifling of a gun tube; the forcing cone allows the rotating band of the projectile to be gradually engaged by the rifling, thereby centering the projectile in the bore.

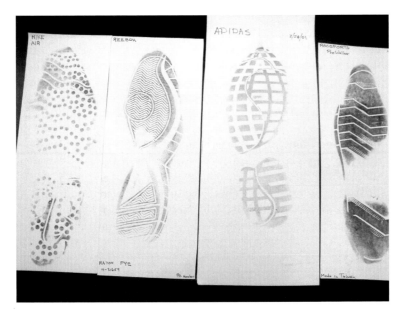

FIGURE F.7 Inked impressions from different styles of sneakers.

Forensic   Analysis of information suitable for use in a court of law.

Forensic anthropology   Application of anthropology theory and methods, primarily human skeletal biology, taphonomy, and archaeological methods, to solve medicolegal problems.

Forensic archaeology   Application of archaeological methods to recover human remains and interpret their spatial associations.

Forensic entomology   The study of insects and related arthropods from a legal aspect.

Forensic evidence   Information generated by the prosecution or defense that satisfies the requirements of state or federal rules of evidence.

Forensic medicine   The use of medicine to determine the cause or time of death, or for other legal purposes (also called *legal medicine, medical jurisprudence*).

Forensic odontology   The study of teeth, dentures, and bite marks for the purpose of obtaining criminal evidence, or identifying physical remains or the source of bite wounds.

Forensic pathology   Pathology that goes beyond the concern for disease to the study of the causes of death — whether from natural, accidental, or criminal agency.

Forensic psychiatry   The study of a criminal's mental state and probable intent.

Forensic psychology   The application of the methods, theories, and concepts of psychology to the legal system. Forensic psychologists may serve as expert witnesses, carry out competence evaluations, and otherwise assist litigations and fact finders.

Forensic sciences   The application of scientific facts to legal problems. The field of science that is used in the judicial process. Some are derived from the physical, medical, and dental sciences, and the best-qualified workers specialize in the court-oriented aspects of each discipline.

Forensic taphonomy   The study of postmortem processes affecting human remains for the purposes of interpreting forensic data.

Forensic toxicology   The examination of all aspects of toxicology (the study of drugs and poisons that may have legal implications).

Forgery (freehand imitation)   A legal term that involves not only a nongenuine signature or document, but also intent on the part of its "marker" to defraud.

Formaldehyde   A readily polymerizable gas. Commercial grades are called *formalin*. Used as embalming fluid, preservative, hardening agent, reducing agent, and durable-press treatment of textile fabrics. Formaldehyde is a highly toxic substance if inhaled or if it comes in contact with the skin.

Format   Size, shape, and general makeup of negatives, slides, photographic prints, camera viewing areas, or video equipment.

Formula   A combination of chemical symbols that expresses a molecule's composition. The reaction formula shows the interrelationship between reactants and products.

Formula weight   The gram-molecular weight of a substance.

Forward spatter   Blood that travels in the same direction as the source of energy or force causing the spatter. Forward spatter is often associated with gunshot wound of exit.

Fouling   The residual deposits remaining in the bore of a firearm after firing. Fouling can change the character of the identifiable striations imparted to the projectile from one shot to another.

Foundation   A required showing to the trial court prior to the admissibility of certain evidence, such as bullet matching, that the party offering it has sufficient knowledge to be able to truthfully testify. One example is a ballistics examiner's rendition of reliable credentials.

Fountain pen   A modern nib pen containing a reservoir of ink in a specially designed chamber or cartridge. After complete filling, the pen may be used to write a number of pages without refilling.

Fourier transform (FT)   A mathematical operation that converts a function of one independent variable to one of a different independent variable. In FT–IR spectrometry, the Fourier transform converts a *time* function (the interferogram) to a *frequency* function (the infrared absorption spectrum). Spectral data are collected through the use of an interferometer that replaces the monochrometer found in the dispersed infrared spectrometer.

Fourier transform infrared (FT–IR) spectrometry   A form of infrared spectrometry, in which an interferogram is obtained; this interferogram is then subjected to a Fourier transform to obtain an amplitude wavelength (or wavelength) spectrum (Figure F.8).

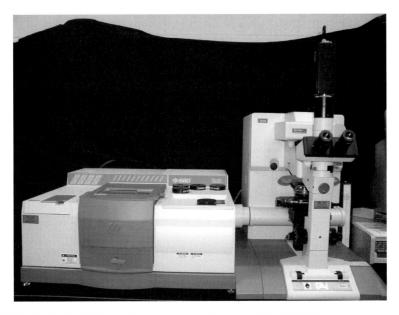

FIGURE F.8 Typical FT–IR micro imaging configuration. The FT–IR instrument is used for the nondestructive acquisition of molecular spectra from various forensic samples.

Foxing A component of the shoe used to reinforce or cover the edge of the shoe where the outsole and the upper join together. Usually a strip of rubber (foxing strip) wrapped around the lower part of the shoe.

Fraction One of the portions of a volatile liquid within certain boiling point ranges, such as petroleum naphtha fractions or gas–oil fractions.

Fragile X syndrome A complex inherited syndrome of mental retardation usually seen in males and associated with a tendency for the X chromosome to break in culture at a trinucleotide repeat site.

Fragment **(DNA analysis)** A piece of DNA cut by a restriction enzyme, also known as a *band on an autorad*. **(Firearms)** A piece of solid metal resulting from an exploding or exploded bomb, or a piece of projectile from a firearm.

Fragmented disk Occurs when there are insufficient contiguous clusters to hold a large file so that it is broken up and spread around the disk, taking advantage of available clusters.

Frame An individual picture on a roll of film or one full onscreen image of displayed computerized information.

Frame buffer A separate area of memory where an image or frame is stored in a computer.

Frame counter A dial on the camera indicating the number of exposures or frames used.

Fraud An intentional misrepresentation or deception employed to deprive another of property or a legal right or to otherwise do them harm.

Fraudulent signature   A forged signature. It involves the writing of a name as a signature by someone other than the person, without his or her permission, often with some degree of imitation.

Freehand simulation   A fraudulent signature that is produced by copying or imitating the style and size of a genuine signature, without the use of physical aids or involving a tracing process.

Freezing point   Temperature at which crystals start to form as a liquid is slowly cooled; alternatively, the temperature at which a solid substance begins to melt as it is slowly heated.

Frequency   **(DNA analysis)** Specifically refers to the number of individuals or measurements in a subgroup of the total group under consideration. The term is often more loosely equated to proportion, that is, to define a fraction or percent. **(Criminalistics)** The number of times per unit time that the magnitude of an electromagnetic wave goes from maximum to minimum, then back to maximum amplitude.

Friction ridge skin   Skin on the soles of the feet, palms of the hands, and fingers of humans and some primates that form ridges and valleys. Friction ridge skin forms classifiable patterns on the end joints of the fingers.

Frye standard   A set of standards established by the Court of Appeals of the District of Columbia in 1923 for *Frye vs. the United States*. The standards in general define when a new scientific test should be admissible as evidence in the court system.

Frye test   A test emphasizing that the subject of an expert witness's testimony must conform to a generally accepted explanatory theory. Named after the case in which the determination was made.

f-stop (f-number)   Focal setting for the diaphragm controlling the size of the aperture; the higher the *f*-stop, the smaller the aperture opening.

Fuel oil   A heavy petroleum distillate ranging from #1 (kerosene or range oil), #2 (diesel fuel), up through #6 (heavy bunker fuels). To be identified as fuel oil, a sample must exhibit a homologous series of normal alkanes ranging from C_9 and upward.

Fully automatic   Term indicates that camera aperture and speed settings can be combined to give complete automatic exposure for a picture.

Fume   Fine particles (typically of a metal oxide) dispersed in air that may be formed in various ways. (e.g., condensation of vapors, chemical reaction). Gas-like emanation containing minute solid particles arising from the heating of a solid body such as lead, in distinction to a gas or vapor. This physical change is often accompanied by a chemical reaction such as oxidation. Fumes flocculate and sometimes coalesce. Odorous gases and vapors are not fumes.

Fume hood   An enclosed laboratory cabinet with a moveable sash or fixed access port on the front, connected to a ventilating system that may incorporate air scrubbing or filtering facilities. In operation it draws in and then exhausts air from the lab to prevent or minimize the escape of air contaminants. It enables employees to manipulate materials in the hood using only their hands and arms (Figure F.9).

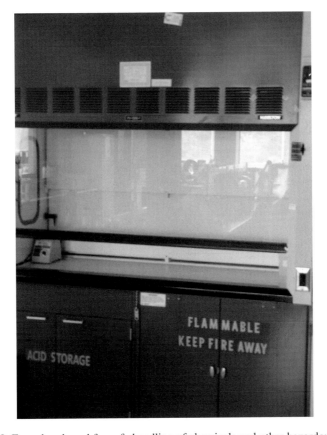

FIGURE F.9 Fume hood used for safe handling of chemicals and other hazardous materials.

Function testing The examination of a firearm concerning its mechanical condition and operation. It is usually performed to determine if all safety features are operable and if the firearm is capable of firing a cartridge.

Fundamental attribution error The belief that behavior is caused by stable factors internal to a person rather than by situational factors external to a person.

G

Gag order   A trial judge's order to the press not to print or broadcast certain information; gag orders of this type are usually found to violate the First Amendment. More common are court orders to attorneys and witnesses not to talk to the press about an upcoming trial; gag orders are entered to prevent pretrial publicity from affecting prospective jurors.

Gage   (**1**) An instrument for measuring or testing. Also spelled *gauge.* (**2**) The interior diameter of the barrel of a shotgun expressed by the number or spherical lead bullets fitting it that are required to make a pound. Thus 12 gauge is the diameter of a round lead ball weighing 1/12 of a pound.

Gain select   Increase sensitivity to light. Used when sufficient illumination is not available for video recording.

Gallops   Relating to cardiac rhythms, an abnormal third or fourth heart sound in a patient experiencing tachycardia. Gallops are indicative of a serious heart condition.

Galvanic skin response (GSR)   The electrical conductance of the skin, one of the physiological responses measured by the polygraph or lie detector to ascertain whether or not a subject is telling the truth.

Gamete   A reproductive cell (egg or sperm). A specialized haploid cell that fuses with a gamete from the opposite sex or mating type to form a diploid zygote.

Gamma   A process that improves the video image by correcting for the lack of picture clarity.

Gangrene   Death of tissue due to lack of blood supply.

Ganser's syndrome   A syndrome often observed in prisoners. Individuals routinely give inaccurate answers to simple questions. Some experts regard this behavior as a form of malingering; others believe that it reflects a distinct syndrome.

Gas   A physical state of matter that has low density and viscosity, can expand and contract greatly in response to changes in temperature and pressure, and readily and uniformly distributes itself throughout any container.

Gas chromatograph   Chromatograms from GCs are used to identify unknown compounds, such as debris collected from arsons, on the basis of the retention time or relative retention time of a peak under certain operating conditions (Figure G.1).

Gas chromatography (GC)   A separation technique involving passage of a gas, as the mobile phase, moving through a column containing a fixed absorbent material; it is used principally as a quantitative analytical technique for volatile compounds or simple gases. The separation of organic liquids, such as gases or drugs into discrete components or compounds that are

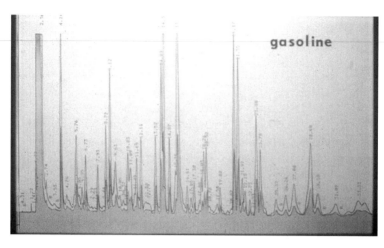

FIGURE G.1 GC chromatogram of gasoline.

seen as peaks on a chromatogram. Separation is done in a column that is enclosed in an oven held at a specific temperature or programmed to change the temperature at a reproducible rate. The column separates the compounds according to their affinity for the material inside the column (stationary phase). Columns can be packed or capillary. Packed columns employ a powdery substance that may be coated with a nonvolatile liquid phase. A capillary column is a glass or quartz tube coated with a nonvolatile liquid (Figure G.2).

Gas cutting (1) An erosive effect in a firearm caused by the high velocity, high temperature propellant gases. (2) The erosion that occurs from the hot gases on the bearing surface and base of a fired bullet.

Gasoline A mixture of more than 20 volatile hydrocarbons in the range of C_4 to C_{12}, suitable for use in a spark ignited internal combustion engine. Regular automotive gasoline has a flash point of -40°F.

Gastric ulcer Erosive-type circumscribed lesion of the lining of the stomach due to the breakdown of the normal mucosal protective layer. May result in hemorrhage due to erosion into underlying blood vessels (Figure G.3).

Gastritis Inflammation of the stomach, characterized by epigastric pain or tenderness, nausea, vomiting, and systemic electrolyte changes if vomiting persists. The mucosa may be atrophic or hypertrophic (Figure G.4).

Gault decision Landmark 1967 Supreme Court decision affirming that juveniles are entitled to the same due process rights as adults the right to counsel, the right to notice of specific charges of the offense, the right to confront and cross-examine a witness, the right to remain silent, and the right to subpoena witnesses in defense. The right to trial by jury was not included.

GC/MS (gas chromatograph/mass spectrometer) A quantitative and qualitative method for the separation and identification of organic materials in complex mixtures or solutions. This method has applications in the examinations of drugs, explosive residues, paints, plastics and inks and can be

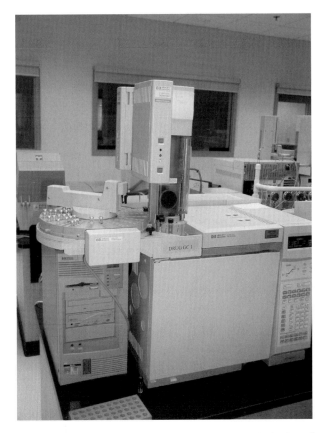

FIGURE G.2 The gas chromatography separates compounds by their size, shape, and reactivity with the chemical coating of the GC column. This GC has a robotic arm and a carousel so the instrument can automatically inject the samples from the glass vials into the column.

used to analyze material to determine if a substance contains gunpowder (Figure G.5).

Gel electrophoresis Using a gel medium to separate charged molecules.

Gel electrophoresis unit and power pack The unit is used for running gel electrophoresis systems. The unit can hold a small polyacrylamide gel, while the power pack supplies the electrical current needed to separate molecules, such as proteins or nucleic acids traveling through the polyacrylamide gel (Figure G.6).

Gene The fundamental physical and functional unit of heredity that carries information from one generation to the next; a segment of DNA composed of a transcribed region and a regulatory sequence that makes transcription possible.

Gene frequency (allele frequency) A measure of the commonness of an allele in a population; the proportion of all alleles of that gene in the population that are of this specific type.

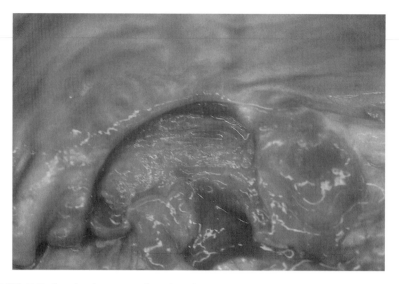

FIGURE G.3 Gastric ulcer extending deep into the inner lining and wall of the stomach. (Courtesy of forensic medical examiner Michael Sikirica, M.D.)

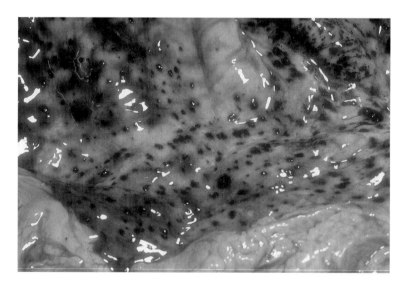

FIGURE G.4 Close-up photograph of gastritis with punctate areas of hemorrhage (dark spots) on the lining of the stomach. (Courtesy of forensic medical examiner Michael Sikirica, M.D.)

General pretrial publicity   Media coverage of issues not specifically related to a particular case but which are thematically relevant to the issues at hand; jurors exposed to pretrial publicity about other crimes are more likely to judge a defendant guilty than jurors who have not been exposed to such publicity.

FIGURE G.5 GC/MS instrument. The gas chromatography (GC) instrument separates the compounds, and the mass spectroscopy (MS) provides information concerning the chemical properties of each of the compounds as it elutes from the chromatographic column.

FIGURE G.6 Gel electrophoresis unit with power supply unit.

General rifling characteristics The number, width, and direction of twist of the rifling grooves in a barrel of a given caliber firearm.

Generic class A group of fibers having similar, but not identical, chemical composition. A generic name applies to all member of a group and is not protected by trademark registration. Generic names for manufactured fibers include, for example, rayon, nylon, and polyester.

Genetic markers Can be divided into two groups based on differences in bio-chemistry, method of detection, and their history of discovery. The two groups are the polymorphic antigen system, which is found on red blood cells and other cell surfaces, and the polymorphic soluble protein markers.

Genus A group of closely related species of organisms. The genus is given as the first part of a scientific name.

Glare Intense light reflected off highly reflective surfaces such as water, glass, and very light-toned objects.

Glass An inorganic substance in a condition that is continuous with, and anal-ogous to, the liquid state of that substance. An inorganic product of fusion that has cooled to a rigid condition without crystallizing. A manufactured fiber in which the fiber-forming substance is glass.

Glaucoma A disease of the eye characterized by abnormal and damaging high pressure inside the eye; usually due to a blockage of the channel that normally allows the outflow of fluid from the eye.

Glue A crude, impure, amber-colored form of commercial gelatin of unknown detailed composition produced by the hydrolysis of animal collagen; gelatinizes in aqueous solutions and dries to form a strong, adhesive layer.

Gooping The accumulation of excessive amounts of ink on the exterior of the point assembly of a ball-point pen as a result of the rotation of the ball; usually transferred to the paper surface immediately after the direction of rotation is substantially changed.

Grain (1) Individual silver particles or groups of particles in the emulsion which, when enlarged, become noticeable and sometimes objectionable. (2) A unit of weight (avoirdupois); 7000 grains equal 1 lb. The grain unit is commonly used in American and English ammunition practice to mea-sure the weight of components.

Graininess The grainy appearance of photographic enlargements. More prom-inent on higher-speed film. The sand-like or granular appearance of a negative, print, or slide resulting from the clumping of silver grains during development of the film. Graininess becomes more pronounced with faster film, increased density in the negative, and degree of enlargement.

Grand jury A group of citizens, usually numbering 23, that are assembled in secret to hear or investigate allegations of criminal behavior. A grand jury has authority to conduct criminal investigations and to charge a crime by indictment; also may have power to issue a report, or presentment, without charging a crime.

Granules The individual particles of propellant powder.

Graphoanalysis A registered trade name that identifies the system of handwrit-ing analysis taught by the International Graphoanalysis Society, Inc.

Graphology   The art of attempting to interpret the character of personality of an individual from his handwriting; also called *Grapho-analysis*.

Graphometry   A method of characterizing a handwriting by measurement of the proportionate values of the angles and ratio of the heights and widths of letters.

Graphonomics   The study of the science and technology of handwriting and other graphic skills (coined in 1982), or the scientific study concerned with the systematic relationships involved in the generation and analysis of writing and drawing movements, and the resulting traces of writing and drawing instruments, either on conventional media such as paper and blackboard, or on electronic equipment.

Grid search   Particular search pattern that involves traversing parallel corridors, perpendicular to the wind if possible, so that the area is covered evenly; also termed *corridor search* or *thorough searches*.

Griess test   A chemical test for the detection of nitrites. It is used by firearms examiners to develop patterns of gunpowder residues (nitrites) around bullet holes.

Grips   A pair of pieces designed to fit the frame of a weapon providing a form-fit gripping surface, usually plastic or wood.

Groove diameter   The major diameter in a barrel that is the diameter of a circle circumscribed by the bottom of the grooves in a rifled barrel.

Grooves   Spiral cuts along the bore of a firearm that cause a projectile to spin as it travels through the barrel, providing stability in flight.

Guide number   An indication of the power of a flash unit, enabling the correct aperture to be selected at a given distance between flash and subject. The number divided by the distance gives the *f*-stop that should be used. A film speed is specified with the guide number and recalculation is needed for different speeds.

Guided-hand signature   A signature that is executed while the writer's hand or arm is steadied in any way. Also known as an *assisted signature*. Under the law in most jurisdictions, such a signature authenticates a legal document provided it is shown that the writer requested the assistance. Guided signatures are most commonly written during a serious illness or on the deathbed.

Guilt   Feeling that one has done something wrong. Also, realization that one has violated principles, accompanied by regretful feeling of lessened personal worth on that account.

Guilty Knowledge Test   A polygraph technique in which the subject is asked a series of questions whose answers would only be known by the perpetrator.

Gun cotton (nitrocellulose)   The principal ingredient of single-base and double-base gun powders. Also known as *cellulose hexanitrate*.

Gunpowder   Any of various powders used in firearms as a propellant charge.

Gunpowder patterns   (**1**) The spatial distribution of gunpowder residues deposited upon a surface. (**2**) The test firing of a firearm for a muzzle to target distance determination (Figure G.7).

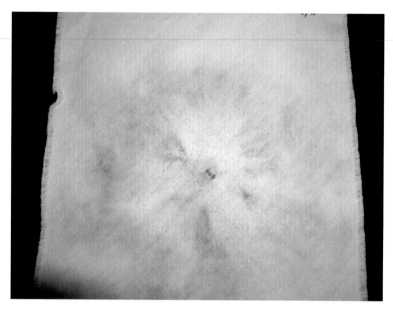

FIGURE G.7 Gunpowder pattern from a distance of 4 in.

Gunpowder residue   Unburned gunpowder, partially burned gunpowder, and smoke from completely burned gunpowder. Gunpowder residues are the largest part of gunshot residues.

Gunshot residue (GSR)   The total residues resulting from the discharge of a firearm. It includes both gunpowder and primer residues, plus metallic residues from projectiles, fouling, etc.

Gyroscopic stability   The ability of a fired bullet to remain stable in flight due to its spin.

H

Habeas corpus A writ that commands that a person be brought before a judge. Most commonly, a writ of *habeas corpus* is a legal document that forces law enforcement authorities to produce a prisoner they are holding and to legally justify his or her detention. After direct appeals have been exhausted, the defendant may petition the trial court claiming that his or her continued detention is unlawful. If sufficient basis exists, the government may be asked to establish the legality of the detention.

Habit Any persistently repeated element or detail of writing that occurs when the opportunity allows.

Hair (1) An appendage of the skin that grows out of an organ known as the *hair follicle*. (2) A thread-like outgrowth of the epidermis of animals, especially a keratinized structure in mammalian skin.

Half-cock The position of the hammer of a firearm when about half retracted and held by the sear so that it cannot be operated by a normal pull of the trigger.

Hallucinogens Drugs like marijuana, LSD, PSP, and ecstasy that produce changes in mood, thought and perception.

Hallux The large toe of the foot.

Hammer A component part of the firing mechanism that gives impulse to the firing pin or primer.

Hand lettering (hand printing) Any disconnected style of writing in which each letter is written separately.

Handguard A wooden, plastic, or metal type of forend/forearm that generally encircles the forward portion of the barrel to protect the hand from heat when firing.

Handgun A firearm designed to be held and fired with one hand.

Haplography The unintentional omission in writing or copying of one or more adjacent and similar letters, syllables, words, or lines.

Hard disk A device used to store large amounts of information. A hard disk maintains the information stored on it after the power is turned off; also referred as a *hard drive*.

Hardy–Weinberg equilibrium In a large random intrabreeding population, not subjected to excessive selection or mutation, the gene and genotype frequencies will remain constant over time. The sum of $p^2 + 2pq + q^2$ applies at equilibrium for a single allele pair where p is the frequency of allele A, q is the frequency of a, p^2 is the frequency of genotype AA, q^2 is the frequency of aa, and $2pq$ is the frequency of Aa.

Hashish Purified resin prepared from the flowering tops of the female cannabis plant and smoked or chewed as a narcotic or an intoxicant.

Hate crimes   Criminal acts that are intended to harm or intimidate people because of their race, ethnicity, sexual orientation, religion, or other minority group status.

Haze filter   Lens filter that reduces the effect of atmospheric haze. Red reduces most, green the least. A blue filter induces haze.

Head   The anterior body region; in insects it bears the mouth parts, antennae, eyes and ocelli (when present).

Head (cartridge case head)   The base of the cartridge case that contains the primer.

Headspace   (Firearms) The distance from the face of the closed breech of a firearm to the surface in the chamber on which the cartridge case bears. (**Criminology**) When fire debris material that is collected from a fire and placed into a container and sealed, the fire debris sits on the bottom of the container and the space above is referred to as *headspace*. This headspace can contain volatile hydrocarbons that, when withdrawn from the sealed container and injected into a gas chromatograph, can reveal the presence of an accelerant if present in the fire debris.

Headspace concentration   A technique for concentration of all or most of the flammable or combustible liquid vapors in a sample onto a tube of charcoal, a wire coated with charcoal, a charcoal-coated polymer, or some other adsorbing material that will later be desorbed in order to analyze the concentrated vapor. This is a primary form of sample preparation in arson debris analysis. This is also known as *adsorption/elution, vapor concentration*, or *total headspace*.

Headspace gage   An instrument for measuring the distance from the breech face of a firearm to the portion of the chamber against which the cartridge bears.

Head stamp   Numerals, letters, and symbols (or combinations thereof) stamped into the head of a cartridge case or shotshell to identify the manufacture, caliber, gauge, or give additional information.

Hearing (legal)   Judicial or legal examination of the issues of law and fact between parties. Also, a formal proceeding where evidence is taken for the purpose of determining an issue of fact and reaching a decision on the basis of that evidence

Hearsay   A statement made during a trial or hearing that is not based on the personal, firsthand knowledge of the witness. Statement made out of court and offered in court to support the truth of the facts asserted in the statement.

Hearsay rule   The regulation making a witness's statement inadmissible if it is not based on personal knowledge, unless it falls within certain exceptions. Oral or written statements are nonadmissible. When witnesses are asked what some other person told them, it is inadmissible if the material being described is for the purposes of determining the truth of the matter asserted. If, however, it is elicited merely to show that the words were spoken, it is admissible.

Heat A mode of energy associated with and proportional to molecular motion that may be transferred from one body to another by conduction, convection, or radiation.

Heel (**Firearms**) **1.** The part of a rifle or shotgun stock at the top of the butt end. **2.** The rear portion of a bullet or its base. (**Foot Impression**) A separate component attached to the rear portion of the outsole. In a one-piece outsole, it is the raised area in the rear portion of the outsole. In a flat shoe, it is the heel area.

Hematology Branch of biology that deals with blood and blood-forming organs.

Hematoma Accumulation of blood in tissue due to internal hemorrhaging. A tumor of blood caused by leakage from damaged blood vessels; it contains enough blood to form a blood-filled space.

Heme Nonprotein portion of hemoglobin and a number of other proteins in the body that possess iron protoporphyrin structures.

Hemizygous The situation in which a chromosomal element has no complement. This is normal for haploid organisms, and for some genetic elements such as mtDNA in diploid organisms.

Hemoglobin (Hb) The iron-containing, oxygen-carrying molecule, pigment of red blood cells composed of two α-chains, two β-chains, and heme group.

Hemoglobin gene Human hemoglobin is a tetramer composed of two α-chains and two β-chains in adults. Other genes and pseudogenes are transcribed during fetal development. The α cluster is on chromosome 16 and the β cluster is on chromosome 11.

Hemolysis Destruction or dissolution of red blood cells in such a manner that hemoglobin is liberated into the medium in which the cells are suspended.

Hemolytic anemia Any anemia resulting from destruction of red blood cells.

Hemophilia A hereditary blood disease characterized by impaired coagulability of the blood and a strong tendency to bleed.

Hemoptysis Coughing and spitting of blood as a result of bleeding from any part of the respiratory tract.

Hemorrhage Escape of whole blood from a blood vessel. Abnormal internal or external bleeding. May be venous, arterial, or capillary from blood vessels into the tissues, or into or from the body.

Heptane An alkane having the formula C_7H_{16}, flash point of 25°F and explosive limit of 1.2 to 6.7%.

Herniation Rupture of tissue into an adjacent space due to internal pressure or swelling.

Heredity The transmission of genetic characteristics from parent to offspring.

Heteroplasmy In particular reference to mtDNA, the situation in which two populations of hemizygous molecules exist in an individual.

Heterozygote An individual with different alleles at some particular locus.

Heterozygote peak height ratio (PHR) The height (RFU-relative fluorescence unit) of the lower peak divided by the height of the higher peak, expressed as a percentage.

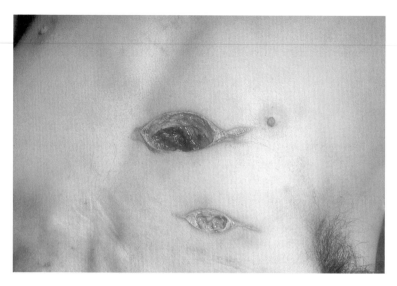

FIGURE H.1 Hilt marks seen on two deep stab wounds to the chest. (Courtesy of forensic medical examiner Michael Sikirica, M.D.)

Hiatus   A gap in a writing stroke of a letter formed when the instrument leaves the paper; an opening; an interruption in the continuity of a line.

High explosives   Explosives that produce an extremely intense explosive effect and a supersonic pressure wave when they detonate.

High-risk crime   Crime committed at time or place that posed a great threat of discovery to the offender. This category of crime is normally attributed to the "disorganized" criminal. The use of alcohol or drugs will greatly enhance the risk potential of the offender by lowering inhibitions.

High-velocity impact spatter   A bloodstain pattern caused by a high-velocity force characterized by a mist-like dispersion, which owing to the low density of the blood particles, has traveled only a short distance in flight. A high-velocity impact is considered to be approximately 100 ft/sec or greater, such as produced by gunshot and high-speed machinery. Individual stains within the mist-like dispersion is usually 0.1 mm or smaller in diameter but may be seen in association with larger bloodstains.

Hilt marks   The handle and guard of a knife or dagger. The hilt of a knife blade where the blade and handle come together. Stab wounds to the body can leave the hilt pattern of abrasion on the skin (Figure H.1).

Hinged frame   Any of a large array of pistols, revolvers, shotguns, and rifles whose frames are hinged to facilitate loading and ejection. Generally, the barrel pivots downward.

HITS   Homicide Investigation and Tracking System. A database at the Washington State Attorney's Office for murder and sexual assault information.

HOLMES   Acronym for the Home Office Large/Major Enquiry System, the U.K. mainframe police computer system.

Holographic document   Any document completely written and signed by one person; also known as a *holograph*. In a number of jurisdictions a holographic may be probated without anyone having witnessed its execution.

Holometabolous   Complete metamorphosis. This is the most complex type of metamorphosis. The developmental life cycle of an insect that goes through four distinct stages of growth: the egg, larva, pupa, and adult.

Holster stock   A holster, usually made of wood, that attaches to the rear of the pistol grip of certain handguns and serves as a shoulder stock.

Homicide   Manner of death; when the death of one person is caused by the actions of another person, including manslaughter and murder.

Homogametic sex   The sex that produces gametes with only one type of sex chromosome. In mammals, each egg carries one X chromosome. Sperm carry an X or a Y chromosome.

Homologous   Refers to the chromosome pairs found in diploid organisms. The human has 22 homologous pairs of autosomes (nonsex chromosomes) plus two sex chromosomes per nucleus. The members of each pair have an identical sequence of genes; however, the alleles at corresponding loci may be identical (homozygous) or different (heterozygous).

Homologous series   A series of similar organic compounds, differing only in that the next higher member of the series has an additional CH_2 group (one carbon atom and two hydrogen atoms) in its molecular structure. Fuel oils are characterized by the presence of identifiable homologous series of normal alkanes.

Homozygote   An individual with the same allele at corresponding loci on the homologous chromosomes.

Homozygous   The presence of identical alleles at corresponding homologous chromosome loci.

Horizontal scent cone   A scent cone formed with wind moving across a source and parallel to the ground, with the cone apex and greatest scent intensity nearest to the source.

Hostile witness   A witness whose testimony is not favorable to the party who calls him or her as a witness. A hostile witness may be asked leading questions and may be cross-examined by the party who calls him or her to the stand.

Hot zone   The area immediately surrounding a chemical hazard incident, such as a spill, in which contamination or other danger exists.

Hue   The name by which one color is distinguished from another (e.g., blue, red).

Hung jury   A jury that cannot reach a verdict.

Hybridization   DNA molecules are composed of two complementary halves that serve as templates for each other. Hybridization occurs when these halves separate and a half of different origin connects with one of the separated halves to form a hybrid molecule.

Hydrocarbon   An organic compound containing only carbon and hydrogen.

Hydrochloric acid Pertaining to or designating a colorless, corrosive, fuming acid, HCL, exceedingly soluble in water. **(Firearms)** A chemical reagent used in the sodium rhodizonate test for lead and other primer residues.

Hydrogen The simplest element. Atomic number of 1. Hydrogen gas has a specific gravity of 0.694 (air = 1), so it is much lighter than air. Hydrogen is highly flammable, forming water upon combustion. Explosive limit is 4 to 75%.

Hydrogen bond A relatively weak bond between a hydrogen (H) atom, covalently bound to a nitrogen (N) or oxygen (O) atom, and another atom. These bonds bind complementary DNA strands together. The bonds can be easily broken by increasing the temperature; a temperature of about 95°C will separate the bonds between double-stranded DNA molecules.

Hydrolytic reaction One in which a covalent bond is broken with the incorporation of a water molecule.

Hydrophilic Groups interact with water, so that hydrophilic regions of protein or the faces of a lipid bilayer reside in an aqueous environment. Having a strong affinity for binding or absorbing water, which results in swelling and formation of reversible gels.

Hydrophobic Groups repel water, so that they interact with one another to generate a nonaqueous environment. Antagonistic to water; incapable of dissolving in water.

Hymen Thin membrane, in females, that separates the external genitalia from the vagina. The outer surface is a dry, squamous epithelium, and the inner surface is a moist mucous membrane.

Hypervariable Some segments of DNA molecules are identical or almost identical in all individuals while others show variability. A hypervariable is a DNA segment that is highly variable and differs in most individuals.

Hypervariable region Locus with many alleles, especially those whose variation is due to variable numbers of tandem repeats.

Hypnosis Trancelike mental state induced in a cooperative subject by suggestion. A sleep-like mental state induced by a person whose suggestions are readily accepted by the subject; because it sometimes releases memories of traumatic events that are otherwise inaccessible, it is sometimes used to discover answers to significant questions, e.g., what was seen or heard during a criminal event.

Hypothermia Having a body temperature below normal.

Hypotheses, alternative and null The two possibilities established by the social scientist before running a statistical test. The null hypothesis means nothing unusual is going on, the independent variable has no significant effect on the dependent variable and the results could have occurred by chance. The alternative hypothesis rejects the null and prophesies that the independent variable will affect the dependent variable.

Hypothesis testing or Significance testing   Process of assessing the statistical significance of a finding. It involves comparing empirically observed sample findings with theoretically expected findings, expected if the null hypothesis is true. This comparison allows one to compute the probability that the observed outcomes could have been due to chance alone.

Hypovolemia   Diminished blood volume.

Hypoxia   Condition in which below-normal levels of oxygen are present in the air, blood, or body tissues, short of anoxia.

I

IAI International Association for Identification, the main professional organization for latent print examiners.

IBIS Integrated Ballistics Information System. A database used for acquiring, storing, and analyzing images of bullets and cartridge casings (Figure I.1).

ICP–MS Inductively coupled plasma–mass spectroscopy. A modern technique for metal analysis that utilizes radio frequency energy for the detection and quantitation of metals.

Icterus A condition characterized by yellowish skin, eyes, mucous membranes, and body fluids owing to deposition of excess bilirubin.

Identifiable striae Striations in the evidence mark that can be identified with reproduced striations in the test marks.

Identification An analytical and classification process by which an entity is placed in a predefined, limited, or restricted class.

Identikit The first packaged system for reconstructing the appearance of a suspect's face, based on a wide choice of drawings of facial features.

IEF (Isoelectric focusing) One of the simplest techniques for separation and characterization of proteins.

Ignition The means by which burning is started.

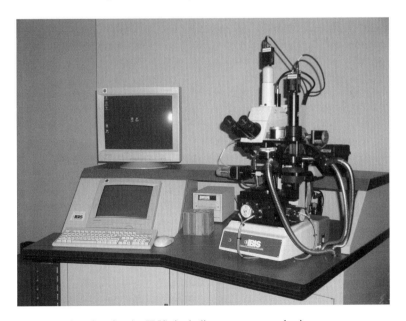

FIGURE I.1 Workstation for the IBIS, including computer and microscope.

Ignition temperature   The minimum temperature to which a fuel must be heated in order to initiate or cause self-sustained combustion independent of another heat source.

Ignition (autoignition) temperature   The minimum temperature required to ignite gas or vapor without a spark or flame being present.

Ignition source   Location of a flame, arc, spark, or chemical reaction that provides sufficient heat energy in the presence of a fuel and an oxidizer to initiate combustion.

Illumination   A specific amount of light present in any given area. Expressed in lux or foot-candles; the lower the lux of equipment, the less light required for a good picture.

Image   (1) The photographic representation of an object or scene formed by optical or chemical action. (2) A two-dimensional array of pixels representing a three-dimensional computer-generated scene.

Image aspect ratio   Ratio of the width to the height of a displayed computer-generated image.

Image resolution   Number of pixels displayed per unit of printed length in an image, usually measured in pixels per inch (ppi).

Immiscible   Describes substances of the same phase or state of matter (usually liquid) that cannot be uniformly mixed or blended.

Immunity   Grant by the court, in which someone will not face prosecution in return for providing criminal evidence.

Immunoassay   A fluorescent antibody technique, used for detection of antigens and antibodies in blood and serum.

Immunochemistry   That branch of chemistry concerned with the various defense mechanisms of the animal organism against infective agents, particularly the response between the body and foreign macromolecules (antigens), and the interaction between the products of the response (antibodies) and the agents that have elicited them. This involves study of the many proteins involved in these responses.

Immunodiffusion   It involves the use of agar plates with wells for both antibodies and antigens. The two reactants diffuse into the gel where immunoprecipitates will form at the point of equivalence for each antigen–antibody pair.

Immunoelectrophoresis   Consists of a combination of electrophoresis and immunodiffusion in a gel. It is based on the fact that in a gel medium, the movement of molecules in an electric field is similar to that in a liquid medium, with the advantage that free diffusion is lessened after electrophoresis.

Impact pattern   Bloodstain pattern created when blood receives a blow or force resulting in the random dispersion of smaller drops of blood.

Impact site   The point on a bloody object or body that receives a blow. Often, impact site is used interchangeably with *point of origin*. Impact site may also refer to an area on the surface of a target that is struck by blood in motion.

Impact spatter   Bloodstain pattern created when blood receives a blow or force resulting in the random dispersion of smaller drops.

Impact velocity   The velocity of a projectile or missile at the instant of impact. Also known as *striking velocity.*

Impetigo   Highly contagious, rapidly spreading skin disorder caused by staphylococcus or streptococcus and characterized by red blisters. Impetigo sometimes occurs as a result of poor hygiene.

Important items (ASCLD)   Standards that are considered to be key indicators of the overall quality of the laboratory but may not directly affect the work product or the integrity of the evidence.

Impramine   The prototype of the tricyclic antidepressant drugs.

Impression   Surface contour variations on an object caused by applying force that is approximately perpendicular to the plane being marked.

Impression evidence   Objects or materials that have retained the characteristics of other objects that have been physically pressed against them.

Impurity   The presence of one substance in another in such low concentration that it cannot be measured quantitatively by ordinary analytical methods.

Inadmissible evidence   The testimony that the judge rules as not proper and hence instructs the jury to disregard.

Inbreeding   Reproduction between related individuals.

In camera   In chambers; in private. The hearing of a case before a judge in private chambers when all spectators are excluded from the courtroom, or when the judge performs a judicial act while the court is not in session.

Incendiaries   Substances or mixtures of substances consisting of a fuel and an oxidizer used to initiate a fire.

Incendiary fire   Fire intentionally set by human hands, often involving the use of an accelerant to spread and increase the rate and intensity of burning.

Incest   Sexual conduct between persons who are closely related by blood. Laws in a number of states define incest as marriage or sexual relationships between relatives who are closer than second (or sometimes more distant) cousins. The most common form of incest is between fathers and daughters.

Incidental accelerants   Flammable or combustible liquids that are usual and incidental to an area where they are detected. Gasoline is incidental to an area where gasoline-powered appliances are kept. Kerosene is incidental to an area where a kerosene heater is kept. Flammable liquids may also comprise a part of a product such as insecticide, furniture polish, or paint. Additionally, certain asphalt-containing building materials may yield detectable quantities of fuel oil components.

Incised wound   Injury produced by a sharp instrument and characterized by lack of surface abrasion and absence of bridging vessels, nerves, and smooth margins (Figure I.2).

Incision   A wound produced by a sharp-edged instrument or object.

Inclusion   A crime suspect's DNA identity profile matching that of a crime evidence sample, or a putative father's DNA identity profile matching offspring paternally derived alleles.

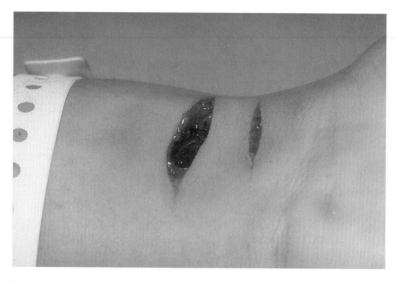

FIGURE I.2 Self-inflicted incised wounds of the wrist. (Courtesy of forensic medical examiner Michael Sikirica, M.D.)

Incompetency Lacking the physical, intellectual, or moral capacity or qualification to perform a required duty.

Incriminating value (IV) The ratio of the probability (x) of a match for the characteristic measured if the suspect and evidence specimens are from the same source to the probability (y) if they are from different sources. $IV = x \div y$.

INDELS Single-base insertion or deletion, also called *SNP* (single nucleotide polymorphism); can be more than one base, e.g., a two-base pair insertion or deletion.

Indented writing Writing impressed into the surface of a page of paper from pressure exerted upon the writing instrument when used on a previous page.

Independent Any two events that have no influence on what happens to each other are independent or unassociated. Therefore, for independent events, the probability of both events happening are the product of the probability for each event.

Indeterminate sentence A sentence of imprisonment to a specified minimum and maximum period of time, specifically authorized by statute, subject to termination by a parole board or other authorized agency after the prisoner has served the minimum term.

Indictment An accusation by a grand jury charging a person with a crime. The process of indictment by grand jury bypasses the filing of a criminal complaint and the holding of a preliminary hearing, so prosecution begins immediately.

Indirect personality assessment (IPA) A behavioral evaluation of a criminal suspect to assist in the determination of the most effective interview, cross-examination, and other investigation techniques. Assessment of a known individual believed to be responsible for the commission of a violent crime.

Individual A unique item, identified as itself to the exclusion of all other items.

Individual characteristics **(1)** A characteristic that is highly personal or peculiar and is unlikely to occur in other instances. **(2)** Traits that define and identify an item as unique, exclusive to all other items.

Individualization Establishment of uniqueness of an item through examination and experimentation; showing that no other item is exactly like the one in question.

Induced damage Damage that was caused by components being squeezed together, causing the sheet to bend outward or inward from its normal position. The damage was not caused by an impact to the particular area of the vehicle.

Induction A process of reasoning based on a set of experiences or observations (particulars) from which a conclusion or generalization based on those specifics is drawn; it moves from the specific to the general.

Inert hand An execution of writing, in which the person holding the writing instrument exercises no motor activity whatsoever, conscious or unconscious. The guide leads the writing instrument through the medium of the hand of the first person. The writer may be feeble or a complete illiterate.

Infinity A distance from which the light appears to reach the lens in parallel rays.

Inflammation Tissue reaction to injury. The succession of changes that occurs in living tissue when it is injured.

Informant An individual who discloses information to an investigator.

Infraction A violation of law not punishable by imprisonment. Minor traffic offenses are generally considered infractions.

Infrared Invisible band of wavelength on the electromagnetic spectrum beyond visible red. The region of the electromagnetic spectrum including wavelengths from 0.78 to 1000 m (wave number range 20,000 to 4000 cm^{-1}).

Infrared absorption The taking up of energy from infrared radiation by a medium through which the radiation is passing.

Infrared examination The examination of documents employing invisible radiation beyond the red portion of the visible spectrum. Infrared radiation can be recorded on specially sensitized photographic emulsions or it can be converted by means of an electronic viewing device into visible light for an on-the-scene study of the evidence.

Infrared luminescence A phenomenon encountered with some dyes used in inks and colored pencils that, when illuminated with a narrow band of light in the blue–green portion of the spectrum, give off a luminescence that can be detected in the far-red or near-infrared range. The technique is useful in distinguishing between certain inks and colored pencils, and in detecting or deciphering erasures.

Infrared photography Recording of images produced by infrared radiation.

Infrared spectrometer Device used to identify and measure the concentration of heteroatomic compounds in gases, in many nonaqueous liquids, and in some solids.

FIGURE I.3 Infrared spectrophotometry instrument. The spectra from the IR instrument are referred to as "fingerprint spectra" of a compound, which aids in classification of the chemical.

Infrared spectrophotometry (IR)   An analytical technique that utilizes an instrument that passes infrared radiation through a sample, or that bounces infrared radiation off the surface of a sample. A very sensitive heat detecting device measures the amount of infrared radiation absorbed as the wavelength of the radiation reaching the detector is changed. IR can give useful information about the type of compounds present in a sample, but it is not capable of precisely identifying a complex mixture. Infrared is very useful in identifying single solvent accelerants. Operates in the IR wavelength range. IR is employed by forensic scientists in the analysis of the following samples: drugs, plastics, fibers, paint, and similar substances (Figure I.3).

Inhibition   The prevention of the normal reaction between an antigen and its corresponding antibody, usually because an antigen of the same specificity, but from another source, is present in the system, hence to inhibit.

Inhibitor   A chemical used to slow or stop a disliked reaction. In manufacturing powder propellants, it is used to decrease the burning rate. Any substance or object that retards a chemical reaction. A major or modifier gene that interferes with a biological reaction.

Injection port   The area on a gas chromatograph or a high-performance liquid chromatography where the sample is introduced into the instrument and onto the column (Figure I.4).

Injunction   A preventive measure by which a court orders a party to refrain from doing a particular act. A preliminary injunction is granted provisionally, until a full hearing can be held to determine if it should be made permanent.

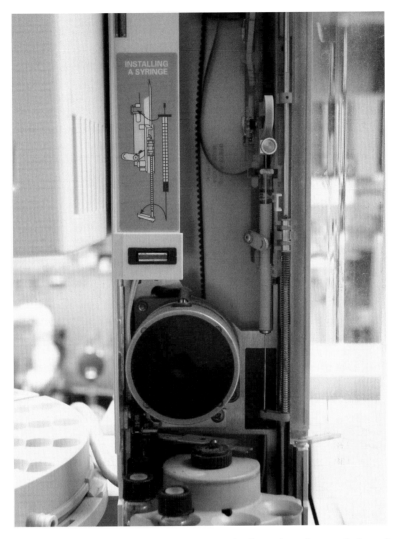

FIGURE I.4 Injection port uses a syringe to automatically aspirate the sample from the vial and inject the sample into the column of the GC/MS instrument.

Ink eradicator   A chemical solution capable of bleaching ink.

Inorganic chemistry   The study of chemical reactions and properties of all the elements and their compounds, with the exception of hydrocarbons, and usually including carbides, oxides of carbon, metallic carbonates, carbon–sulfur compounds, and carbon–nitrogen compounds.

Inorganic fiber   A class of fibers of natural mineral origin (e.g., chrysotile asbestos) and man-made mineral origin (e.g., fiberglass).

Inorganic pigment   A natural or synthetic metal oxide, sulfide, or other salt used as a coloring agent for paints, plastics, and inks.

Insanity   A social or legal term indicating a condition in which a person lacks responsibility or capacity due to mental illness. As stated in the American Law Institute Penal Code, "A person is not responsible for criminal conduct, if at the time of such conduct as a result of mental disease or defect he or she lacks substantial capacity either to appreciate the criminality or wrongfulness of his or her conduct or to conform his or her conduct to the requirements of the law."

Insect   Any arthropod characterized by having mandibles and six legs at some stage in its life.

Insertion   The addition of writing and other material within a document such as between lines or paragraphs, or the addition of whole pages to a document.

Instamatic   A designation of a particular brand-name camera normally associated with 126-size film.

Instar   Each of the successive incremental growth steps terminated by a molt.

Instrument linearity   Straight-line relationship between concentration of analyte and instrument response, in which a change in concentration causes a proportional change in response.

Insurance fraud   Act intended to deliberately deceive an insurance carrier into paying a claim for a loss or issuing a policy based on false evidence. This may include a claim for the loss of a structure due to an intentionally set fire or a claim for reimbursement for items of greater value than those present in a fire-damaged structure.

Integrated Ballistics Identification System (IBIS)   Combines specially designed imaging and correlation software with motors, cameras, a microscope, and computer equipment. The elements of this system work together to improve the way bullet and cartridge case evidence is stored and analyzed. IBIS is used to acquire images of cartridge cases and bullets found at the crime scene or obtained from test fires. These images are stored in a database and correlated against one another. IBIS looks for similarities between these images and ranks likely candidates for matches (Figure I.5).

Interference colors   Colors produced by the interference of two out-of-phase rays of white light when a birefringence material is observed at a nonextinction position between crossed polars. The retardation at a particular point in a birefringent fiber may be determined by comparing the observed interference color to the Michel–Levy chart.

Interfering substance   Substance other than the analyte that gives a similar analytical response or alters the analytical result.

Interlineation   The act of inserting writing or typewriting between two lines of writing.

Internal proficiency testing program   Proficiency testing program managed and controlled within the laboratory system.

Internal reflection spectroscopy (IRS)   The technique of recording optical spectra by placing a sample material in contact with a transparent medium of greater refractive index and measuring the reflectance (single or multiple) from the interface, generally at angles of incidence greater than the critical angle.

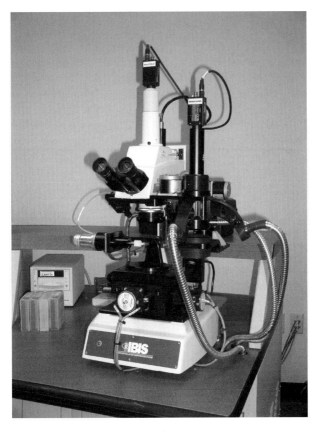

FIGURE I.5 The microscope used for the IBIS.

Internal standard   Addition of a fixed amount of a known substance that is not already present as a constituent of the specimen or sample in order to identify or quantify other components. The physico-chemical characteristics of the internal standard should be as close as possible to those of the analyte.

Interpretation   Explanation of what analytical results mean based on chemical, pharmacological, toxicological, and statistical principles.

Interrogatories   Set of specialized questions sent by one attorney to another concerning requested information of their clients or respective companies, such as maintenance and accident history of the vehicle, pre-existing medical problems of the occupants, and other pertinent information with respect to the accident itself.

Intumescent char   In plastics, the swelling and charring that results in a higher ignition point. Used in the preparation of flame retardant materials.

In vitro   Means "in glass" and refers to a biological process carried out in the laboratory separate from an organism.

In vivo   Refers to a biological process within a living organism.

Iodine fumes   The oldest method for visualizing latent fingerprints at a crime scene.

Ion   An atom, molecule or radical that has lost or gained one or more electrons, thus acquiring an electric charge. Positively charged ions are *cations*; negatively charged ions are *anions*.

Iris   The opening of a camera lens that controls the amount of light let in.

Iron–gallotannate ink   This ink is found in fountain pens, was used as early as the eighth century and with substantial improvement is still in use today. Iron salts are combined with gallotannic acid in an aqueous solution. This solution when applied to paper is first colorless but darkens quickly when oxidized by air.

Ischemia   Obstruction of blood flow (usually by arterial narrowing) that causes lack of oxygen and other bloodborne nutrients.

Ischemia necrosis   Death of cells as a result of decreased blood flow to affected tissues.

Isothermal   A type of gas chromatographic analysis wherein the column is maintained at a uniform temperature throughout the analysis.

Invertebrate   Any species of animal lacking a back bone.

J

Jacket Cylinder of steel covering and strengthening the breech end of a gun; the envelope enclosing the lead core.

Jaggies The undesirable "stair-stepping" (aliasing) effect of diagonal edges in a computer image. Reduced by *anti-aliasing*.

Jaundice Yellowing of the skin and whites of the eyes due to an accumulation of bile pigments (e.g., bilirubin) in the circulating blood. Another cause is liver damage caused by hepatitis.

Jig A mechanical device that holds the correct position relationship between a piece of work and a tool or two pieces of work.

Joint or juncture The point or position at which two or more strokes meet within a letter.

Judgment The final disposition of a lawsuit.

> **Consent judgment** Occurs when the provisions and terms of the judgment are agreed upon by the parties and submitted to the court for its sanction and approval.
>
> **Default judgment** A judgment rendered because of the defendant's failure to answer or appear.
>
> **Judgment n.o.v.** Literally a judgment *non obstante verdicto*, which translates as "judgment notwithstanding the verdict"; it is a judge's decision to decide a case contrary to the verdict of the jury. It may be made in a civil or criminal case.
>
> **Summary judgment** Judgment given on the basis of pleadings, affidavits, and exhibits presented for the record without any need for a trial. It is used when there is no dispute as to the facts of the case and one party is entitled to judgment as a matter of law.

Judicial review Authority of a court to review the official actions of other branches of government; also, authority to declare unconstitutional the actions of other branches.

Jurisdiction The nature and scope of a court's authority to hear or decide a case. Inherent power and authority of a particular court to hear and determine cases, usually involving certain categories of persons or allegations. Jurisdiction should be distinguished from *venue*, which is the particular county or district where a court with jurisdiction may hear and determine a case.

Jury A certain number of persons selected according to law and sworn to inquire into matters of fact and declare the truth about matters laid before them.

Grand jury Traditionally composed of 23 people who decide whether the facts of a criminal case are sufficient to issue an indictment charging a person with a crime.

Petit jury An ordinary or trial jury, composed of 6 to 12 persons that hears either civil or criminal cases.

Jury commissioner The court officer responsible for choosing the panel of persons to serve as potential jurors for a particular court term

Jury nullification An option for the jury that allows it to disregard both the law and the evidence and acquit the defendant if the jury believes that an acquittal is justified.

Justice Fairness, or providing outcomes to each party in line with what they deserve.

Justification In type composition, the adjustment of spacing in each line of type so that all lines are filled out to the same desired length.

Juvenile Characteristic of youth, or a young person. In a majority of states, youth means under the age of 18 years; minor.

Juvenile court A court to decide criminal charges brought against children under the age of 18; these courts often handle cases of abused or neglected children.

K

Karyotype An individual's set of chromosomes. Chromosomes arranged in order of length and according to position of centromere; also the abbreviated formula for the chromosome constitution, such as 47, XX + 21 for human trisomy-21.

Kb (kilobase) An abbreviation for 1000 base pairs of DNA.

Kelvin Unit of temperature (K) measurement used to measure the color temperature of light.

Kernechtrot solution A reddish stain that is used in conjunction with picroindigocarmine solution in the identification of human sperm. The solution will turn the head of the sperm a reddish-pink color (Figure K.1).

Kerning The spacing of two letters closer together than customary when their designs leave too much intercharacter white space.

Kerosene (#1 fuel oil) Flash point generally between 100° and 150°F with explosive limits of 0.7 to 5.0%. Kerosene consists mostly of C_9 through C_{17} hydrocarbons. In order to be identified as kerosene, a sample extract must exhibit a homologous series of five consecutive normal alkanes between C_9 and C_{17}. Kerosene is the most common "incidental" accelerant, as it is used in numerous household products ranging from charcoal lighter fluid to lamp oil to paint thinner to insecticide carriers; also used as jet fuel. K-1 kerosene has a low sulfur content required for use in portable space heaters.

Ketone A type of organic compound having a carbonyl functional group (C=O) attached to two alkyl groups. Acetone is the simplest example of a ketone.

Keyboard search A manual search of the National DNA Index System (NDIS) initiated by the NDIS custodian.

Kinetics A dynamic process involving motion.

Knit fabric A structure produced by interloping one or more ends of yarn or comparable material.

Known sample technique A quality assurance procedure in which a previously identified substance is submitted to a laboratory for examination to determine the reliability of the laboratory's procedures.

Known standard A specimen of an identified source acquired for the purpose of comparison with an evidence sample; synonymous with *exemplar.*

Knurls or **knurling** Regularly spaced ridges or rectangles used on a metal surface to assist in the prevention of slippage, usually on a knob.

Korsakoff's Syndrome Named after a Russian neurologist, it describes a personality characterized by psychosis with polyneuritis (inflammation of two or more nerves), delirium, insomnia, illusions, and hallucinations. Frequently occurs as a sequel to chronic alcoholism.

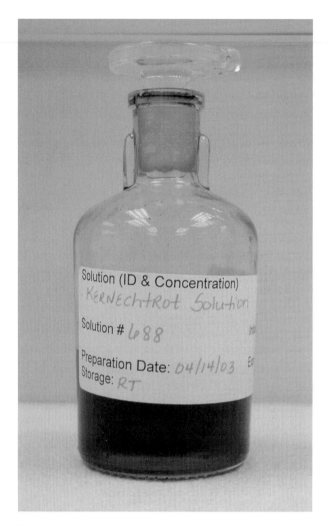

FIGURE K.1 The Kernechtrot chemical solution is used in staining sperm cells. The red-color reagent will stain the sperm head a two-tone red color.

L

Labia majora Outer lips to the vagina that are covered by pubic hair after menarche (onset of menstruation).

Laboratory satellite A member of a laboratory system that is managed by, but is physically separated from, a parent laboratory.

Laboratory system An organization containing at least two physically separate laboratory facilities that are independently managed under the control of a single laboratory director.

Laceration A wound produced by a tear in the skin due to application of blunt force in crushing or shearing.

Lacquer A sealant used by some ammunition manufacturers to seal the primer and/or bullet in the cartridge case. It is used as a waterproofing agent.

Land The raised portion between the grooves in a rifled bore.

Land and grooves impressions (right and left turn) The negative impressions on the surface of a bullet caused by the rifling in the barrel from which it was fired (Figure L.1A and B).

Lane of gel The path in the gel within which DNA fragments migrate.

FIGURE L.1A Looking down through a section of a barrel, the cuttings in the barrel are referred to as the lands and grooves.

FIGURE L.1B A wooden model of a bullet is used to show how the lands and grooves on a bullet can line up.

Langer's lines   Structural orientation of the fibrous tissue of the skin that forms the natural cleavage line present in all body areas but visible only in certain areas such as the creases of the palm.

Larceny   The crime of taking another person's property without consent and with the intent of depriving the owner of the property.

Larvae   The primary feeding and growth stage of invertebrates. Usually it is the stage following hatching of the egg.

Laser   A device that uses the maser principle of amplification of electromagnetic waves by stimulated emission of radiation, and operates in the optical or infrared regions.

Latent image   The invisible image left by the action of light on photographic film or paper. The light changes the photosensitive salts to varying degrees depending on the amount of light striking them. When processed, this latent image will become a visible image either in reversed tones (as in a negative) or in positive tones (as in a color slide) (Figure L.2).

Latent print   Generally used to describe any type of print found at the scene of a crime or on evidence associated with a crime. Latent prints are normally not visible. Some means of development is generally required for their visualization (Figure L.3).

Lateral axis   The short axis of the vehicle, from the right side to the left side.

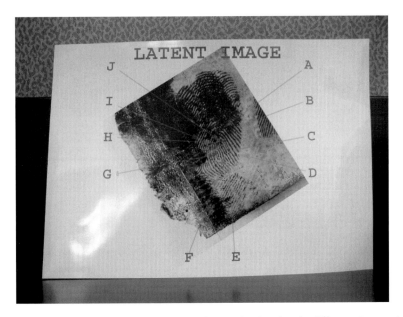

FIGURE L.2 A poster model of a latent image fingerprint showing the different characteristics of a fingerprint.

Lateral expansion The horizontal dimension of writing produced by the width of letters, the space between letters and words, and the width of margins.
Lateral writing Writing characterized by wide letters and spacing.
Lattes crust method This method relies upon the presence of the agglutinins in a bloodstain, and it is an application only to the ABO system. Adding indicator cells to the blood crust or bloodstain and testing for agglutination is a convenient way to detect the presence of agglutinin.
LCMS (liquid chromatography–mass spectrometry) A technique that replaces a gas chromatograph with a liquid chromatograph. The technique is generally applicable to solutes that are soluble in organic solvents and not ionized (Figure L.4).
Lead Element with the chemical symbol Pb and atomic number 82. Used in the fabrication of bullet and shot for its formability and lubrication properties.
Lead agency The Federal department or agency assigned lead responsibility to manage and coordinate a special function — either crisis management or consequence management. Lead agencies are designated on the basis of their having the most authorities, resources, capabilities, or expertise relative to accomplishment of the specific function. Lead agencies support the overall lead federal agency during all phases.
Lead glass Glass into which lead oxide is incorporated to give high refractive index, optical dispersion, and surface brilliance; used in optical glass.
Leading The accumulation of lead in the bore of a firearm from the passage of lead shot or bullets. Also called *metal fouling.*

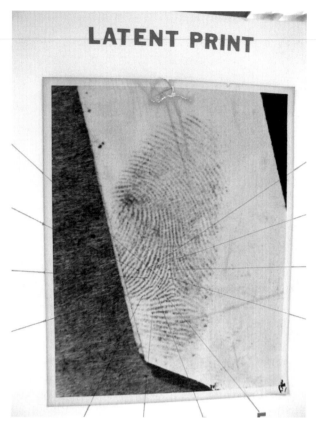

FIGURE L.3 An enlargement of a latent fingerprint poster used for teaching new police recruits.

Leading question (**1**) A question that suggests the answer desired of the witness. A party generally may not ask one's own witness leading questions; leading questions may be asked only of hostile witnesses and on cross-examination. (**2**) Queries that direct the interviewee to talk about an area that he or she did not intend to talk about. A leading question may engender in the mind of the listener a specific visual image that would not have been produced had the question not been asked. (**3**) Queries with implied directions that leads the witness toward a conclusion that supports the argument of the attorney asking the question.

Learning theory A form of criminological theory that emphasizes how specific criminal behaviors are learned directly from reinforcement and modeling influences.

Least-squares Statistical method of determining a regression equation, that is, the equation that best represents the relationship among the variables.

Left-handed curve A stroke that is made in a counterclockwise direction.

Left-handed or wrong-handed writing Any writing executed with the opposite hand from that normally used. Sometimes referred to as writing "with the

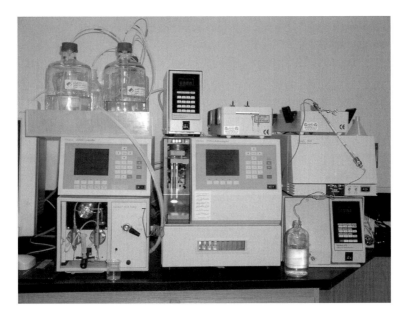

FIGURE L.4 The LCMS utilizes a closed system and pumps to pressurize the solvent (mobile phase) and to force the liquid through the column.

awkward hand." It is an attempt to disguise handwriting. Thus, the writing of a right-handed person written with his left hand accounts for the common terminology for this class of disguise as "left-handed writing."

Legal custody Right and responsibility to make the decisions regarding the health, education, and welfare of a child.

Legibility The ease with which a reader recognizes individual letter and character shapes.

Leniency Recommendation by the prosecutor to the judge regarding the sentence that may be imposed in a criminal case.

Lens cap A cover used to protect a lens from dust and damage when not in use.

Letter Any drawn, written, printed, or typed character, lowercase or uppercase, that can be recognized as an allograph of the alphabet of any language.

Leucomalachite green (leuco) test A catalytic test that is used for the detection of blood and blood stains. The test depends upon an oxidation reaction in which an oxidant, such as hydrogen peroxide, oxidizes a colorless material such as phenolphthalein or malachite green to a colored one. The test is named after the compound oxidized that is the leuco base of malachite green. Malachite green structurally resembles phenolphthalein and the leuco prefix merely refers to the colorless or reduced form of the compound. The term *leuco* comes from the literature of biological stains and dyes. A positive reaction will produce a bluish-green color (Figure L.5).

FIGURE L.5 A chemical screening test for the presence of blood; a bluish-green reaction indicates a positive result.

Level of significance Probability that a result would be produced by chance alone, i.e., the probability of incorrectly rejecting the null hypothesis. It is, therefore, the probability of making a type I error.

Lever action A design wherein the breech mechanism is cycled by an external lever generally below the receiver.

Lexical Pertaining or related to the words of a language (hence *dyslexia*, meaning a disturbance of the ability to read).

Liable Responsible or answerable for some action.

Ligature A group of connected characters treated typographically as a single character; sometimes a stroke or bar connecting two letters.

Light (**1**) The natural condition or medium permitting vision. (**2**) Any one of a number of known forms of radiant energy that travels with a wave motion. (**3**) A form of radiant energy that makes up the visible part of the electromagnetic spectrum.

Light microscope A microscope that employs light in the visible or near-visible portion of the electromagnetic spectrum.

Light source General term for any source of light used in photography, whether natural or artificial.

Likelihood A statistical measure of the correctness of a hypothesis given certain observations.

Likelihood ratio The probability of a random drawing of a specified sample from a population, assuming a given hypothesis about the parameters of the population, divided by the probability of a random drawing of the

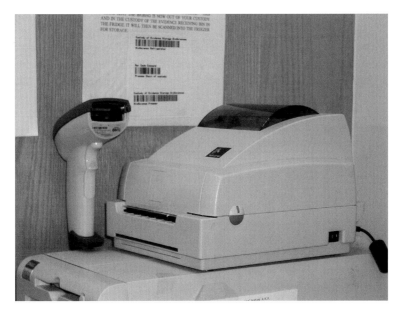

FIGURE L.6 The LIMS uses a bar code method for the identification of evidence. The picture shows the bar code labelmaker and a handheld scanner.

same sample, assuming that the parameters of the population are such that this probability is maximized.

Limit   Prescribed or specified maximum or minimum amount, quantity, or number.

Action limit Corresponds to a three standard deviation from the mean. If an observed value falls outside the action limit, the cause must be identified and remedial action taken.

Confidence limit The limits of the confidence interval.

Control limit The limits, on a control chart, that are used as criteria for action or for judging whether a set of data does or does not indicate lack of statistical control.

Detection limit Smallest measured content from which it is possible to deduce the presence of analyte with reasonable statistical certainty.

Quantitation limit The smallest measured content from which it is possible to quantitate the analyte with an acceptable level of accuracy and precision.

Warning limit Corresponds to a two standard deviation from the mean. Even if the method is under statistical control, approximately 5% of results may be expected to fall outside the warning limits.

LIMS (Laboratory Information Management System) Software package for collating, calculating, controlling, and disseminating analytical data. It can perform a variety of functions, from specimen or sample registration and tracking to processing captured data, quality control, and financial control and report generation. This system uses a bar code label for identification and tracking of various specimen or samples (Figure L.6).

Line quality   Appearance of a written stroke determined by a combination of factors, such as speed, shading, pen position, and skill; ranges from smooth and legible to tremulous and awkward.

Linear regression   Method of describing the relationship between two or more variables by calculating a best-fitting straight line or graph.

Lineup   The practice of placing a suspect within a group of people lined up for the purpose of being viewed (and possibly identified as the perpetrator) by eyewitnesses (also called *identification parade*).

Linkage   A measure of association between loci. Loci on different chromosomes are nonlinked. Those close together on the same chromosome are closely linked and are usually inherited together.

Linkage analysis   The comparison of crimes to determine whether they were committed by the same offender. Linkages can be established through physical evidence, eyewitnesses, or behavioral similarities such as *modus operandi* (MO) and signature. Also known as *crime pattern analysis*.

Linkage disequilibrium   The phenomenon of a specific allele of one locus being associated or linked to a specific allele or marker of another locus, on the same chromosome, with a greater frequency than expected by chance.

Linkage equilibrium (LE)   When two or more genetic loci appear to segregate randomly in a given population. The genotypes appear randomly with respect to each other.

Liquid accelerant   Combustible or flammable liquid used to accelerate ignition and spread of a fire.

Litigation   A case, controversy, or lawsuit.

Livor mortis   A coloration of the skin of the lower parts of a corpse caused by the settling of the red blood cells as the blood ceases to circulate (Figure L.7).

Locard's exchange principle   According to Edmond Locard, when two objects contact each other, materials are transferred from one object to another; the basis for proving contact by the analysis of microscopic evidence.

Locus (*plural*, loci)   The site on a chromosome where a gene or a defined sequence is located. The position on a chromosome occupied by a gene.

Logbook   Book that records laboratory activities, e.g., instrumentation, maintenance, or instrumentation, sample preparation, and reagents.

Longitudinal axis   The long axis of the vehicle that runs from the front (or hood) to the rear (or trunk) of the vehicle.

Low explosive   Explosives having a detonation less violent than high explosives (above) and that produce a subsonic pressure wave.

Low-velocity impact spatter   Bloodstains produced on a surface when the blood source has been subjected to a low-velocity force approximately 5 ft/sec or less.

LSD (lysergic acid diethylamide)   A drug that can induce a psychotic-like state. A psychotomimetic drug synthesized from compounds derived from ergot.

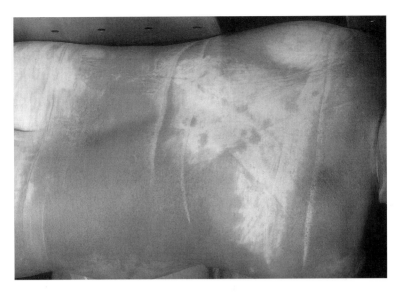

FIGURE L.7 Posterior lividity of the back of a person, with blanching due to the pressure effect of deceased's position and clothing. (Courtesy of forensic medical examiner Michael Sikirica, M.D.)

Luger A German automatic pistol widely used in Europe as a military sidearm, manufactured in various calibers, most commonly 7.65 mm, and 9 mm.

Lumen (Photography) Photometric unit equal to the luminous flux on 1 ft² of surface from a standard candle 1 ft away. **(Microscopy)** The cavity or central canal that is present in many natural fibers (e.g., cotton, flax, ramie, jute, hemp). Its presence and structure are often a useful aid in identification.

Lumigraph A sheet of x-ray film with the results of quantified DNA that is measured in ng/uL.

Luminesce To absorb illumination and re-emit it at a wavelength different from the incident light; akin to fluorescence, luminescence is useful to criminal investigation in that latent fingerprints become visible because organic solids in perspiration can be detected by lasers due to their luminescence.

Luminescence The visible glow of certain substances (e.g., components of some inks) when subjected to stimulation by electromagnetic radiation, electric fields, or heat. Luminescence embraces fluorescence and phosphorescene.

Luminol A substance that can be sprayed onto furnishings at a crime scene to reveal traces of blood as spots of bright light.

Luminol test A method of choice for the detection of occult (usually not noticeable to the naked eye) blood at a crime scene that was cleaned up or escaped detection for extended periods of time.

Luster The gloss or shine possessed by a fiber, resulting from its reflection of light. The luster of manufactured fibers is often modified by use of a delustering pigment.

Lymphocyte   A general class of white blood cells that are important components of the immune system of vertebrate animals.

Lyocel   A manufactured fiber composed of precipitated cellulose and produced by a solvent extrusion process where no chemical intermediates are formed.

Lysis   The process by which cells are broken apart and/or the process of disintegration or destruction of cells.

Lysis agent   A chemical used to open cell membranes and the cell's nucleus, which will allow DNA from the cell to go into the extraction solution.

M

Machine defect Any defect in typewriting resulting from the malfunctioning of the machine rather than the typebar or type element. Normally, these defects include improper escapement spacing (that is, each letter under space or over space a fraction of the basic unit) and defects in printing brought about by improper alignment of the typing unit and the roller. In other words, machine defects tend to affect all the characters on the machine rather than any particular character.

Machine gun Bipod- or tripod-mounted or handheld automatic weapon whose ammunition is fed from a magazine or a belt (Figure M.1).

Macro lens Lens designed to work at close distance, permitting image magnification.

Macrophotography Photography usually involving close-up capabilities, whether with lens or bellows, with a magnification from life size (110) up to 50 times (501).

Magazine clip A container for cartridges that has a spring and follower to feed the cartridges into the chamber of a firearm.

Magenta A reddish-blue (minus green) color.

FIGURE M.1 A popular automatic weapon used in the 1920s and 1930s.

FIGURE M.2 Maggots on a decomposed body. (Courtesy of forensic medical examiner Michael Sikirica, M.D.)

Maggot   The larva of a higher fly. It sheds its skin twice and has three growth instars prior to pupariation. A legless larva without a well-developed head capsule (Figure M.2).

Magistrate   Judicial officer exercising some of the functions of a judge; also, refers in a general way to a judge, as in the phrase "neutral magistrate."

Magnesium (Mg)   A silvery metal used in some metal incendiaries. The dust is highly explosive, with an ignition point of 650°F.

Major case management system   A computer system designed to store, collate, compare, and analyze investigative information in serious crimes.

Major criminal prints   A recording of all of the friction ridges skin that covers the hands. Major criminal prints include fingers, palm, tips of the fingers, and middle joints of the fingers on both sides.

Malfeasance   The commission of an unlawful, wrongful act; any wrongful conduct that affects, interrupts, or interferes with the performance of official duties.

Malpractice   Improper or unethical conduct by the holder of a professional or official position. Professional misconduct or improper practice. The professional's action or lack thereof must be below the minimum standards for the profession, and the patient or client must be harmed because of the professional's actions or failure to act.

Mandible   A mouth organ of invertebrates (especially in the arthropods and insects) used for seizing, biting, and manipulating food. With vertebrate organisms, it is recognized as the lower jaw (Figure M.3).

Manner of death   A typology of deaths according to whether they are due to homicide, suicide, accident, or natural causes. Death occurs in one of four manners: *natural*, if caused solely by disease; *accidental*, if it occurs

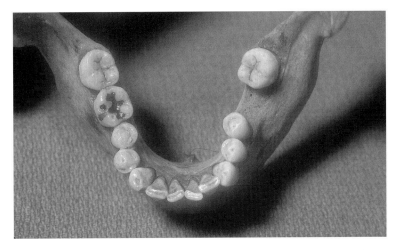

FIGURE M.3 Mandible with restorations and old molar loss on left side. (Courtesy of forensic medical examiner Michael Sikirica, M.D.)

without apparent intent; *suicidal*, if caused by the deceased; and *homicidal*, if someone other than the deceased caused it.

Mannlicher-type bolt   A bolt-action rifle that was designed for the receiver bridge; has a gap at the top to allow passage of the bolt handle.

Manslaughter   The unlawful killing of another without intent — expressed or implied — to effect death; may be voluntary or involuntary.

Manual typewriter   A machine whose operation depends solely upon the mechanical action set in motion by striking a letter or character key. During the first 50 or more years in typewriting history, all such machines were manually operated (Figure M.4).

Manufactured fiber   A class name of various families of fibers produced from fiber-forming substances that may be synthesized polymers, modified or transformed natural polymers and glass.

Manuscript writing   A disconnected form of script or semiscript writing. This type of writing is taught to young children in elementary schools as the first step in learning how to write.

Marijuana   Popular name for the dried flowers and leaves of *Cannabis sativa*.

Marker (DNA-genetic)   **(1)** A fragment of known size used to calibrate an electrophoretic gel. **(2)** Any allele of interest in an experiment.

Mass murder   A murder incident in which several victims are killed simultaneously, or within a relatively short time period in the same general area.

Mass spectrometer   A mass spectroscope in which a slit moves across the paths of particles with various masses, and an electrical detector behind it records the intensity distribution of masses.

Mass spectrometry   An analytical technique for identification of chemical structures, determination of mixtures, and quantitative elemental analysis, based on application of the mass spectrometer. A method of chemical analysis which vaporizes, then ionizes the substance to be analyzed, and

FIGURE M.4 Manual Corona™ typewriter.

then accelerates the ions through a magnetic field to separate the ions by molecular weight. Mass spectrometry can result in the exact identification of unknown compounds, and is a very powerful analytical technique, especially when combined with chromatography. The instrument used for this analysis is referred to as a gas *chromatograph/mass spectrometer detector* (GC/MSD).

Master   A high-quality tape that serves as the source for subsequent copies; also, a video unit that is used for playback in a dubbing operation.

Match   When genetic profiles show the same types at all loci tested and no unexplainable differences exist.

Match criteria   A set of empirically derived, laboratory-specific data that is used to set limits on the amount of difference within which two DNA fragments can be considered the same size in RFLP or PCR/STR analysis.

Match report   After CODIS determines that two or more DNA profiles match; an electronic report is generated by CODIS and automatically distributed to the laboratories responsible for the matching profiles.

Match stringency   CODIS software supports three match stringency levels: low, moderate, and high. The match stringency determines whether or not two DNA profiles match. Low stringency matches occur when one or more bands/alleles match between the target and candidate profiles at a given locus. Moderate stringency matches require all bands/alleles to match, but the target and candidate profiles can contain a different number of bands/alleles. That is, if the target profile has three bands/alleles and the sample profile has two, the two bands/alleles must match. High stringency matches all bands/alleles to match.

Matching probability   The number of individuals that may be surveyed before finding the same DNA pattern in a randomly selected individual. The combined matching probability for more than one locus is the product of

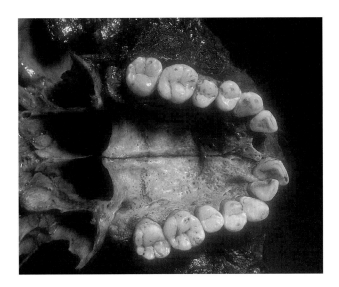

FIGURE M.5 Maxilla (upper jaw) with a missing tooth.

the individual matching probability at each locus, assuming that they are not linked. Also known as *probability of match* (pM).

Material safety data sheet (MSDS) Documents prepared by the chemical industry to transmit information about the physical properties and health effects of chemicals and about emergency response plans.

Maternal Pertaining to, or related to, a mother.

Maternal inheritance Describes the preferential survival in the progeny of genetic markers provided by one parent. A type of uniparental inheritance in which all progeny have the genotype and phenotype of the parent acting as the female.

Matrix (DNA analysis) Consists of at least five fluorescently labeled DNA fragments for each dye that are run and analyzed in separate lanes. **(Drug analysis)** The composition of the biological sample being analyzed, consisting of proteins, lipids, and other biomolecules that can affect analyte recovery.

Maxilla The upper jawbone in vertebrates. One of the pair or pairs of jaws behind the mandibles of an arthropod (Figure M.5).

Mean (arithmetic) A statistical measure of central tendency equating to an arithmetic average of a group of values.

Measurement scale An object showing standard units of length (e.g., ruler) used in photographic documentation of an item of evidence (Figure M.6).

Mechanical pipettes Hand-held pipettes that can deliver a specific volume of liquids; one can use the dial on the pipette to select the desired volume. There are different types of pipettes depending on what volume of liquid is needed (Figure M.7).

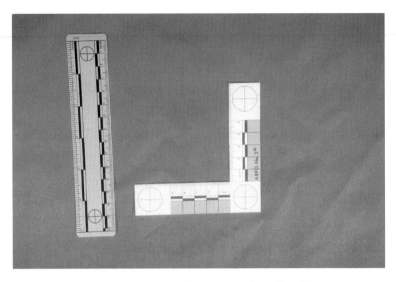

FIGURE M.6 Different types of rulers used to measure forensic evidence.

Mechanism of death   Biochemical or physiologic abnormality produced by the cause of death and is incompatible with life, e.g., ventricular fibrillation or exsanguination.

Median   A statistical measure of central tendency equating to the mid-value in a ranked series.

Mediation   Process by which individuals voluntarily discuss and try to settle disputes, often with the assistance of an attorney or mental health professional trained in mediation skills. Mediation is commonly used with parents to resolve issues related to child custody and visitation.

Medical examiner   Government official, always a physician and often a forensic pathologist, charged with investigating sudden and unexpected deaths or deaths from injuries.

Medical neglect   Failure to seek medical or dental treatment for a health problem or condition that, if untreated, could become severe enough to represent a danger to the individual.

Medium-velocity impact spatter   Bloodstains produced on a surface when the blood source has been subjected to a medium-velocity force between approximately 5 and 25 ft/sec. A beating typically causes this type of spatter. The preponderance of individual spots of blood produced in this manner are usually 1 to 3 mm in diameter, but larger and smaller spots can occur.

Medulla   Marrow of bones; central part of an organ or tissue; pith or central portion of stem. The central portion of a hair composed of a series of discrete cells or an amorphous spongy mass. A cellular column that runs through the center of the cortex. It may be air-filled, and if so, will appear opaque or black using transmitted light or white using reflected light. In

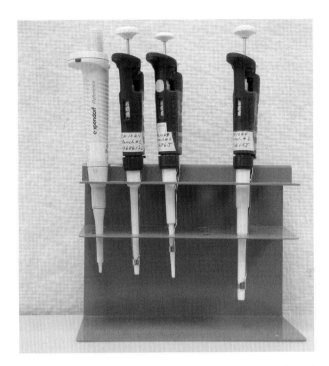

FIGURE M.7 Handheld mechanical pipettes that can deliver a specific volume of liquid. Each pippette contains an adjustable dial that can be set for a specific volume measured in microliters.

animal hair, several types have been defined as uni- or multi-serial ladder, cellular or vacuolated, and lattice.

Mega-   A prefix meaning 10^5 units (symbol M). One megagram equals 1,000,000 grams.

Meiosis   The process whereby a sex cell nucleus, after chromosomal replication, divides twice to form four nuclei each with one half the original chromosome number.

Melanin   Black or dark-brown pigment most frequently seen in skin and hair (Figure M.8).

Melting   The denaturation point in referring to DNA.

Melting temperature (Tm)   The midpoint of the temperature range over which DNA is denatured.

Membranes   Consist of an asymmetrical lipid bilayer that has lateral fluidity and contains proteins. The coating of a biological cell, in and through which the osmotic mechanism of nutrient supply operates.

Mendel's law   (Segregation) During meiosis, only one member of each homologous chromosome pair is transferred to a specific gamete. **(Independent assortment)** During meiosis, the members of the different homologous chromosome pairs assort independently when transferred to a specific

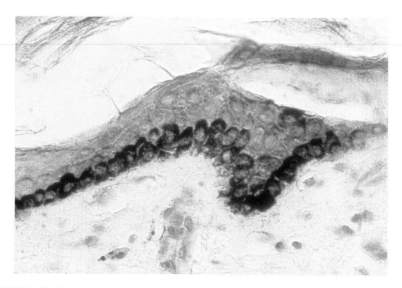

FIGURE M.8 Photomicrograph of the skin showing melanin pigments. (Courtesy of forensic medical examiner Michael Sikirica, M.D.)

gamete; for an example, AA′ and BB′ homologous chromosome pairs could give rise to AB, AB′, A′B or A′B′ possible gametes.

Meningitis   Brain infection involving an acute inflammation of the membranes that cover the brain and spinal cord, characterized by drowsiness, confusion, irritability, and sensory impairments (Figure M.9).

Mental status interview   Interview that evaluates appearance and behavior, speech and communications, content of thought, sensory and motor functioning, cognitive functioning, temperament, emotional functioning, and insight and judgment. It may be conducted as part of the intake interview.

MEOS   The microsomal ethanol oxidizing system, an enzyme system in liver that converts ethanol to acetaldehyde.

Meperidine hydrochloride   A fine, white, odorless, crystalline powder; very soluble in water, soluble in alcohol, and used in medicine as a narcotic.

Mercerized cotton   Cotton that has been strengthened by passing through a 25 to 30% solution of sodium hydroxide under tension, and then washed with water while under tension. This causes the fibers to shrink, increasing their strength and attraction for colors, as well as imparting luster.

Mercuric iodide   Red, tetragonal crystals, turning yellow when heated to 150°C. Used in medicine and analytical reagents (Nessler's reagent and Mayer's reagent).

Mercury bath   A process using mercury for the removal of lead residue from a barrel.

Metabolism   The chemical change, constructive and destructive, occurring in living organisms. The chemical transformations occurring in an organism from the time a nutrient substance enters it until the nutrient has been utilized and the waste products eliminated.

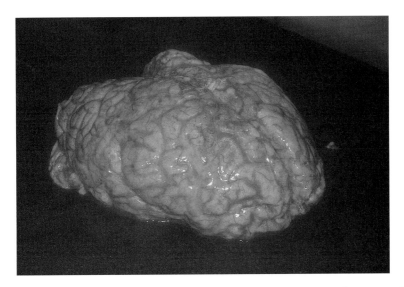

FIGURE M.9 Cloudy-appearing meninges (membrane covering the brain) due to acute bacterial meningitis. The cloudiness is caused by the accumulation of inflammatory white cells. (Courtesy of forensic medical examiner Michael Sikirica, M.D.)

Metabolite An intermediate material produced and used in the processes of a living cell or organism. Metabolites are used for replacement and growth in living tissue and are also broken down to be a source of energy in the body.

Meta-ethyltoluene (*m*-ethyltoluene) A chemical compound that can be found in gasoline.

Metal fouling Metallic bullet material left in the bore after firing.

Metallic paint Paint used for covering metal surfaces; the pigment is commonly iron oxide.

Metallic pigment Thin, opaque aluminum or copper alloy flakes that are incorporated into plastic masses to produce metal-like effects.

Metameric Two or more materials that appear the same color under one type of illumination and different under another. Spectral analyses can differentiate metameric pairs.

Metamorphosis The process in arthropods of changing from one life stage into another.

Metaphysis Wide areas at both ends of an immature long bone shaft or diaphysis that contain growth zones and are attached and eventually united to epiphyseal discs.

Metatarsal bones The long bones of the foot that join with the phalanges (toes).

Meter The basic unit of length of the metric system, abbreviated with the letter *m*.

Methadone hydrochloride A synthetic narcotic. Used medicinally as a sedative and also useful in treating heroin addiction.

Methamphetamine   Colorless, volatile liquid; characteristic strong odor and slightly burning taste. Highly toxic, flammable, as well as a dangerous fire risk. Basis of a group of hallucinogenic, habit-forming drugs that affect the central nervous system.

Methane   The simplest hydrocarbon and the first member of the paraffin (alkane) series, having a formula CH_4. Methane is the major constituent of natural gas. Methane has a heating value of 1000 BTU/ft^3. Its explosive limits are 5 to 15%.

Methanol   Methyl alcohol or wood alcohol. The simplest alcohol that is water soluble and has a flash point of 54°F and an explosive limit of 6 to 36.5%.

Method traceability   Property of a method whose measurements give results that can be related with a given uncertainty to a particular reference, usually a national or international standard, through an unbroken chain of comparisons.

Methyl silicone   A nonvolatile oily liquid used in gas chromatography to separate nonpolar compounds. Methyl silicone columns typically separate compounds according to their boiling point.

Michel–Levy chart   A chart relating thickness, birefringence, and retardation so that any one of these variables can be determined for an anisotropic fiber when the other two are known.

Micro-   A prefix representing 10^6, or one-millionth.

Microanalysis   Application of a microscope and microscopy techniques to the observation, collection, and analysis of microevidence.

Microcrystal tests   A reaction between the compound of interest and chemical reagent that results in the formation of unique crystals that can be observed with the microscope.

Microfuge   A high-speed (usually 10,000 rpm and faster) centrifuge for the centrifugation of small (usually <2 ml) specimens.

Micrometer   An instrument for measuring very small distances or dimensions. A caliper or gauge arranged to allow minute measurements. Abbreviated as (m). Also known as *micron* (μm).

Micrometry   A device utilizing a scale calibrated with stage micrometer for measurement of the physical dimensions of material viewed with a microscope.

Microphone   A device used to accept audio and video signals.

Microphotography   The term used in Europe for the making of large photographs of small objects, usually through a microscope. In the United Kingdom and the United States this is called *photomicrography*, and microphotography is used to refer to the technique of making microscopically small photographs by the process of optical reduction.

Microsatellite   Short tandem repeat or simple sequence length polymorphism composed of di-, tri-, tetra-, or pentanucleotide repeats of nucleotides.

Microscope   An optical instrument consisting of a combination of lenses that allows the operator to view a magnified image of a small object (Figure M.10).

Microscopic marks   Striae or patterns of minute lines or grooves in an object. In firearm and toolmark identification these marks are characteristic of the object that produced them and are the basis for identification.

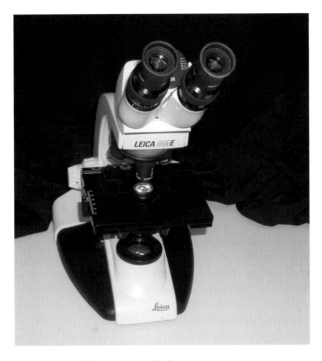

FIGURE M.10 Transmitted-light compound microscope.

Microscopist An individual who uses a microscope to examine minute particles, hairs, fibers, and objects unable to be seen by the naked eye.

Microsomal enzymes Detoxifying enzyme associated with certain membranes (smooth endoplasmic reticulum) within cells.

Microspectrophotometry Instruments that generate transmission, reflection, or absorption spectra from various translucent and opaque samples. The principal types are visible and infrared.

Microtome An instrument for making very thin sections for microscopic observations.

Midsole A component found on some shoes that is often different in color, density, or materials, and is located between the outsole and the shoe upper.

Mineral spirits A medium petroleum distillate ranging from C_8 to C_{12}. The flash point of mineral spirits is generally around 100°F. Mineral spirits, sometimes known as *mineral turps*, is commonly used as a solvent in insecticides and certain other household products. Many charcoal lighter fluids are composed almost entirely of mineral spirits.

Minisatellites Regions of tandem repeats sequence DNA scattered throughout animal (and probably plant) genomes. Simple sequence tandem repeat polymorphism in which the core repeat unit is usually 10 to 50 nucleotides long; variable number of tandem repeats.

Minutiae The characteristics that make each fingerprint capable of being differentiated from any other print by a different area of friction skin.

Comparison of latent prints with known prints begins with the overall pattern. The ridge detail of fingerprints, including the ends of the ridges, their separations, and their relationships to one another, constitute the bases for fingerprint comparison.

"Miranda warning"   Requirement that police tell a suspect in their custody of his/her constitutional rights before they question him/her, so named as a result of the *Miranda v. Arizona* ruling establishing such requirements. Law enforcement procedure that forewarns suspects of their right to remain silent when in police custody. A statement of confession made by the suspect is usually inadmissible as evidence in court proceedings if the suspect was not informed of this right before the confession was disclosed.

Mirror writing   Writing that runs in the opposite direction to the normal pattern; starts on the right side of the page and proceeds from right to left, with reversed order in spelling and turning of the letter images.

Miscible   Having the ability to mix (but not chemically combine) in any ratio without separating into two phases (e.g., water and alcohol).

Misdemeanor   Criminal offenses considered less serious than felonies. Misdemeanors generally are punishable by a fine or a limited local jail term but not by imprisonment in a state penitentiary.

Misfire   Failure of the primer mixture to ignite.

Misting   Blood which has been reduced to a fine spray as the result of the energy or force applied to it.

Mistrial   A trial that is terminated before its normal conclusion and declared invalid prior to the returning of a verdict. A judge may declare a mistrial due to an extraordinary event (e.g., death of a juror), for a fundamental, prejudicial error that cannot be corrected by instructions to the jury, or because of the jury's inability to reach a verdict (hung jury). In a criminal case, a mistrial may prevent a retrial under the doctrine of double jeopardy.

Mite   Any arthropod in the order *Acari*. These are very small to minute animals having four pairs of legs in the adult stage, but only three pairs in the larva. All mites have chelicerated mouth parts and lack mandibles.

Mitigating circumstances   Factors such as age, mental capacity, motivation, or duress that lessen the degree of guilt in a criminal offense and thus the nature of the punishment.

Mitochondria   A DNA-containing cytoplasmic organelles of eukaryotes. Mitochondria are referred to as the powerhouse of the cell because of the site for ATP production. The DNA in the mitochondria has a maternal inheritance (Figure M.11).

Mitosis   The cell division that produces daughter cells with the same number of chromosomes as the original cells. All cell division, with the exception of that which produces mature sex cells, is mitotic.

Mixture   A heterogeneous blend of elements or compound that may or may not be uniformly dispersed. All solutions are uniformly dispersed mixtures.

M'Naghten rule   In most jurisdictions, the test applied for the defense of insanity. Under this test, an accused is not criminally responsible if suffering from a mental disease or defect at the time of committing the act and not

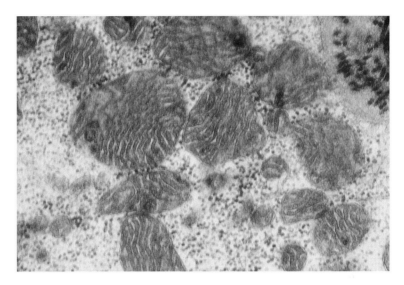

FIGURE M.11 Mitochondria within a cell visualized by electron microscopy. (Courtesy of forensic medical examiner Michael Sikirica, M.D.)

understanding the nature and quality of the act or that what was done was wrong. To be considered "sane," and therefore legally responsible for the act committed, the defendant must know and understand the nature and quality of the act and be able to distinguish between right and wrong at the time the offense was committed.

Mobile phase   The movement of the liquid phase used for development of drugs spotted on thin-layer chromatography silicon plates. In gas chromatography, the mobile phase is the inert carrier gas that moves the volatile analytes through the length of the column.

Modacrylic fiber   Generic name for a manufactured fiber in which the fiber-forming substance is any long-chain synthetic polymer composed of less than 85% but at least 35% by weight of acrylonitrile units. Characterized by moderate tenacity, low water absorption, and resistance to combustion, it also is self-extinguishing.

Modality   In physiology, any of the various types of sensations, such as vision, hearing, taste, smell, or touch.

Mode   In statistics, the value or values occurring most frequently in a set of data.

Modem (Modulator/demodulator)   A device that converts digital signals to analog signals for transmission over the telephone system.

Modification ratio   A geometrical parameter used in the characterization of noncircular fiber cross-sections. The modification ratio is the ratio in size between the outside diameter of the fiber and the diameter of the core. It may also be called *aspect ratio*.

***Modus operandi* (MO)**   Manner or mode of behavior; a criminal's typical pattern of performing crimes. Method of operation of a criminal. The principle that a criminal is likely to use the same technique repeatedly and that any analysis and record of the technique used in every serious crime will provide a means of identification in a particular crime.

Moiré The imprecision with which the habits of the writer are executed on repeated occasions (Huber), or the divergence of one execution from another in an element of an individual's writing that occurs invariably in the graph but may also occur in the choice of the allograph (Huber), or normal or usual deviations found between repeated specimens of any individual's handwriting or in the product of any typewriter or other record making machine (Hilton).

Molal A concentration in which the amount of the solute is stated in moles and the amount of the solvent in kilograms.

Molar A concentration in which one molecular weight in grams (one mole) of a substance is dissolved in one liter of solution. Molarity is indicated by an italic capital M. Molar quantities are proportional to the molecular weight of the substance.

Molecular biology A subdivision of biology that approaches the subject of life at the level of molecular size. This applies to phenomena occurring within the cell nucleus, where the chromosomes and genes are located.

Molecular genetics The study of the molecular processes underlying gene structure and function.

Molecular weight (MW) The sum of the atomic weights (q.v.) of all of the atoms within a molecule. Generally, molecules of the same type have higher boiling points if the molecular weight is higher.

Molecule The smallest particle into which a substance can be divided without changing its chemical properties. A molecule of an element consists of one atom or two or more atoms that are similar. A molecule of a compound consists of two or more different atoms.

Molt The process of shedding of the exoskeleton of outer body wall in arthropod growth: also termed *ecdysis*.

Mongoloid Of or pertaining to the so-called "yellow race," with skin color varying from light yellow to light brown, hair straight to wavy, sparse body hair, broad nose, high cheek bones, and dark eyes with marked epicanthic folds.

Monochrome Single colored; for instance, black-and-white photographs and sepia- or other-toned images in one color. Similar light rays of one color wavelength (i.e., a single, pure color).

Monomer The simplest unit of a polymer. Ethylene is the smallest of polyethylene. Styrene is the smallest unit of polystyrene.

Monozygotic Twins produced from a single zygote that later splits and develops identical genomes.

Moot A subject for debate; unsettled; undecided. A case is moot when a determination on a matter is sought that when rendered has no practical effect on the matter under dispute. A moot case or a moot point is one not subject to a judicial determination because it involves an abstract question or a pretended controversy that has not yet actually arisen or has already passed. Mootness usually refers to a court's refusal to consider a case because the issue involved has been resolved prior to the court's decision, leaving nothing that would be affected by the court's decision.

Moral dilemmas Hypothetical scenarios that require an individual to choose a specific moral action and then justify why that particular resolution was the right thing to do; used to assess levels of moral reasoning.

Morphine White crystalline alkaloid, slightly soluble in water, alcohol, and ether; highly toxic, narcotic, habit-forming drug.

Morphology The science of form and structure of plants and animals, as distinct from consideration of functions.

Mortality The death rate; ratio of number of deaths to a given population.

Mosaic An individual composed of two genetically different cell lines originally derived from the same zygote.

Motion An application for a rule or order, made to a court or judge. An application to the court requesting an order or a rule in favor of the applicant.

Motor drive Device for advancing the film and retensioning the shutter by means of an electric motor.

Mourning Act or social expression of deprivation associated with the loss of someone through death. Mourning includes rituals and behaviors specific to various cultures and religions.

Movement An important element of handwriting. It embraces all the factors related to the motion of the writing instrument — skill, speed, freedom, hesitation, rhythm, emphasis, tremor, and the like. The manner in which the writing instrument is moved, i.e., by finger, hand, or arm action, may influence each of these factors.

mtDNA Maternally inherited mitochondrial DNA; present in 1000 to 10,000 copies per mammalian cells.

Multi-locus probe A DNA probe that detects genetic variations at multiple sites; an autoradiogram of a multi-locus probe yields a complex, stripelike pattern of 30 or more bands per individual. This pattern was originally called a "DNA fingerprint" by its originator Alec Jeffreys.

Multiple flash The use of more than one flash unit, usually operating simultaneously.

Multiple personality Type of dissociative disorder characterized by the development of two or more relatively independent personality systems in the same individual.

Mummification The drying, shrinking, and hardening of dead flesh due to extreme dehydration

Murder The unlawful killing of a human being with malice aforethought. Murder in the first degree is characterized by premeditation; murder in the second degree is characterized by a sudden and instantaneous intent to kill or to cause injury, without caring whether the injury kills or not.

Mushroom **(Drugs)** Umbrella-shaped fungus, some varieties of which contain a drug that can cause hyperventilation, tremors, and hyperactivity when the fungus is chewed, smoked, or ground and infused in water and drunk as a tea. **(Firearms)** Also used to describe the expansion of a projectile upon impacting a target (firearms).

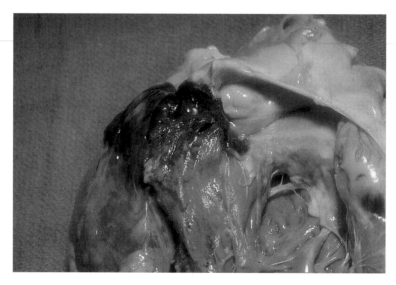

FIGURE M.12 Hemorrhage in the heart muscle caused by myocardial ischemia. (Courtesy of forensic medical examiner Michael Sikirica, M.D.)

Musket A firearm with a long barrel and forend or forearm extending nearly to the muzzle.

Mutation Any change in the sequence of genomic DNA. May result from one or many base pair changes. A change in a gene's DNA sequence resulting in the formation of another allele.

Mutation rate Number of mutation events per gene per unit of time (for example, per cell generation); the proportion of mutations per cell division in bacteria and single-celled organisms or the proportion of mutations per gamete in higher organisms.

Muzzle The end of a firearm barrel from which the bullet or shot emerges.

Myiasis The invasion of any living vertebrate animal, including people, by fly larvae, especially maggots. The description may be further refined to indicate location affected (e.g., nasal myiasis, rectal myiasis) or the predisposing cause (e.g., traumatic myiasis in a suppurating wound). Myiasis may be classified as either primary or secondary (facultative), q.v.

Myocardial ischemia Insufficient oxygen supplies to meet the metabolic demands of heart muscles (Figure M.12).

Myocarditis Inflammation of the muscles of the heart.

Myoclonus Involuntary spasm or twitching of a muscle or group of muscles.

Myoglobin The oxygen-transporting, pigmented protein of muscle resembles blood hemoglobin in function.

Myotomy Cutting of muscle; in forensic odontology, cutting facial muscles to release postmortem *rigor mortis*.

N

NAA Neutron activation analysis. A technique for metal analysis utilizing the characteristics of emitted radiation for the detection and quantitation of metals.

Nanogram (ng) One billionth (10^{-9}) of a gram.

Nanometer A term for millimicron, as used in UV and infrared measurements. A unit of length equal to one-billionth of a meter or 10^{-9} meters.

Naphtha An ambiguous (and obsolete) term that may mean high-flash naphtha (mineral spirits), or low-flash naphtha (petroleum ether, low boiling ligroin) or something altogether different. Flash points and explosive limits may vary.

Narcotic Pharmacologically, any substance that produces narcosis, a stuporous state resembling sleep, and characterized by loss of sensation. Addictive substance that reduces pain, alters mood and behavior, and usually induces sleep or stupor.

Natatorial Adapted or specialized for swimming.

Natural cause Event, such as lightning, flood, tornado, earthquake, etc. that is not under the control of humans.

Natural fibers A class of fibers of vegetable (e.g., cotton, flax, ramie), animal origin (e.g., silk, wool, and specially fur), or mineral origin (e.g., asbestos).

Natural gas A mixture of low-molecular-weight hydrocarbons obtained in petroleum-producing regions throughout the world. Natural gas consists of approximately 85% methane, 10% ethane with the balance propane, butane, and nitrogen. Because it is nearly odorless, an odorizing agent is added to most natural gas prior to final sale.

Natural size A photograph enlarged to the true size of the content; a photograph of a shoe or tire impression is enlarged so the shoe or tire impression is life size.

Natural writing Any specimen of writing executed normally without an attempt to control or alter its identifying habits and its usual quality of execution. It is the typical writing of an individual.

NDIS The National DNA Index System. NDIS is the FBI-administered, centralized system of DNA identification records contributed by all state and local participating laboratories. NDIS receives records from every lower-level index and supports the searching functions of CODIS.

NEAFS Northeast Association of Forensic Scientists.

Near point The closet object to the camera in focus for a given distance.

Necrophilous Having a dietary fondness for dead flesh.

Necrosis Death of one or more cells or a portion of a tissue or organ.

Negative   Photographic image in which the amount of silver present is more or less based on the reflectivity from the original object. Black is white, white is black. The developed film that contains a reversed-tone image of the original scene.

Neglect   Form of child maltreatment characterized by failure to provide for the child's basic needs. Neglect can be physical, educational, or emotional/psychological.

Neglectful abuse   Injury or mistreatment by not nurturing or caring for a more or less helpless person.

Negligence   An act or omission that causes harm despite a duty to behave otherwise. Failure to exercise that degree of care that a reasonable person would exercise under the same circumstances.

Neoplasm   A new and abnormal formation of tissue such as a tumor or growth.

Neurogenetics   The study of the relationship between genetics and neurology.

Neuropathy   A disorder of the nervous system; in contemporary usage, a disease involving the cranial or spinal nerves.

Neuroticism   A major dimension of personality involving the tendency to experience negative emotions such as anxiety, anger, and depression, often accompanied by distressed thinking and behavior.

Neurotoxin   A poisonous substance in snake venom that acts as a nervous system depressant. Toxic substance that affects the brain and its neural pathways, causing psychological and physical problems.

Neutralize   To make a solution neutral pH of 7 (either acidic or basic) by adding a base to an acidic solution, or by adding an acid to a basic solution.

Neutron activation analysis   Technique for identifying substances by bombarding a sample with neutrons in a nuclear reactor and measuring the energies and intensities of the resulting gamma rays.

Nicad   Nickel cadmium (NiCd) rechargeable battery.

Ninhydrin (triketohydrindene hydrate)   A strong oxidizing agent that causes the oxidative deamination of the α-amino function. The products of the reaction, which are the resulting aldehyde, ammonia, carbon dioxide, hydrindantin, and reduced derivatives of ninhydrin. The ammonia produced in this way can react with the hydrindantin and another molecule of ninhydrin to yield a purple product.

NIST   National Institute of Standards and Technology. Federal agency responsible for setting, approving, and maintaining measurements and materials standards in the United States.

Nitrate   To treat or combine with nitric acid or a compound, to change into a nitro derivative.

Nitrite   A salt of nitrous acid.

Nitrocellulose   Pulpy, cotton-like, amorphous solid (dry), colorless liquid to semisolid (solution). Used for fast-drying automobile lacquers, high explosives, and leather finishing.

Nitrogen A gaseous element that makes up approximately 80% of the Earth's atmosphere. Nitrogen is relatively inert and does not support either combustion or life. Nitrogen is usually found in the molecular N_2 form.

Nitroglycerin A high explosive used in some propellant gases.

Nocturnal Active at night.

Nodule A small, rounded mass or lump of ink caused by an excessive deposit; the result of "gooping" in some ballpoint pens.

Nonaqueous ink Ink in which the pigment or dye is carried in any vehicle other than water. Inks of this class are found in ballpoint pens, typewriter ribbons, and stamp pads, and are widely used in the printing industry.

Nonce word A word coined to fit a special situation.

Noncoding A region of DNA that lacks the capacity to produce a protein.

None detected (ND) Indicates the absence of an analyte within the specification of the test performed.

Nonsperm cell fraction In a differential extraction, the portion of a sample containing DNA isolated from nonsperm cells.

Nonsperm cells Any cell not derived from a male gamete.

Nonverbal communication Messages unwittingly sent through changes in facial expressions, voice quality, body movements, and the distancing of one's self from the other speaker.

Normal lens A lens that makes the image in a photograph appear in a perspective similar to that of the original scene.

Normal saline U.S. Pharmacopoeia title for a sterile solution of sodium chloride in purified water, containing 0.9 g of sodium chloride in 100 ml; isotonic with body fluids. Also known as *isotonic sodium chloride solution.*

Normality (N) Measure of the number of gram-equivalent weights of a compound per liter of solution.

Nortriptyline The mono-*N*-desmethyl metabolite of amitriptyline, and is itself an active antidepressant agent.

Notes The documentation of procedures, standards, controls and instruments used, observations made, results of tests performed, charts, graphs, photos, and other documents generated that are used to support the examiner's conclusions.

Notification law A law that notifies citizens that a sex offender has been released in their area or community.

Nuclear DNA The DNA contained within the nucleus of a cell. It constitutes the vast majority of the cell genome.

Nuclear fast red Biological stain used to differentially stain spermatozoa to aid in their identification. It stains their nuclear material a dark red.

Nuclear magnetic resonance (NMR) A phenomenon exhibited by a large number of atomic nuclei, in which in a static magnetic field absorbs energy from a radio frequency field at certain characteristic frequencies.

Nuclease An enzyme that can degrade a DNA molecule by breaking its phosphodiester bonds.

Nucleic acid A general class of molecules that are polymers of nucleotides. DNA is a nucleic acid.

Nucleotide A molecule composed of a nitrogen base, a sugar, and a phosphate group; the basic building block of nucleic acid. A building block of DNA or RNA.

Nucleotide pair A pair of nucleotides (one in each strand of DNA) that are joined by hydrogen bonds.

Nucleus A complex, spheroidal body surrounded by a thin membrane and embedded in the protoplasm of most plant and animal cells. It contains the chromatin that is essential in the processes of heredity, and is the directive center of all the vital activities of the cell, as assimilation, metabolism, growth, and reproduction.

Nylon A manufactured fiber in which the fiber-forming substance in any long-chain synthetic polyamide in which less than 85% of the amide linkage is attached directly to two aromatic rings.

Nylon membrane The nylon membranes are used in the Southern blotting method. The DNA to be analyzed is exposed to restriction enzymes and after being separated by agarose gel electrophoresis, the DNA fragments in the gel are denatured with an alkaline solution and transferred onto a nitrocellulase filter or nylon membrane by blotting, thus preserving the distribution of the DNA fragments in the gel.

O

Objection The process by which one party takes exception to some statement or procedure. An objection is either sustained or overruled by the judge. If the judge overrules the objection, the witness may answer the question. If the judge sustains the objection, the witness may not answer the question.

Objective The first lens, lens system, or mirror through which light passes or from which it is reflected in an optical system.

Objectivity Degree to which interviewers are open to what they see, hear, and feel during the interview and do not prejudge the interviewee.

Oblique lighting examination An examination with the illumination so controlled that it grazes or strikes the surface of the document from one side at a very low angle; also referred to as a *side light examination.*

Obliteration/Obliterated Most often used to refer to serial numbers on firearms that are no longer readable. The blotting out or smearing over of writing to make the original invisible or undecipherable (Figure O.1).

Obturation The act of sealing or preventing the escape of propellant gases from the breech of a gun.

Occipital condyles Pair of small, slightly rounded projections of the occipital bone, at the base of the cranium near the spinal cord opening, that form a joint with the first cervical vertebra.

Occlusal surface Surface of a tooth that during chewing comes in contact with teeth from the opposing jaw.

Octane (1) An alkane having the formula C_8H_{18} and with a flash point of 56°F and explosive limits of 1 to 3.2%. (2) A measure of the resistance of a sample of gasoline to premature ignition (knocking), 100-octane fuel has the knocking resistance of 100% iso-octane (2,2,4-trimethyl pentane). Zero-octane fuel has the knocking resistance of *n*-heptane; 89-octane fuel has the knocking resistance of a mixture of 89% iso-octane and 11% *n*-heptane.

Odontologist An individual who studies the structure development and abnormalities of teeth.

Odorant A substance possessing a perceptible odor.

Ohm adapter, 330/75 TV antenna wire is either 300 ohm (flat, twin-lead ribbon type) or 75 ohm (round, shielded coaxial cable). TV sets and VCRs are able to accept both types of antenna connections.

Olfaction The act of detecting scent, generally by respiration, transmitting impulses from the mucous membranes in the upper part of the nose via the olfactory nerve to the forebrain, where the information is translated into perceived odor.

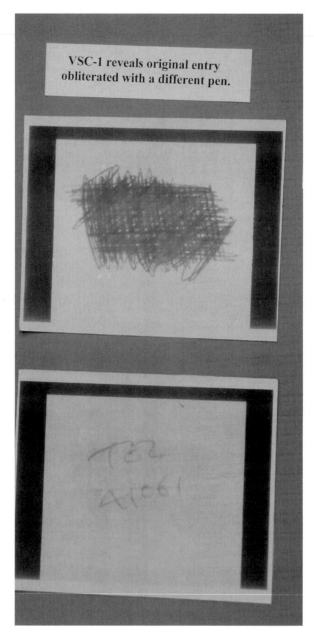

FIGURE O.1 Using different light sources writing that has been obliterated can now be revealed showing the message.

Oligonucleotide   A polymer composed of a few, usually less than 100 nucleotides. Oligonucleotides are usually synthesized by automated machinery and used as primers in PCR and as probes.

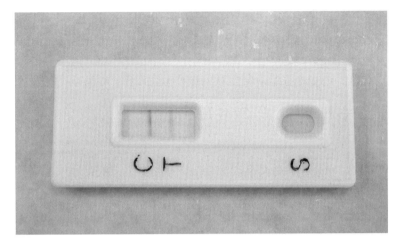

FIGURE O.2 OneStep Abcard®, Hema Trace® membrane is used as a confirmatory test for the presence of blood.

Omnibus hearing (legal)   Hearing held in criminal court to dispose of appropriate issues, such as whether evidence is admissible, before trial so as to ensure a fair and expeditious trial and avoid a multiplicity of court appearances.

OneStep ABAcard® Hema Trace® membrane test   This membrane test device was developed originally for the detection of occult blood in human feces, often associated with gastrointestinal pathologies. In forensic serology this membrane test provides a sensitive, reproducible, and reliable test for determining whether the blood stains found on criminal evidence are of human origin. The species specificity of the reaction is based on the recognition by antibodies of antigens displayed on human hemoglobin. A positive result produces a pink colored line at the test area; absence of this color line suggests a negative result (Figure O.2).

Open flash   Method of using the flash in which the shutter is opened, the flash is fired, and then the shutter is closed. It is used when the shutter speed is unimportant because existing lighting is poor or nonexistent.

Open grid search   Pattern in which a dog works 25 to 50 ft ahead of its handler quartering the wind.

Open surveillance   Surveillance in which there is little or no attempt at concealment; the subject may be and most likely is aware of the surveillance, but must not be lost (also called *rough surveillance*).

Open up   The term used in reference to changing to a larger aperture (*f*-stop) opening.

Opening statements   Not part of the evidence, these orations made by the lawyers on each side give an overview of the evidence that will be presented during the trial. Speech made by an attorney at the start of the trial or at the beginning of his or her presentation in court, summarizing the attorney's case, what he or she plans to prove, and the evidence to be presented.

Operant conditioning Shaping a particular behavior by pairing a particular stimulus and response with a reinforcement.

Opiates Natural, semi-synthetic, or synthetic substances with morphine-like effects in the body. They are primarily employed as analgesics and can be considered narcotic in their effects.

Opinion (legal) **(1)** Conclusion reported by a witness who qualifies as an expert on a given subject. **(2)** Judge's statement of the reason for a court's judgment, as opposed to the judgment itself.

Opium A highly toxic plant alkaloid that is a habit-forming narcotic; one source of opium is morphine.

Optical analysis Study of properties of a substance or medium, such as its chemical composition or the size of particles suspended in it, through observation of effects on transmitted light, such as scattering, absorption, refraction, and polarization.

Optical disk A permanent, usually removable, data storage device that uses a laser to read and write the information it contains. These devices are not subject to erasure when exposed to a magnetic field.

Optical microscope An instrument used to obtain an enlarged image of a small object, utilizing visible light; in general, it consists of a light source, a condenser, an objective lens, and an ocular or eyepiece that can be replaced by a recording device. Also known as a *light microscope* (Figure O.3).

Order A taxon in classification between class and family that includes related families of organisms.

Order (legal) Any written directive of a court or judge other than a judgment.

Order to show cause (OSC) Order to appear in court and present reasons why a particular order should not be executed. If the party fails to appear or to give sufficient reasons why the court should desist, the court will take the action requested.

Organic chemistry The study of the carbon atom and the compounds it forms, mainly with the 20 lightest elements, such as hydrogen, oxygen, and nitrogen. Some 3,000,000 organic compounds have been identified and named.

Organic compounds Class of chemical compounds with carbon bases; all hydrocarbons are organic compounds.

Organized offender Exhibits a great deal of thought and planning. The offender maintains control over himself and the victim. Little or no material of evidentiary value is present. Organized crime is carried out in a sophisticated and methodical manner.

Orient The aligning of two bullets that were fired from the same barrel on the comparison microscope so that the land and groove impressions on those bullets, which were produced by the same lands and grooves in the barrel, are opposite each other. Sometimes called *phasing* or *indexing*.

Origin determination Observing a fire scene, collecting and analyzing evidence, and conducting interviews with witnesses to determine where the fire began.

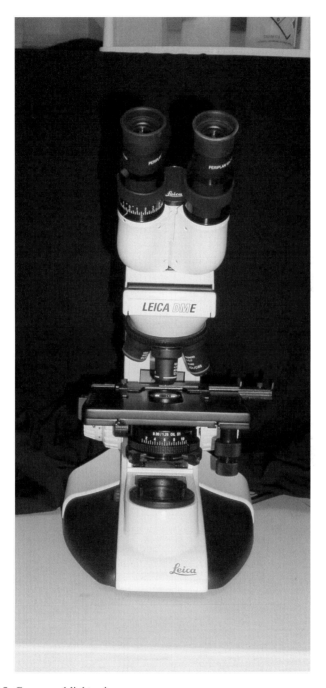

FIGURE O.3 Compound light microscope.

Orthography The principles by which the alphabet is set into correspondence
   with the speech sounds; the art of spelling.

Osmolality   The osmotic concentration of a solution determined by the ionic concentration of dissolved substances per unit of solvent.

Ossification   Formation of bone from cartilage or other fibrous tissue.

Ossification center   The area of bone where development and growth occur, gradually replacing cartilage.

Osten   Basic unit of structure of compact bone, with concentrically arranged lamellae around a haversian canal.

Osteoarthritis   Deterioration in joint integrity connected with use–wear, exacerbated by inflammation and related to reduction in bone density.

Osteology   The study of skeletal biology.

Osteomyelitis   Inflammation of the bone — especially the marrow — caused by a pathogenic organism.

Osteoporosis   Increased porosity of the bone, seen most often in the elderly.

Outsole   The outermost sole of a shoe. The portion of the shoe that contacts the ground and is exposed to wear.

Overdose   An excessive dose of medicine or narcotic substance.

Overkill   Administering more trauma than necessary to end a life; overkill indicates personalized anger and suggests the offender knew the victim.

Overlay   A scale drawing with only specific data shown. It can contain the vehicles as the investigator determines the point of impact (POI) or just the measured data taken from the scene. Electronically in a computer-assisted design (CAD) program, these overlays are easily removed or laid over the base drawing as required. In court exhibits the base drawing is on opaque paper and all the overlays are on clear, partial see-through Mylar film.

Overrule   **(1)** Judge's decision not to allow an objection. **(2)** Decision by a higher court finding that a lower court decision was in error.

Oviposit   To lay or deposit eggs.

Oviposition   The act of depositing eggs.

Oxidation   Originally, oxidation meant a chemical reaction in which oxygen combines with another substance. Usage of the word has been broadened to include any reaction in which electrons are transferred. The substance that gains electrons is the *oxidizing agent*.

Oxygen   A gaseous element that makes up approximately 20% of the Earth's atmosphere. It is usually found in the molecular O_2 form. Oxygen is the most abundant element on earth.

P

Packed column   A metal tube evenly filled with a solid support material that is coated with a liquid stationary phase of low vapor pressure (Figure P.1).

Paint Chemistry

> **Binder**   The actual film-former that binds the pigments particles to one another and to the substrate.
>
> **Drier**   A material that promotes or accelerates the drying, curing, or hardening of oxidizable coating vehicles. The principal driers are metal soaps of a monocarboxylic acid
>
> **Drying oils**   Naturally occurring triglycerides that form films principally by air oxidation. The same oils may be used as feed stocks for varnishes, alkyd resins, epoxy ester resins, oil-modified urethane resins, and some plasticizers.
>
> **Enamel**   The term *enamel* does not intimate the chemical nature of the coating, but implies a pigmented coating that dries to a hard gloss. Increasingly, the term has come to mean a cross-linked thermosetting resin.
>
> **Extender**   A low-cost white inorganic pigment used with other white pigment to modify the gloss, texture, viscosity, and other properties, and to reduce the cost of the finished product.
>
> **Latex**   A suspension of a pigment in a water-based emulsion of any of several resins, for example, acrylic polymers, vinyl polymers, or styrene–butadiene polymers.

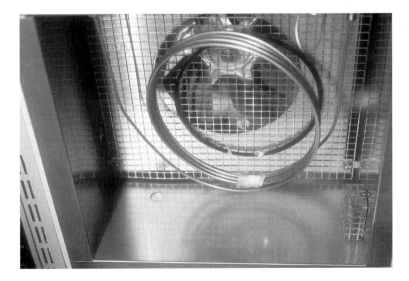

FIGURE P.1 Inert material packed into capillary columns used in gas chromatography.

Paint   A suspension pigment in an oil vehicle. It applies to virtually any surface coating designed for protection of a surface or for decoration, or both. Sometimes the word *paint* may be a general term and the term *surface coating* is more specific.

Pigment   A finely powdered solid that is essentially insoluble in the medium in which is dispersed. Pigments may be inorganic, such as titanium dioxide, or organic, such as phthalocyanine. White pigments are primarily intended to hide the underlying surface. A pigment is distinguished from a dye in that a dye is soluble in the vehicle while a pigment is not.

Plasticizer   A material incorporated into a polymer to increase its flexibility or workability.

Solvent   Organic liquids of various types having the function of dissolving the binder and thereby providing a consistency to the coating that is more suitable for application.

Stain   A solution of a dye or a suspension of a pigment in a vehicle designed to impart a color to wood surface rather than to form a protective coating.

Thermoplastic polymer   A resin that polymerizes without the necessity of heat. If the resin is heated below its decomposition temperature it softens and hardens again upon cooling; hence, the term *thermoplastic* .

Thermosetting polymer   A resin that can be made to form cross-linkage when baked.

Varnish   A homogenous solution of drying oils and resins in organic solvents. The resins may be naturally occurring, such as rosin or dammar, or synthetic.

Vehicle   The portion of a surface coating other than the pigment, the purpose of which is to enable the pigment to be distributed over the surface. The vehicle includes solvents, binders, and other additives. The term *vehicle* is frequently used to indicate the oil or resin that forms a continuous film and binds the pigment to the substrate.

Palindrome   A DNA site where the base order in one strand is the reverse of that in the complementary strand, e.g., 5′GAATTC3′, 3′CTTAAG5′.

Palmar zone   The elevated area just behind the fingers and above the center of the palm. Papillary ridges (friction ridges). The fingerprint ridges that can be observed on the inner surfaces of the hand. Friction ridge skin is a highly specialized organ and differs from the skin on the rest of the body in more than simply its ridged appearance. This zone has no hair follicles and, thus, no apocrine or sebaceous glands.

Pan-and-tilt head   Tripod head with separate locks for horizontal (pan) and vertical (tilt) movements of the camera.

Panning   The movement from left to right and right to left of the camera; normally associated with movie and video cameras.

Parabellum   A Latin term meaning *for war*. Used as a cartridge designation, i.e., 9-mm parabellum.

Paraffin   A translucent, waxy, solid mixture of hydrocarbons, indifferent to most chemical reagents; it is a constituent of peat, soft coal, and shale but is

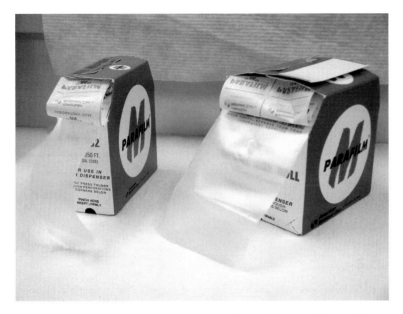

FIGURE P.2 A translucent, waxy, solid paper of various widths can be used for wrapping around the top of glass or plastic tubes to prevent the liquid inside the tube from spilling out.

derived principally from the distillation of petroleum. Can come in rolls that are 2 or 4 in. wide and used to cover the top of glass test tubes or small plastic tubes (Figure P.2).

Paralinguistics The study of the variations in the quality of the voice (pitch, intonation, loudness, softness) and their effect on the meaning conveyed.

Parallax Difference between the image seen in a viewfinder and that recorded by the taking lens. Most pronounced at close distance with twin-lens reflex and rangefinder cameras. Single-lens reflex and studio cameras are free from parallax error.

Parallelogram method Graphic method by which vectors can be added. The two vectors are laid off graphically to scale in proper directions from a common starting point. They form two adjacent sides of a parallelogram. Drawing the two opposite sides meeting at the far end of the diagram then completes the parallelogram. The diagonal of the parallelogram is the resultant of the two original quantities both in length and in direction.

Paraphilia A condition in which sexual arousal and gratification are dependent on fantasizing about and engaging in sexual behavior that is atypical and extreme; it is thought that sexual offenders who are paraphiliacs are likely to reoffend.

Pardon A form of executive clemency preventing criminal prosecution or removing or extinguishing a criminal conviction.

Patching Retouching or going back over a defective portion of a writing stroke. Careful patching is a common defect in forgeries.

Patent Documented exclusive legal right to a process.

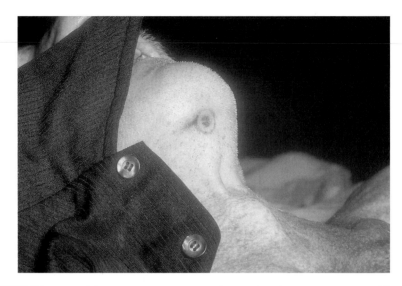

FIGURE P.3 Pattern injury due to a button on the deceased's shirt collar. (Courtesy of forensic medical examiner Michael Sikirica, M.D.)

Paternity   Refers to the biological father of an offspring.
Paternity index (PI)   The ratio of the probability (x) that the putative father is the biological father to the probability (y) that any random man is the biological father. Represented by the equation PI = $x + y$.
Pathogen   An organism that causes disease in another organism.
Pathology   The medical science that treats morbid conditions, their causes, the nature, and the effects of diseases and other abnormalities.
Pattern   The distribution of a series of shots fired from one gun or a battery of guns under conditions as nearly identical as possible to that which occurred at the crime scene. The points of impact of the projectiles being dispersed about a single point are called the *center of impact* .
Pattern area   The area that displays the patterns of the fingerprint and is surrounded by the type lines.
Pattern injury   The imprint of either the offending object, such as a pipe, or an intermediary material, such as clothing, is imprinted or stamped on the skin by the crushing effect of the blunt object (Figure P.3).
Pattern theory   A multidisciplinary approach that combines rational choice and routine activity theory to explain the distribution of crime and criminal behavior. Offender target choice is affected by their interactions with the physical and social environments. Also known as *crime pattern theory* .
Paurometabolous   The type of metamorphosis where the young and adults look similar and live in the same habitat; the adults are winged.
Payout   The term given to a condition where the length of the webbing of the seat belt increases due to a malfunction of the retractor mechanism.
PDOF   Principal direction of force. Many computer simulation programs today require an input telling it the principal direction from which the force was

being applied to the vehicle. The clock directions usually do this, with the front of the vehicle being 12 o'clock.

Peak   The visual image representing an allele on an electropherogram.

Pedigree   A "family tree," drawn with standard genetic symbols, showing inheritance patterns for specific phenotypic characters.

Peer   An individual having expertise in a specific discipline gained through documented training and experience.

Peer review   A comprehensive review and evaluation of analytical data, reports, notes, and other documents to ensure an appropriate and adequate basis for the scientific conclusions in the corresponding case report.

Peer to Peer   A method of networking that allows every computer on the network to share its resources with all other users. This method makes good use of available hardware in exchange for data security.

Pellet   (**Chemistry**) The button of particulate material formed after a suspension has been centrifuged. (**Firearms**) A pellet is a common name for the smooth, spherical projectiles loaded into shotshells, also referred to as *shot*. Also, a nonspherical projectile used in air guns.

Pen   Any writing instrument used to apply ink to the paper.

Pen lift   An interruption in a stroke caused by removing the writing instrument from the paper.

Pen position   The relationship between the pen point and the paper. Specifically, the angle between the nib of the pen and the line of writing and between the pen point and the paper surface are the elements of pen position. Either condition may be reflected in the writing, but is not always revealed except when the writing was prepared with the point of the pen.

Pencil   A writing instrument in which the marking portion consists of a compressed stick of graphite or colored marking substance usually mixed with clays and waxes.

Pencil grade   A qualitative description of the hardness or softness of a pencil, i.e., how dark a stroke it is capable of making.

Pencil lead   Not really lead, but a mixture of various types of waxes, clays, graphite, and carbon.

Pentane   An alkane having the formula C_5H_{12}, with a flash point of -40°F, and with an explosive limit of 1.4 to 8%. Pentane is frequently used to extract flammable or combustible liquid residues from fire debris samples.

Pentobarbital   A derivative of barbituric acid that produces depression of the central nervous system and consequent sedation; this drug may be toxic and habit-forming when not taken as prescribed.

Perception time   The time it takes the human body to perceive that a situation that requires some action is about to take place, or is taking place on the highway ahead.

Percussion cap   A small metal cap with a priming mix that is placed on the nipple of a percussion lock.

Perimortem   At or near the time of death.

Permanent defect   Any identifying characteristic of a typewriter that cannot be corrected by simply cleaning the typeface or replacing the ribbon. Actually, this term is not absolutely accurate, since all defects in typewriters undergo modification and change with time.

Permeation The passage of chemicals, on a molecular level, through intact material, such as protective clothing.

Perpetrator The individual who commits a crime. The identity of a perpetrator may or may not be known to the police.

Personal protective equipment (PPE) Articles such as disposable gloves, masks, and eye protection that are utilized to provide a barrier to keep biological or chemical hazards from contacting the skin, eyes, and mucous membranes and to avoid contamination of the crime scene.

Perspective grid target A 2 ft^2 (or other predetermined size) target used in the scale mapping of scene documentation.

Petechiae Pinhead-sized (red) dots which are minute hemorrhages found inside the eyelids and the facial skin; considered by pathologists to be a sign of strangulation.

Petition (legal) Formal application to the court for judicial action on a certain matter, stating allegations that, if true, form the basis for court intervention. A petition may be filed in juvenile or family court at the beginning of cases involving neglect, abuse, termination of parental rights, or delinquency.

Petroleum distillates By-products of the refining of crude oil. Low-boiling or light petroleum distillates (LPD) are highly volatile mixtures of hydrocarbons. These mixtures are sometimes called *ligroin*, *petroleum ether*, or *naphtha*. LPDs are used as cigarette lighter fluids, copier fluid, and solvents. Medium-boiling petroleum distillates (MPDs) are sometimes known as *mineral spirits*, and are used as charcoal starters, paint thinners, and solvent for insecticides. High-boiling or heavy petroleum distillates (HPDs) are combustible liquids such as kerosene and diesel fuel.

Peyote The common name for the small Mexican cactus, *Lophophora williamsii,* which contains the hallucinogen, mescaline.

pH The pH value of an aqueous solution is a number describing its acidity or alkalinity. A number used to represent the acidity or alkalinity of an aqueous solution. A solution with a pH of 7 is considered to be neutral; those solutions with pH below 7 are classified as acids. Bases have a pH above 7; the higher the pH, the solutions become more basic or alkaline.

pH electrode Membrane-type glass electrode used as the hydrogen-ion sensor for most pH meters; the pH response electrode surface is a thin membrane made of a special glass (P.4; pH electrode on left).

pH meter An instrument used to measure the degree of the acidity or the alkalinity of a solution: pH 7 (neutral), pH less than 7 (acidic), pH greater than 7 (alkaline) (Figure P.5).

Phadebas™ reagent Commercial chemical consisting of a dye cross-linked to an insoluble starch. Upon digestion of the starch by amylase, the dye is released into solution. The intensity of color relates to the level of amylase present. This reagent is used for the detection of saliva stains on forensic evidence.

Pharmacodynamics The study of the relationship of drug concentration to drug effects.

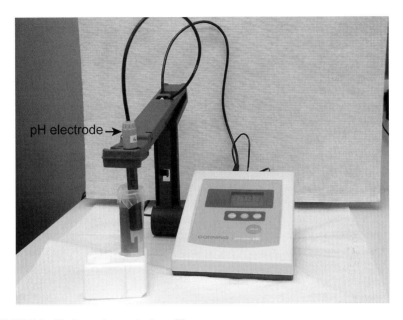

FIGURE P.4 pH electrode attached to pH meter.

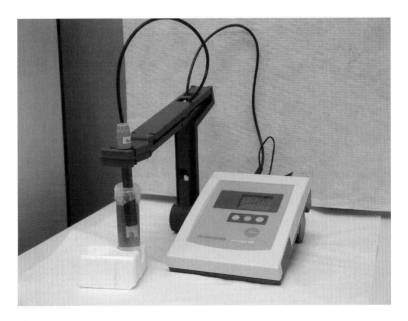

FIGURE P.5 pH meter.

Pharmacokinetics   The study of the time course of the processes (absorption, distribution, metabolism, and excretion) a drug undergoes in the body.

Pharmacologic   Relating to the study of drugs and their origin, natural properties, and effects on living organisms.

Phencyclidine (PCP)   Has an anesthetic activity and is manufactured legitimately for use as a veterinary anesthetic. It has no legitimate use in humans because of its hallucinogenic actions. The effects on humans are considered euphoric, but at times depression or anxiety and aggressive behavior are produced. Common street names are *PCP*, *peace pill*, *hog*, and *angel dust*.

Phenol (carbolic acid)   A poisonous and caustic organic compound, used in the isolation of DNA from cellular proteins.

Phenolphthalein   Pale yellow powder; forms an almost colorless solution in neutral or acid solution in presence of alkali, but colorless in the presence of a large amount of alkali. Used in dyes, acid-base indicator, and in medicine as a laxative.

Phenotype   The physical makeup of an individual as defined by genetic and nongenetic factors. Appearance of an inherited characteristic; the same appearance may be produced by different sets of alleles, and the same allele set may produce different appearances as a result of environmental and the interaction effects on gene expression.

Phosphatase   An enzyme that removes phosphate groups from different substrates.

Photo flash lamp   An electronic lamp working at higher than the normal voltage, giving brighter light.

Photoelectric cell   Light-sensitive cell used in exposure meters and for remote triggering of the shutter.

Photoflood   Photographic lamp designed to produce a high output of light during a comparatively short life (Figure P.6; lamps hanging at an angle).

Photogrammetry   The process of surveying or mapping through analysis of photographs. A scientific method used to determine from photographs the length of skid marks, width of roadways, or any other types of measurements needed.

Photographic negative   A transparency produced when black-and-white film is exposed in a camera and then developed. The term is derived from the appearance of the transparency, in which white areas of the original appear the darkest or most opaque, while the darkest portions of the original are almost clear. With color film the light–dark reversal is coupled with a change of colors to the complements of those in the original material.

Photographic positive   A print made by passing light through the negative generally onto photographic paper. In this print the tonal values are directly proportional to those of the original; i.e., light areas of the original appear light, and the dark areas are dark.

Photography   To write or draw with light. Recording with light is closer to the modern meaning of the word.

Photoionization detector (PID)   A type of detector used in chromatography that employs ultraviolet radiation rather than a flame to ionize compounds

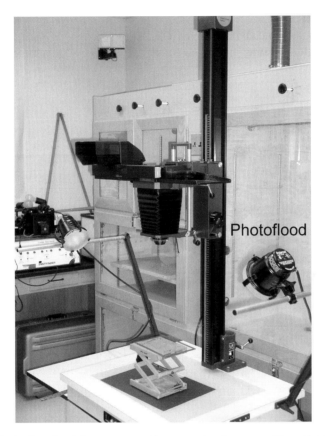

FIGURE P.6 A photoflood lamp setup with an overhead camera. The photoflood lamps provide the needed lighting for taking pictures.

as the particles pass through a detector. Photoionization detectors are particularly sensitive to aromatic compounds.

Photomicrographs   Photographs that are made through a compound microscope and may be a greatly enlarged image of a small area. Similarly, enlarged photographs, which may be prepared with only a lens of very short focal length, are accurately termed *photomacrographs* . It is extremely difficult to distinguish between photographs made by these two processes, and both are often incorrectly referred to as a photomicrograph.

Phylum   A taxon in classification between kingdom and class.

Physical abuse   Injury or mistreatment by a deliberately inflicted physical means.

Physical dependence   A state that develops in parallel with chronic tolerance and is revealed by the occurrence of serious disturbances (abstinence syndrome) when drug intake is terminated.

Physical evidence   Any tangible article that tends to prove or disprove a point in question. Physical evidence must usually be authenticated by a witness who testifies to the connection of the evidence with other facts in the case.

Pica **(Questioned documents)** A unit of measure of printer's type, approximately $^1/_6$ in. or 12 points, typically used for vertical measurement. Also, a term used to denote conventional monotone typewriter typeface that has a fixed character width of 10 to the inch. **(Hematology)** A perversion of appetite associated with ingestion of material not fit for food such as starch, clay, ashes, or plaster.

Picking Adherence of a drug to the face of the punch used to produce a tablet. Picking creates holes in the surfaces of pressed tablets, usually near letters such as A or R.

Pico A prefix used in the metric system to signify 10^{-12}; picogram is used in reporting the mean corpuscular hemoglobin.

Picroindigocarmine solution A greenish stain that is used in conjunction with Kernechtrot solution, for the identification of human sperm. This solution will stain the tail of the sperm cell a greenish–blue color (Figure P.7).

Pigment A finely divided insoluble material used to deluster or color fibers (e.g., titanium dioxide, iron oxide).

Pipette A small glass or plastic tube, sometimes graduated, used for the removal of small portions of fluid and can be also used for measuring the volume of liquids (Figure P.8).

Pistol (automatic, semi-automatic, single shot) A small firearm having a stock that fits in the hand and contains a short barrel. Firearm designed to be fired with one hand and with a chamber that is integral to the barrel.

Pitch, rifling The angle at which the rifling is cut in relationship to the axis of the bore. It is usually stated as the number of inches required for one revolution. Also known as *rate of twist* .

Pixel Picture element. The smallest unit of information that can be seen on a computer screen.

Plain view An exception to the requirement for a search warrant, when there is evidence of a crime in plain view by a person who sees it lawfully.

Plaintiff The complaining party in litigation.

Plant **(Arson investigation)** An ignition device that ignites the first fuel, or assists the initial flame to build in intensity; it may include a timing mechanism. **(Surveillance)** A technique in which the surveillant remains essentially in one position or locale (also called *stakeout, fixed surveillance*).

Plantar Pertaining to the sole of the foot.

Plasma The liquid portion of whole blood containing water, electrolytes, glucose, fats, proteins, and gases. Contains all the clotting factors necessary for coagulation but in an inactive form. Once coagulation occurs, the fluid is converted to serum.

Plaster A very general term, including all gypsum casting materials. Also used to define the softer gypsum materials having a lower compressive strength.

Plaster of Paris A gypsum material produced by heating crushed gypsum in an open oven at high temperatures. Can be used as dental and tool mark impressions (Figure P.9).

Plea In a criminal proceeding it is the defendant's declaration in open court that he or she is guilty or not guilty — the defendant's answer to the charges

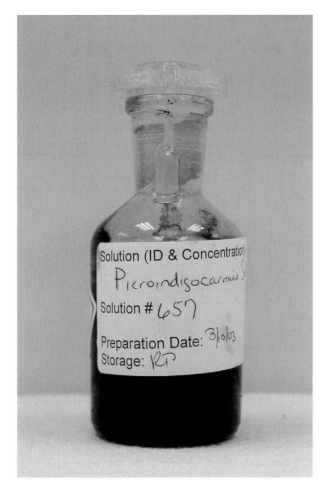

FIGURE P.7 A chemical reagent used in staining sperm cells, this solution will stain the tails of the sperm cells a greenish color.

made in the indictment or information. A plea can be *dilatory* (contests grounds other than the merits of the plaintiff's case, such as improper jurisdiction, wrong defendant, or other procedural defects) or *peremptory* (answers to plaintiff's contention).

Plea bargaining The process through which an accused person and a prosecutor negotiate a mutually satisfactory disposition of a case. Usually it is a legal transaction in which a defendant pleads guilty in exchange for some form of leniency. It often involves a guilty plea to lesser charges or a guilty plea to some of the charges if other charges are dropped.

Pleochroism The property, exhibited by double-refracting colored crystals, of showing different colors when the transmitted light is viewed along different axes. The color depends on the orientation of the substance and arises because of differential absorption of light in the different orientations.

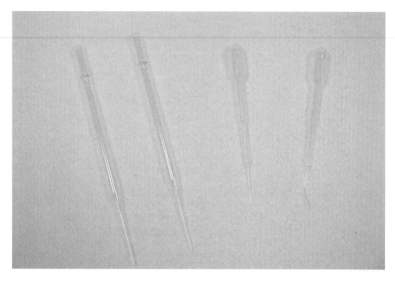

FIGURE P.8 Various types of plastic pipettes.

FIGURE P.9 A gypsum material used to develop a cast impression of a shoe print left at the scene.

Plumb bob A conical metal weight suspended from the end of a string. This
      device is used to generate a perfectly vertical line (Figure P.10).

Ply The number of single yarns twisted together to form a piled cord; also
      referred to as an individual yarn in a piled yarn or cord.

PMI Abbreviation for *postmortem interval* . The time period between death and
      the discovery of the body.

PMSI Abbreviation for *postmortem submersion interval*. The time period the body
      remained under the water surface before surfacing due to natural means.

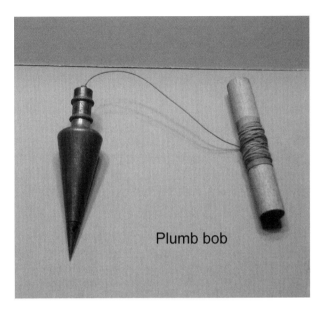

Plumb bob

FIGURE P.10 The weight used at the end of a plumb line.

Pneumonitis Inflammation of the lungs.

Poach To trespass on another's property for the purpose of illegal taking or killing of wildlife.

Poacher An offender who sets out specifically to search for a victim, basing the search from an activity site other than his or her residence, or who travels to another city during the victim search process.

Poikilothermic (Cold-blooded) An animal whose body temperature fluctuates with environmental temperature.

Point The basic typographic unit of measurement of fonts, line spacing, rules, and borders; there are 12 points to a pica and 72 points to the inch; typically used for vertical dimensions.

Point mutation An alteration of one complementary nucleotide pair in chromosomal DNA that consists of addition, deletion, or substitution of paired nucleotides.

Point of convergence A point to which a bloodstain pattern can be projected. This point is determined by tracing the long axis of well-defined bloodstains with the pattern back to a common point or source.

Point or area of origin The three-dimensional point or area from which the blood that produced a bloodstain originated. This is determined by projecting angles of impact of well-defined bloodstains back to an axis constructed through the point or area of convergence.

Polar coordinates Methods of crime scene measurement; measurement of items of evidence based upon their distances and angles from a fixed position.

Polarity The measure of an electrical charge on a molecule. Most flammable or combustible liquids are nonpolar. Many water-soluble compounds, including alcohols and acetone, are polar solutions.

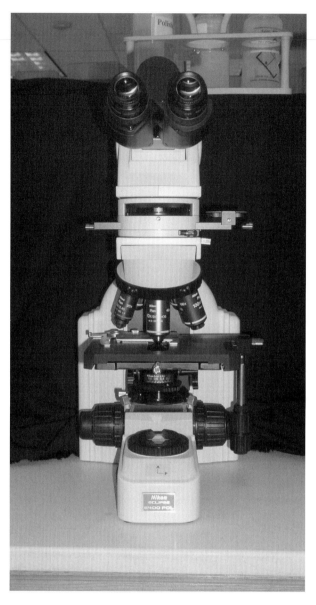

FIGURE P.11 Polarized light microscope with polarizing filters.

Polarized light microscope (PLM) A refined biological microscope stand to
    which several special purpose features have been added. These features
    should include, at a minimum, a polarizer, an analyzer, a rotatable circular
    stage, a cross-hair ocular, and a compensator slot. Quarter- and full-wave
    compensators should be part of the standard equipment. The most versatile

of all for obtaining in-depth information from a sample, especially samples of transfer or trace evidence (Figure P.11).

Polarizer   Two lenses used together to cut off all phases of light waves but one, eliminating glare in varying degrees.

Polarizing filter   Filter that passes on only polarized light and can be rotated to block polarized light reaching it, cutting down glare from polished surfaces or from blue sky.

Polyacrylamide   A chemical used in the preparation of electrophoretic gels, these gels used for the separation of mixtures of macromolecules. A polymer that is used to separate relatively small DNA fragments. In forensic DNA analysis, used in AMP–FLP and STR analyses.

Polyester fiber   A synthetic fiber of high tensile strength made by the esterification of ethylene glycol and other organic compounds.

Polyethylene terephthalate   A polyester formed from ethylene glycol by direct esterification or by catalyzed ester exchange between ethylene glycol and dimethyl terephthalate. Uses are: blended with cotton, for wash-and-wear fabrics, blended with wool for worsteds and suitings, packaging films, and recording tapes.

Polygonal rifling   Helical grooves in the bore of a firearm barrel to impart rotary motion to a projectile.

Polygraph   "Lie detector"; an instrument for recording variations in several physiological functions that may indicate whether a person is telling the truth or lying.

Polymarker   Common usage for a commercial kit called *AmpliType* ® PM; group of five different bi- and tri-allelic loci exhibiting sequence variation. Available as a kit for forensic DNA analysis.

Polymer   A large molecule consisting of repeating units of a monomer. Polymers may be natural, such as cellulose, or synthetic, such as most plastics. A compound composed of many smaller subunits; results from the process of polymerization.

Polymerase   An enzyme believed to catalyze the formation of messenger DNA in the cell.

Polymerase chain reaction (PCR)   A technique in which cycles of denaturation, annealing with a primer, and extension with DNA Polymerase, are used to amplify the number of copies of a target DNA sequence more than a millionfold using thermal stable *Taq* Polymerase. Oligonucleotide primers must be annealed to the target DNA sequence 5' flanking regions. The PCR may be likened to a molecular copy machine.

Polymorphic probe   A known DNA sequence that recognizes a specific locus on a chromosome that is polymorphic.

Polymorphism   Occurrence in a population of two or more genetically determined alternative phenotypes with frequencies greater than could be accounted for by mutation or drift. The occurrence of different forms, stages, or types in individual organisms, or in organisms of the same

species, independent of sexual variation. In microchemistry, it is crystallization of a compound in at least two distinct forms.

Polypeptide A long chain of amino acids linked by peptide bonds forming a
protein.

Polypropylene (C_3H_5)n A synthetic crystalline thermoplastic polymer, with a
molecular weight of 40,000 or more.

Polyurethane (PU) A family of resins produced when di-isocyanate reacts with
organic compounds containing two or more active hydrogens. It is used
in both the outsoles and midsoles of shoes.

Population (Theoretical) entity defined as an entire group of people, things, or
events that have a least one trait in common.

Population genetics The study of the frequency of genes and alleles in various
populations.

Population sample A biological sample containing DNA, typically a blood
sample from an anonymous individual that is subjected to DNA analysis.
The results of the DNA are examined along with many other samples for
statistical purposes. The statistical analysis then is applied to the interpretation of forensic DNA results. The population samples form a basis of
the analyst's opinion as to the significance of a DNA match.

Population statistics Statistical descriptors of the population, e.g., mean,
median, mode, or standard deviation.

Portal hypertension Increased pressure in the portal vein as a result of obstruction of the flow of blood through the liver.

Positive coercion bias The tendency for jurors to conclude that a suspect is guilty
when he or she has been promised leniency for confessing to the crime.

Positive control Those samples, which when run in a chemical reaction, give
a positive result. Those samples give the same result each time.

Positivist school of criminology A point of view that emphasizes that criminal behavior by a person was determined, rather than a product of free
will.

Postconviction hearing Hearing granted upon a motion raising evidentiary
issues. Such hearings often occur a significant time after conviction and
are typically unsuccessful.

Postfeeding larva The wandering, fasting phase of the third instarmaggot, ter-
minating in purpariation.

Posthypoxic encephalopathy Condition in which the brain has been damaged
as a results of insufficient oxygen.

Postmortem After death, occurring after death, or pertaining to a postmortem
examination, an autopsy.

Postmortem artifact Alteration to the body that occurs after death that is not
related to antemortem injury (Figure P.12).

Postmortem interval The period of time between death and corpse discovery.

Postoffense behavior Behavior of a suspect within hours, days, and weeks after
a crime. Such behavior distinguishes the offender from the rest of the
suspect population.

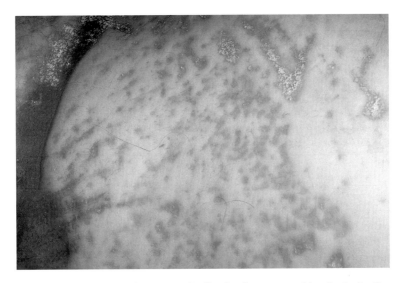

FIGURE P.12 Postmortem artifact due to feeding by fire ants on skin of a body discovered outdoors in Texas. (Courtesy of forensic medical examiner Michael Sikirica, M.D.)

Post-traumatic stress disorder An anxiety disorder in which the victim experiences a pattern of intense fear reactions after being exposed to a highly stressful event.

Potassium chlorate ($KClO_3$) Transparent, colorless crystals or white powder; used as an oxidizing agent in explosives, matches, percussion caps, and textile printing.

Potassium ferricyanide ($K_3FeCN)_6$ Bright red, lustrous crystals or powder. Used for tempering steel, etching liquid, production of pigments, electroplating, and fertilizer compositions.

Potassium nitrate (KNO_3) Transparent, colorless or white crystalline powder or crystals. Used in pyrotechnics, explosives, matches, metallurgy, and glass manufacture.

Potassium oxalate ($K_2C_2O_4 \cdot H_2O$) Colorless transparent crystals, odorless, soluble in water and highly toxic if inhaled or ingested. Can be a strong irritant to tissue cells. Used to remove stains from textiles and photography.

Potassium perchlorate ($KClO_4$) Colorless crystals or white, crystalline powder. Decomposed by concussion, organic matter, and agents subject to oxidation. Used in explosives, medicine, oxidizing agents, photography, pyrotechnics, and flares.

Potassium permanganate ($KMnO_4$) Dark-purple crystals, with blue metallic sheen, sweetish astringent taste, and odorless. Used as an oxidizer, disinfectant, and deodorizer; for dye tanning, radioactive decontamination of skin; and as a reagent in analytical chemistry.

Power of discrimination (P_d) Used in reference to a genetic marker or combination of markers. Defines the potential power of a system to differentiate between any two people chosen at random. Can be calculated from the allele frequencies in a defined population.

Precipitant Any substance, as a reagent, that when added or applied to a solution results in the formation of a precipitate.

Precipitate A substance separating in solid particles from a liquid as the result of a chemical or physical change.

Precipitin An antibody produced in the blood serum by inoculation with a foreign protein and capable of providing immunity against specific bacteria.

Precision Closeness of agreement between independent test results obtained under prescribed conditions. It is generally dependent on analyte concentration, and this dependence should be determined and documented. The measure of precision is usually expressed in terms of imprecision and computed as a standard deviation of the test results. Higher imprecision is reflected by a larger standard deviation. Independent test results refer to results obtained in a manner not influenced by any previous results on the same or similar material. Precision covers repeatability and reproducibility.

Preliminary hearing In criminal law, the hearing at which a judge determines whether there is sufficient evidence against a person charged with a crime to warrant holding him or her for trial. The Constitution bans secret accusations, so preliminary hearings are public unless the defendant asks otherwise; the accused must be present, accompanied by legal counsel.

Preponderance of the evidence The standard for a verdict in a civil suit; the evidence for one side outweighs that of the other by even a slight margin.

Pressure The amount of force exerted on the point of the writing instrument, technically termed *point load*. Pressure may manifest itself in line quality, i.e., thickness and shading of the stroke; also noted in the amount of indentation in the paper surface.

Presumption An inference resulting from a rule of law or the proven existence of a fact that requires such rule or action to be established in the action. Presumptions can be irrebuttable, such as the presumption of incapacity in a person under 7 years of age to act, or rebuttable, in which case it can be disproved by evidence.

Presumptive Describes things that are based on presumptions about what is probably true rather than on certainty.

Presumptive negative Specimen or sample that has been flagged as negative by screening. Usually no further tests are carried out, so there is no certainty about its content.

Presumptive positive Specimen or sample that has been flagged as positive by screening but that has not yet been confirmed by an adequately sensitive alternate chemical method.

Pretrial conference A meeting between the judge and the lawyers involved in a lawsuit to narrow the issues in the suit, agree on what will be presented at the trial, and make a final effort to settle the case without a trial. Also, refers to a meeting between the expert witnesses and the prosecutor to formulate a line of questioning that will be used during the trial.

Preview button A button or lever on the camera lens permitting the photographer to see the actual light level and depth of field while using an automatic lens.

Prima facie **evidence** Evidence that, in the judgment of the law, is good and sufficient to establish a given fact or a chain of facts making up a party's claim or defense. If such evidence is unexplained or uncontradicted, it is sufficient to sustain a favorable judgment for the issue it supports; may be contradicted by other evidence.

Primary crime scene The place where the corpse is discovered and homicide or suicide is suspected.

Primary deviance Behavior that violates a law or norm for socially acceptable conduct.

Primer (ballistics) The ignition component of a cartridge.

Primer cratering The extrusion of the primer into the firing pin hole; this phenomenon can produce identifiable marks. Also known as primer *flowback*.

Primer DNA A short, perhaps 20-mer, oligonucleotide annealed to the $5'$ end of a DNA template. The primer provides an initiation point for addition of deoxyribonucleotides in DNA replication.

Probability Mathematical measurement of how likely it is that something will happen, expressed as a fraction or percentage. Values for statistical probability range from 1 or 100% (always) to 0 or 0% (never). The relative frequency obtained after a long run of measurements or results will give good approximations to the true probability. It is also understood in other ways as expressing in some indefinable way a "degree of belief," or as the limiting frequency of an occurrence in an infinite random series.

Probable cause A reasonable ground for suspicion, supported by the circumstances sufficiently strong to justify the issuance of a search warrant or to make an arrest. Reasonable ground for believing that a crime has been committed or that the person committed a crime.

Probation An alternative to imprisonment allowing a person found guilty of an offense to stay in the community, usually under conditions and under the supervision of a probation officer. A violation of probation can lead to its revocation and to imprisonment.

Probe **(DNA analysis)** A specific sequence of DNA that attaches to unzipped DNA. A single-stranded segment of DNA, or mRNA, capable of being tagged with a tracer, such as ^{32}P, and hybridized to its complementary sequence. **(Human remains recovery)** A device used to penetrate the ground to a depth of one or more feet in order to release odor for perception by a dog in the search for buried remains.

Procedure Specified way to perform an activity. For quality assurance purposes, procedures should be written.

Processed data Raw data that have been acted upon to make them clearer or more readily usable.

Product gel Diagnostic tool used in PCR analysis to determine if a DNA sample has been successfully amplified.

Product rule **(DNA analysis)** A calculation based on population genetics that allows individual allele frequencies and genotype frequencies to be multiplied together to generate an overall profile frequency. **(Forensic psychology)** Another name for the Durham rule, a legal definition of insanity that states the accused is not criminally responsible if his or her unlawful conduct was the product of mental disease or defect.

Proficiency testing Ongoing process in which a series of proficiency specimens or samples, the characteristics of which are not known to the participants, are sent to laboratories on a regular basis. Each laboratory is tested for its accuracy in identifying the presence (or concentration) of an unknown substance using its usual procedures. An accreditation body may specify participation in a particular proficiency-testing scheme as a requirement of accreditation.

Proficiency tests Tests to evaluate the competence of analysts and the quality performance of a laboratory. In open tests, the analysts are aware that they are being tested; in blind tests, they are not aware. Internal proficiency tests are conducted by the laboratory itself; external proficiency tests are conducted by an agency independent of the laboratory being tested.

Profile Description of the results of an investigative analysis of an unsolved crime of violence; may cover victimology, crime reconstruction, significant facts of the autopsy, characteristics and traits of the offender, post-offense behavior, and investigative suggestions.

Profiling The psychological assessment of a crime, in which the personality type of the perpetrator is surmised through the recognition and interpretation of visible or spoken evidence at the crime scene.

Programming A method of gas chromatographic analysis that reproducibly raises the temperature of the column so as to allow better resolution of the components over a wide range of boiling points.

Projected blood pattern A pattern created when a force other than a low-velocity impact acts upon a quantity of blood approximately 0.10 ml or greater.

Projected prints A print made by focusing light from the negative on the printing paper by means of a lens system. These positives are generally enlargements. Some workers refer to them as *bromides* because of the type of paper emulsion originally used.

Projective test Psychological test based on the notion that if an individual is shown an ambiguous stimulus and asked to respond, his or her responses will reveal aspects of his or her personality, including inner thoughts, wishes, conflicts, and feelings.

Prokaryote A cell lacking a nucleus or any other subcellular organelle. Prokaryotes are all bacteria.

Proof mark A stamp applied at or near the breech of a firearm after it has passed a proof test.

Proof test The firing of a deliberate overload to test the strength of a firearm barrel and/or action.

FIGURE P.13 Gunshot residue (GSR) is a mixture of organic and inorganic materials originating from the projectile, cartridge case, propellant, and primer of a firearm that emerge from the barrel and other openings of a firearm and are deposited on the hand of the person firing the weapon.

Proofload, provisional proof (historical)   A cartridge loaded to specified pressures higher than service loads to test firearms barrels during manufacture, but before assembly; sometimes called a *blue pill*.

Propane   An alkane having the formula C_3H_8. Propane is the major constituent of LP gas, with an explosive limit of 2.4 to 9%. One cubic foot of propane has a heating value of 2500 BTU.

Propellant   In a firearm, the chemical composition, which when ignited by a primer, generates gas. The gas propels the projectile. Also called *powder*, *gunpowder*, or *powder, smokeless*.

Propellant gases   The gases created by the burning powder that force the projectile from the gun (Figure P.13).

Propensity evidence   Evidence of a defendant's past wrongdoings that suggest the defendant had the propensity, or inclination, to commit a crime.

Proportional-spacing typewriter   A modern form of typewriting resembling printing in that letters, numerals, and symbols do not occupy the same horizontal space as they do with a conventional typewriter. For example, the "i" occupies two units, the "o" three, and the "m" five.

Propoxyphene   A mildly effective narcotic analgesic, somewhat less potent than codeine, that bears a close structural relationship to methadone.

Prosecutor   A trial lawyer representing the government in a criminal case.

Prostatic-specific antigen (PSA)   A protease enzyme secreted by epithelial cells of the prostate that is used in the diagnosis of prostate cancer. Antigen-specific membrane tests are currently used in clinical settings

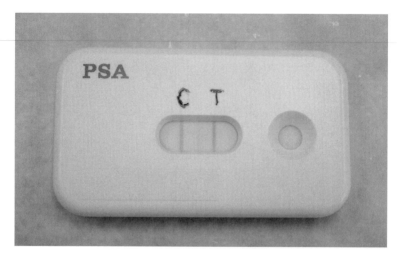

FIGURE P.14 A membrane test used to confirm the presence of prostatic-specific antigen.

to screen a patient's serum for the presence of PSA. In forensic serology this PSA membrane test is used when the acid phosphatase test is positive and microscopic examination for sperm cells is negative (Figure P.14).

Protective custody The confinement or guardianship of an individual by law enforcement with the objective of preventing an assault or other crimes against him or her.

Protein The agents of biological function, they are also the expression of genetic information. A biological molecule composed of amino acids. Proteins serves as the "building blocks" of body structures or as the enzymes that initiate specific biochemical reactions.

Proteinase K A hydrolytic enzyme used in the digestion of proteins to amino acids.

Protocol A directive listing the procedures to be followed in performing a particular laboratory examination or operation — the overall plan for analysis of a particular type of evidence.

Proximal Relatively nearer to the central portion of the body or point of origin.

Proximate cause A cause that constitutes an obvious or substantial reason why a given harm occurred.

Prying tool A tool that can be used to forcibly open a locked door/cover by applying leverage to the door/cover at one of its edges.

Pseudocumene A component of gasoline (1,2,4-trimethly benzene).

Pseudomalingering A phenomenon whereby a mentally ill individual feigns the mental illness he or she actually has. The behavior is considered a temporary ego-supportive device that allows the individual to feel he or she has control over the illness.

Psychological autopsy An attempt to determine the mode of death (whether an accident, suicide, homicide, or natural causes) by an examination of what was known about the deceased.

Psychological stress evaluator A device that analyzes vocal characteristics to determine if the person is lying.

Psychological theory of crime The approach to explaining criminal behavior that uses factors within the person such as motivation, ability level, and aspirations.

Psychopathy A long-term pattern of unsocialized or criminal behavior by a person who feels no guilt about such conduct.

Psychosis A mental disorder characterized by derangement of personality and loss of touch with reality. Severe mental disorder, with or without organic damage, characterized by deterioration of normal intellectual and social functioning and by partial or complete withdrawal from reality.

Pubic symphysis Immovable joint formed by fibrous tissue and cartilage where the pubic bones (left and right pelvis) meet in the middle front of the abdomen.

Public defender Government lawyer who provides free legal defense services to a poor person accused of crime.

Pull-up Specifically related to ABI GeneScan® software, a peak seen in one color that is not due to the presence of DNA, but to incorrect compensation for the spectral overlap of the four dyes used in detecting multiple loci in one reaction.

Pulmonary edema Accumulation of extravascular fluid in the lungs that impairs gas exchange; usually due to either increased intravascular pressure or increased permeability of the pulmonary capillaries.

Pulp Neurovascular tissue in the center of a tooth.

Pump action A firearm that features a movable forearm that is manually actuated in motion parallel to the barrel by the shooter. Also known as *slide action*.

Pupa That immature stage between the larva and adult in insects having complete metamorphosis. This is a stage of major transformation. Among higher flies the pupa is inside the puparium.

Pupariation The immobilization of the postfeeding maggot with the shrinking, hardening, and darkening of its outer skin.

Purpura A condition with various manifestations and diverse causes, characterized by hemorrhages into the skin, mucous membranes, internal organs, and other tissues.

Putative father A man accused but not proven to be the biological father of an offspring.

Putrescine Malodorous chemical compound produced during decomposition.

Putrifaction The foul-smelling, anaerobic decomposition of moist or wet organic matter by microorganisms. The breakdown of tissues, particularly proteins, due to enzyme action.

Pyridine   A colorless liquid, nitrogenous compound, C_5H_5N, with a pungent, noxious odor. Used in organic synthesis, as a disinfectant, antiseptic, and alcohol denaturant.

Pyrimidine   An organic compound, $C_4H_4N_2$, resulting from the acid hydrolysis of a nucleic acid. A type of nitrogen base; the pyrimidine bases in DNA are cytosine and thymine.

Pyrolysis   Decomposition by the application of or as a result of heat. The breaking apart of complex molecules into simpler units by the use of heat, as in the pyrolysis of heavy oil to make gasoline.

Pyromania   An irresistible impulse or compulsion to start a fire or set something on fire.

Pyrophoric distillation   The slow drying and passive pyrolysis of wood materials.

Q

QUAD   Professional 2-in. reel-to-reel format videotape.

Qualification   The professional experience, education, and ability of an analyst to perform his or her duties. Before being permitted to testify as an expert witness, the court must rule that a scientist is qualified as an expert in the specific scientific field of concern.

Qualified analyst   A forensic scientist who has passed the appropriate competency test and has exhibited current proficiency in the relevant examination.

Qualify the witness   Process of establishing the qualifications of the witness to give a particular type of testimony; includes expert testimony of the handler and the "expertise" of the trained K-9.

Qualitative test   A test that determines the presence or absence of specific drugs or metabolites, proteins, or enzymes in the specimen or sample.

Quality assessment   Overall system of activities whose purpose is to provide assurance that the overall quality control job is being done effectively. It involves a continuing evaluation of the products produced and of the performance of the production system.

Quality assurance (QA)   System of activities whose purpose is to provide to the producer or user of a product or a service the assurance that it meets defined standards of quality with a stated level of confidence.

Quality assurance management   All activities of the overall management function that determine and implement quality policies, objectives, and responsibilities.

Quality assurance manager   An individual designated by top management who has the defined authority and obligation to ensure that the require- ments of the quality assurance activities and results comply with planned arrangements and whether these arrangements are implemented effec- tively and are suitable to achieve objectives.

Quality assurance program   Internal control system designed to ascertain that the studies are in compliance with the principles of good laboratory practices.

Quality control (internal)   Set of procedures undertaken by a laboratory for continuous monitoring of operations and results in order to decide whether the results are reliable enough to be released. Quality control of analytical data primarily monitors the batchwise trueness of results on quality control specimens or samples and precision on independent replicate analysis of test materials.

Quality manual   Document stating the general quality policies, procedures, and practices of an organization.

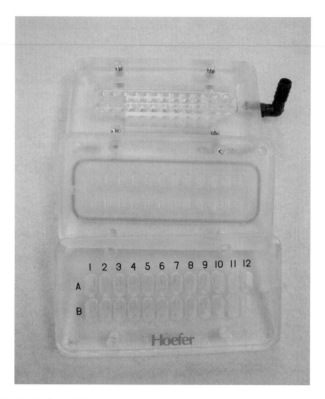

FIGURE Q.1 Hoefer® slot blot setup.

Quality policy Statements by top management regarding the laboratory's adherence to principles of quality. It may set forth codes of practice or ethics.

Quality system The organizational structure, responsibilities, procedures, processes, and resources for implementing quality management. In a laboratory it refers to the total features and activities of a laboratory aimed at producing accurate work and a high-quality product.

Quantiblot® A slot blot technique that is used to obtain information about the quantity of human DNA extracted from evidence samples (Figure Q.1).

Quantitative inheritance Inheritance of measurable traits (height, weight, color intensity) that depends on the cumulative action of many genes, each producing a small effect on the phenotype.

Quantitative test Chemical analysis to determine the amounts or concentrations of one or more components of a mixture.

Quartering the wind Search pattern that involves traversing a path perpendicular to wind direction.

Quartz lens A special lens used for ultraviolet photography.

Questioned document Any document about which some issue has been raised or that is under scrutiny.

Questioned (sample)   Material collected as or from items of evidence that have a known location but an unknown originating source.

Quid pro quo   Something for something, as in making a deal, e.g., plea-bargaining.

Quinine   Bulky, white, amorphous powder or crystalline alkaloid; very bitter taste; odorless and levorotatory. Used in medicine as an antimalarial drug.

R

Race As applied to the human species (*Homo sapiens*), a population subgroup with a gene pool characteristic only of that group.

Racial profiling The police practice of using race as a factor in determining actions such as traffic stops, arrests, and questioning of suspects.

Radial A loop formed as part of a fingerprint pattern that opens toward the thumb.

Radial fractures Fractures that form a star shape when a bullet pierces a sheet of glass, and which originate on the side opposite to the initial impact.

Radiation (1) Transfer of heat through electromagnetic waves from hot to cold. (2) Electromagnetic waves of energy having frequency and wavelength. The shorter wavelengths (higher frequency) are more energetic. The electromagnetic spectrum is comprised of gamma rays, x-rays, visible light rays, infrared, microwave, and radio waves, cosmic rays and ^{32}P ultraviolet rays.

RAM (random access memory) Computer chips that provide rapid access to information. This information can be read and written. RAM memory requires power to maintain the information it contains. RAM is not used for permanent storage, and data are lost when the power is turned off.

Random "man" Any individual in the population whose DNA profile matches a crime-specimen DNA profile or an offspring's paternally derived DNA profile.

Random sample Sample taken in such a way that all the members of the population have an equal chance of being included; that is, each is chosen entirely by chance or at random.

Range Concentration interval for which acceptable accuracy and precision can be achieved (adapted from). Statistically, it is the difference between the minimum and the maximum values of a set of measurements. **(Firearms)** The range is the horizontal travel of a projectile from the weapon to the target; a location where firearms are used for testing the weapon's integrity; skill of the shooter; practice or competitive events.

Rangefinder A viewer system found on cameras without a through-the-lens viewing capacity (SLR cameras).

Rape Sexual intercourse between a man and a woman without the woman's consent. This may occur by deception or by force.

Rape shield laws Laws that prevent or restrict the questioning of an alleged rape victim during that person's time on the witness stand; specifically, questioning about the alleged victim's past sexual activities is prohibited or limited.

Rape trauma syndrome A collection of behaviors or symptoms that are frequent aftereffects of having been raped.

Raster image The representation of an image by colors as a two-dimensional grid of pixels.

Rate of twist The distance required for the rifling to complete one revolution.

Rational choice theory A proposition that, if the rationale for committing a crime exceeds that for not committing it, the likelihood of the crime being committed increases.

Rational crime theory The theory that some illegal behavior "makes sense" because of the reward and unlikelihood of detection.

Raw data Data that are in their original state and have not been processed.

Ray tracing A technique to generate an image from a geometric model of an object. For each pixel in an image, a theoretical ray is cast from the observer's viewpoint into the model to determine what part of the model should be displayed at that point in the resulting image.

Reaction time How long it takes the human body to react to a perception that requires some action. It could be a brake application, or turning the steering wheel to move the vehicle out of the line of the action taking place ahead.

Reactivity Ability of a substance to chemically interact with other substances.

Reading the dog Observing a dog's behavior closely to detect an attitude change when it encounters a target odor.

Reagent blank control This control consists of all reagents used in the test process minus any sample. This is used to detect DNA contamination of the analytical reagents and materials.

Reagent chemicals High-purity chemicals used for analytical reactions, for testing of new reactions where the effect of impurities are unknown, and in general, for chemical work where impurities must either be absent or at a known concentration.

Real time Continuous motion of a computer system with no noticeable movement between images. Television broadcasts in the United States are recorded at 30 frames per second, at which the human eye perceives no delay. If a computer can keep up with this motion it is said to be in *real time*.

Reannealing Spontaneous realignment of two single DNA strands to re-form a DNA double helix that had been denatured.

Reasonable doubt (legal) Doubt that arises from evidence or lack thereof and would be entertained by a reasonable or prudent person. Reasonable doubt requires acquittal.

Reasonable suspicion A term referring to police officers' justification for stopping and, perhaps, frisking persons; a reasonable suspicion is one that can be described in terms of specific facts that a judge deems to be reasonable; a mere hunch is not reasonable suspicion.

Rebuttal The presentation of evidence to counter or disprove facts previously introduced by the adverse party.

Recess   An adjournment of a trial or a hearing that is temporary and occurs after the commencement of the trial. If there is going to be substantial delay, it is called a *continuance*. A temporary dismissal is called *sine die*.

Recognition   The act of remembering an event after some cue is provided that assists in its recollection, as when a mug shot is picked from a rogues' gallery file or an individual from a lineup.

Recoil   The backward movement or thrust of a gun caused by the pressure of the propellant gases in the process of pushing the projectile forward through the bore. Also, the distance that a firearm recoils.

Recoil operation   An operating principle of automatic and semiautomatic firearms. When the weapon is fired, the barrel and breechblock initially recoil together. After traveling a short distance, the barrel and breechblock unlock and the breechblock continues to travel to the rear, extracting and ejecting the expended cartridge.

Record   Document that furnishes objective evidence of activities performed or results achieved.

Record/review   Automatically rewinds and plays back the last few seconds of videotape recording. Provides a smooth transition from one segment to another.

Recovery   Percentage of the drug, metabolite or internal standard originally in the specimen or sample that reaches the end of the procedure.

Recovery expansion search   Type of canine cadaver search where some remains have already been discovered and additional remains are sought from that area.

Recross   To cross-examine a witness a second time after redirect examination.

Re-direct examination   Opportunity to present rebuttal evidence after one's evidence has been subjected to cross-examination.

Redirect questioning   Questioning by the original attorney that follows the opposing counsel's cross-examination.

Reference collections   (Questioned documents) Collections of typewriting, check-writer specimens, inks, pens, pencils, paper, etc. compiled and organized by the document examiner as standards of the products. **(Firearms)** A collection of various types of firearms and ammunition used by the firearms examiner for the purposes of test firing weapons, for identification of ammunition and firearms (Figure R.1).

Reference line   An extension of the reference point (RP) from which the X or Y direction measurement is taken. Generally speaking, the RP is a pole or hydrant set back from the street or road. A straight line is drawn from the RP to the curb or edge of the road. The line from the pole to the curb is the vertical reference line. A second line is then drawn on the outside of the curb and is the horizontal reference line.

Reference material   Material or substance, one or more properties of which are sufficiently well established to be used for calibrating an apparatus, assessing a measurement method, or assigning values to materials.

FIGURE R.1 Different types of long rifles stored in a reference collection.

Reference material (in-house) Material whose composition has been established by the user laboratory by several means, by a reference method,
   or in collaboration with other laboratories.
Reference method or standard consensus method Method developed by
   organizations or groups that use collaborative studies or similar approaches
   to validate a new method or a new instrument. A method's value depends
   on the authority of the organizations that sponsor it.
Reference shoes Shoes known to belong to an individual that are used as a
   known comparison standard in a barefoot comparison.
Reference standard A standard, generally of the highest quality available at a
   given location, from which measurements made at that location are
   derived.
Refind Trained behavior when a canine finds a scent, comes to the trainer, gives
   some indication it has found the target scent, and is cued to take the
   handler back to the target.
Reflection The bouncing back of rays of light striking a surface.

Reflex camera   A camera in which the image can be seen right side up and full size on the ground-glass focusing screen.

Refraction   The bending of a light ray when passing obliquely from one medium to a medium of different density.

Refractive index (N)   The change in direction (apparent bending) of a light ray passing from one medium to another of different density, as from air to water or glass. The ratio of the sine of the angle of incidence to the sine of the angle of refraction is the index of refraction of the second medium. Index of refraction of a substance may also be expressed as the ratio of the velocity of light in a vacuum to its velocity in the substance.

Regression analysis   Method of explaining or predicting the variability of a dependent variable using information about one or more independent variables. Also, techniques for establishing regression equations.

Regression curve   Curve that comes closest to approximating a distribution of points in a scatter diagram.

Reinforcement   Anything that affects behavior due to association with that behavior; in canine training, reinforcement provides information to the dog about the correctness of what it is doing.

Relative judgment   An eyewitness's process of deciding, when looking at a simultaneous lineup, which of the people shown in the lineup looks most like the perpetrator.

Relative retention time (RRT)   Ratio of the retention time of the substance of interest divided by the retention time of an internal standard run on the same gas or liquid chromatographic system at the same time.

Release on recognizance   A court order releasing a defendant from custody on the defendant's written promise to appear in court when the defendant's case is scheduled for a hearing, trial, or other proceeding; a defendant who is released on recognizance is not required to deposit money or other property with the court in order to be released.

Reliability   Processing the quality of being dependable; may refer to personnel, materials, and equipment.

Reload   A cartridge that has been reassembled with a new primer, powder, projectile, or other components. Also, to place fresh ammunition into the firearm.

Remote   An action originating from another location, as in a surveillance situation.

Renaturation   The reassociation of denatured complementary single strands of a DNA double helix. The restoration of the DNA molecule back to its double helix form. Repeating unit in a tandem cluster is the length of the sequence that is repeated and appears circular on a restriction map.

Rendering   Generating an image on a computer screen that is a precise scene.

Repeatability   Closeness of agreement between the results of successive measurements during a short time (within one standard deviation).

Reproducibility   Closeness of agreement between the results of measurements of the same measurable quantity on different occasions, made by different observers, using different calibrations, at different times (between one standard deviation).

Request standards   Writing samples written at the request of another person.

Res gestae   All of the things done or words spoken in the course of a transaction or event; a record of what was said or done in the first moments of an investigation.

Resolution   (Chromatography) A measure of the separation of components; in thin-layer chromatography (TLC), the ability to visually separate spotted drug samples on a glass plate. **(Spectroscopy)** A measure of the ability of the instruments to detect individual absorbance peaks. **(Microscopy and photography)** The capability of an optical device to separate into two or more objects (or points) what to the unaided eye appears to be one object (or point), thus yielding details not otherwise perceptible. Measurement in units per inch of the amount of detail in an image file: dpi = dots per inch; ppi = pixels per inch; lpi = liners per inch.

Respiratory depression   Slowing or cessation of breathing due to suppression of the function of the respiratory center in the brain.

Rest   A party is said to "rest" or "rest its case" when it has presented all of the evidence it intends to offer.

Restoration   Any process in which erased writing is developed or brought out again on the document itself.

Restriction endonuclease   Enzymes (molecular scissors) that cleave double-stranded DNA at specific palindromic base recognition sequences. These sequences are usually different for each enzyme. Restriction enzymes are named according to the bacterial species of origin.

Restriction enzyme   An enzyme that cuts DNA internally at a specific, known sequence site.

Restriction fragment length polymorphism (RFLP)   The different-length fragments of DNA produced by the action of a restriction enzyme at a specific polymorphic site. If the restriction endonuclease recognizes the variable site, then two fragments are produced; if not, only one is formed. An individual may be homozygous or heterozygous, i.e., the site may be present or absent on both chromosomes of the homologous pair, or it may be present on one chromosome and absent on the other chromosome of the heterozygous pair.

Retardation (r)   The actual distance of one of the doubly refracted rays behind the other as they emerge from an anisotropic fiber. Dependent upon the difference in the two refractive indices, n_2 - n_1 and the thickness of the fiber.

Retardation factor (RF)   The ratio of the distance traveled by the solute spot's center on a thin-layer chromatography glass plate, divided by the distance traveled by the solvent front, both measured from the origin.

Retention index   In gas chromatography, the relationship of retention volume with arbitrarily assigned numbers to the compound being analyzed, used to indicate the volume retention behavior during analysis.

Retention time   The length of time required for a compound or component of a mixture to pass through a chromatographic column.

FIGURE R.2 Swing-out cylinder revolver.

Retouching   Going back over a written line to correct a defect or improve its appearance; synonymous with patching.

Retracing   Any stroke that goes back over another writing stroke. In natural handwriting there may be many instances in which the pen doubles back over the same course, but some retracing in fraudulent signatures represents a reworking of a letter form or stroke.

Reversal   A positive film such as slide film (either color or black-and-white).

Revolver   A type of pistol with a revolving cylinder in the breech chambered to hold several cartridges so that the revolver may be fired in succession without reloading (Figure R.2).

Rhythm   The element of the writing movement marked by regular or periodic recurrences. It may be classed as smooth, intermittent, or jerky in its quality.

Ribbon condition   Cloth or multiple-use typewriter ribbons gradually deteriorate with use, and the degree of deterioration is a measure of the ribbon condition.

Ribbon impression   Typewriting made directly through a cloth or carbon film ribbon is called a ribbon impression. Original typewriting is made in this way.

Ricochet   The deflection of a projectile after impact.

Ricochet or secondary splash   The deflection of large volumes of blood after impact with a target surface that results in staining of a second surface. Ricochet does not occur when small drops of blood strike a surface.

Ridge characteristics of fingerprints

Angle – An angle results from two or more ridges converging with one another at a point.

Bifurcation (fork) – A single ridge, splitting or forking into two braches.

Bridge – A short ridge that interconnects two other parallel ridges.

Converging ridges – Two or more ridges that meet at a point are converging, and the point at which they meet is called the point of convergence.

Diverging ridges – Diverging ridges are parallel for some distance but then swing out away from each other.

Dot – A very short ridge and means exactly what the word dot implies.

Island (enclosure) – An island is formed by a single ridge which, after bifurcating for a short distance, reconverges and continues as a single ridge. An enclosure usually refers to a larger island.

Ridge ending – The point of the ridge's termination. It is considered an ending ridge only if it terminates within the pattern area.

Short ridge – A relative term used to denote a ridge that is not as long as the average ridge in that specific print.

Trifurcation – One single ridge splitting into a three-pronged, fork-shaped pattern.

Rifle   A firearm having rifling in the bore and designed to be fired from the shoulder.

Rifle slug   A single projectile with spiral grooves and hollow base, intended for use in shotguns. The theory of the grooves is that after leaving the gun barrel's muzzle the slug will rotate and thus reach its target much more accurately.

Rifling methods

Broach, gang – A tool having a series of cutting edges of slightly increasing height used to cut the spiral grooves in a barrel.

Broach, single – A nonadjustable rifling cutter that cuts all of the grooves simultaneously and is used in a series of increasing dimensions until the desired groove depth is achieved.

Button – A hardened metal plug, called a button, with a rifled cross section configuration. It is pushed or pulled through a drilled and reamed barrel so as to cold form the spiral grooves to the desired depth and twist. When the carbide button was first introduced it was described as a swaging process or swaged rifling.

Electro-chemical rifling (ECR) – The use of electric current that passes through a conductive fluid.

Hook – A cutting tool that has a hook shape and cuts only one groove at a time.

Scrape – A cutting tool that cuts two opposing grooves at a time.

Swage – An internal mandrel with rifling configuration that forms rifling in the barrel by means of external hammering. Also known as *hammer forging*.

Rigor mortis   The stiffness of the body after death that helps in reconstructing the time at which death occurred. The progressive rigidity of a corpse following death, caused by an accumulation of lactic acid in dying muscle tissues. This is a temporary condition lasting 12 to 36 h.

Rim   The flanged portion of the head of a rimfire cartridge, certain types of centerfire rifles and revolver cartridges, and shotshells. The flanged portion is usually larger in diameter than the cartridge or shotshell body diameter and provides a projecting lip for the extractor to engage. In a rimfire cartridge, the rim provides a cavity into which the priming mixture is placed.

River   Gaps in the writing or printing pattern that form a straggling white stream down the page.

Robbery   Felonious taking of another's property from his person or immediate presence and against his will by means of force or fear.

Rogues' gallery   A file of photographs of arrested individuals; usually includes fullface and profile photographs (mug shots) along with detailed physical description, age and place of birth, Social Security number, fingerprint classification, nicknames and aliases, *modus operandi*, etc. (also called *mug shot file*).

Roller pen   A type of ball-point pen that uses aqueous ink.

ROM (Read only memory)   Computer chips that provide rapid access to information. This information can only be read. ROM memory does not need power to maintain the information it contains. It is primarily used for the special programs required to start a computer.

Rough sketch   A relatively crude, freehand representation of all essential information (including measurements) at a crime scene; it is made while at the scene.

Router   A device attached to a network cable to connect two unlike topologies.

RP (Reference point)   Chosen by the on-scene investigator, from which to take all measurements in an X and Y or north and south direction.

Rule 702   A federal rule of evidence that permits an expert who is qualified by experience, training, or education to offer an expert opinion if the scientific, technical, or other specialized knowledge will assist the trier of fact to understand the evidence or to determine a fact in issue. This rule was amended in 2000.

Rules of evidence   Standards governing whether evidence in a civil or criminal case is admissible.

S

Sabot A device, "shoe," which enables a subcaliber projectile to be fired in a larger caliber barrel.

Sacrum Portion of the lower part of the spine below the lumbar vertebrae and above the coccyx that forms a joint with the left and right pelvis.

Safety A type of device that locks a weapon to prevent accidental discharge.

Safety manager An individual designated by the director of a laboratory who has the defined authority and obligation to ensure that the requirements of the safety system are implemented and maintained.

Safety manual A document stating the safety policy and describing the various elements of the safety system of an organization.

Saliva Oral secretion comprised of water, mucus, proteins, salts, and enzymes. Its primary functions are to moisten the mouth, lubricate chewed food, and aid in digestion.

Sample A selected, representative portion of the whole. Representative fraction of material tested or analyzed in order to determine the nature, composition, and percentage of specified constituents, and possibly their reactivity.

Saponification The conversion of corpse body fat into a curdlike foul-smelling product called *adipocere* .

Saprophagous Feeding on dead or decaying plant or animal material, such as carrion, corpses, dung, or rotting wood.

Sarcoma Cancer arising from connective tissue such as muscle or bone. It may affect the bones, bladder, kidneys, liver, lungs, parotids, and spleen.

Satellite DNA Highly repetitive eukaryotic DNA mainly located around centromeres and found in other places in the genome. Consists of many tandem repeats (identical or related) of a short basic repeating unit, usually 4 to 7 base pairs in length. The repetitive DNA forms a satellite or off-the-bell-curve fraction in a density gradient because of the base compositions of the repetitive regions.

Satellite spatter Small droplets of blood that are projected around or beside a drop of blood upon its impact with a surface. A wave castoff is also considered a form of satellite spatter.

Scale The enlargement or reduction of an object or texture.

Scallop pattern A bloodstain produced by a single drop that is characterized by a wave-like, scalloped edge.

Scanning electron microscope (SEM) A microscope that is used to study the surface morphology of different types of samples. The images produced are striking and often give the illusion of being three dimensional. A microscope that utilizes an accelerated focused electron beam to image particulate samples (e.g., gunshot residue) at high magnification, with

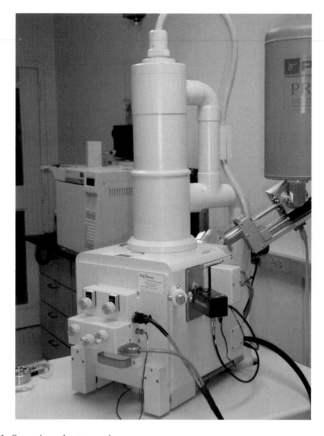

FIGURE S.1 Scanning electron microscope.

great depth-of-field, while providing size, shape, morphology, and chemical information in both manual and automated modes (Figure S.1).

Scent cone The patterned distribution of scent molecules that have diffused from a source, generally becoming less concentrated and more dispersed the further they diffuse from the source.

Schlieren optics Imaging system in which the transparent or translucent object to be examined is placed between two spherical mirrors. The illuminant is a point light source placed at the focal point of one of the mirrors. Parallel light rays from the mirror pass through the object to the second mirror, which projects the image onto a screen. A knife edge is placed at the focal point of the second mirror to block unrefracted light rays. Only light rays refracted by the object reach the screen. Schlieren optics can produce images of thickness, density, and refractive index differences.

Schutzen A type of competitive training for dogs, emphasizing both obedience and endurance.

Scoliosis A lateral curvature of the spine (Figure S.2).

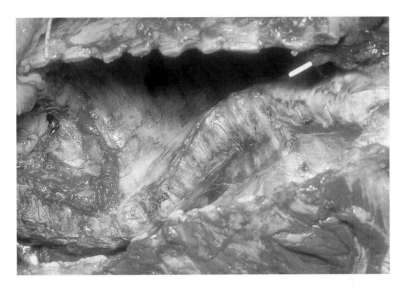

FIGURE S.2 Scoliosis of the spine in an elderly adult. (Courtesy of forensic medical examiner Michael Sikirica, M.D.)

Screen A series of initial tests designed to separate samples containing drugs at or above a particular minimum concentration from those below that minimum concentration (positive vs. negative).

Script Handwriting as distinguished from printing or lettering; cursive writing.

Scurvy A deficiency disease characterized by hemorrhagic manifestations and abnormal formation of bones and teeth.

Search and rescue Search, often by dog–handler teams, for individuals who are missing and may need to be rescued; frequently includes the possibility the missing individuals are dead.

Search and seizure Form of investigation covered by the Fourth Amendment, requiring the area searched to be free from the reasonable expectation of privacy unless there is a search warrant.

Search baseline An arbitrary boundary of an area to be searched, perpendicular to the route of travel and parallel to the backline.

Search warrant A written order of consent issued by a court that specifies the place where a search is to be made and the seizable property that is to be looked for, and directs that when such property is found, it should be brought before the court.

Seating The positioning of a primer or bullet in a cartridge case.

Seating lines The circumferential striae parallel to the axis of the projectile, generated on the surface of the bullet by the cartridge case.

Secobarbital A barbiturate derivative of short duration of action; used as either a sedative or hypnotic.

Secondary contamination Transfer of a harmful substance from one body (primary body) to another (secondary body), thus potentially permitting adverse effects to the secondary body.

Secondary splash or ricochet   The deflection of a large volume of blood after impact with a target surface to another target surface.

Secret ink   A material used for writing that is not visible until treated by a developing process; also referred to as *sympathetic ink* .

Secretor   An individual whose genetic markers can be detected by using their saliva and testing for a polymorphic antigen that adheres to the cell surfaces, such as in the Lewis system.

Sector   A portion of a track (an arc) on a floppy or hard disk.

Seizable property   Contraband, or the fruits or instruments of crime (e.g., a weapon or other relevant evidence); its nature, as well as where it is to be discovered, must be specified in a search warrant.

Selenium   Nonmetallic element sensitive to light; used as a coating on drums of photocopying machines.

Self-contained breathing apparatus (SCBA)   Protective equipment consisting of an enclosed facepiece and an independent, individual supply (tank) of air; used for breathing in atmospheres containing toxic substances or underwater.

Self-defense   A claim that an act otherwise criminal was legally justifiable because it was necessary to protect a person or property from the threat or action of another. A legal defense relied upon by criminal defendants typically charged with homicide; it asserts that the defendant's actions were justified by a reasonable belief that he or she was in imminent danger of death or bodily harm from an attacker.

Self-timer   A timing device permitting the photographer to delay shutter function.

Selvage   The narrow edge of woven fabric that runs parallel to the wrap. It is made with stronger yarns in a tighter construction than the body of the fabric to prevent raveling.

Semen   Sperm cells plus the seminal fluid. Complex mixture of organic and inorganic substances produced in the postpubertal male genital tract. The term *semen* is applied to the fluid that is ejaculated.

Semi-automatic   A firearm that uses the forces of combustion to extract and eject a cartridge and to chamber a new cartridge from the ammunition source with each pull of the trigger.

Seminal fluid   The impregnating fluid of male animals.

Sentence   A court's determination of the punishment to be inflicted on a person convicted of a crime.

Sentencing (legal)   Last stage of criminal prosecution in which a convicted defendant is imprisoned, fined, ordered to pay restitution, or granted a conditional release from custody. Sentencing is the equivalent of disposition in a juvenile case.

Sepsis   Pathologic state, usually febrile, resulting from the presence of micro-organisms or their poisonous products in the bloodstream.

Septicemia   Bacteria in the blood system with signs and symptoms of disease.

Sequela (*plural,* sequelae)   A condition that follows as a consequence of injury or disease.

Sequence of strokes   The order in which writing strokes are placed on the paper.

Sequestration   Keeping all of the jurors together during a trial to prevent them from being influenced by information received outside the courtroom. Sequestered jurors are usually housed in a hotel, have their meals together, and are given edited copies of newspapers and magazines, all in an attempt to keep them from outside influences.

Sequestration of witnesses   Keeping all witnesses (except plaintiff and defendant) out of the courtroom except for their time on the stand, and admonishing them not to discuss their testimony with other witnesses. Also called *separation of witnesses* . Prevents a witness from being influenced by the testimony of a prior witness.

Serial arson   Three or more separate arson events with an emotional cooling-off period between fires.

Serial murder   Three or more separate murder events with an emotional cooling-off period between homicides.

Serial rape   Three or more separate rape events with an emotional cooling-off period between attacks.

Serologist   An individual who, through their examination of evidence, characterizes and identifies blood and body fluids.

Serology   The science of serums and their actions.

Serrations   Roughness along the edges of an ink line seen under a microscope.

Serum   The watery, straw-color fluid that separates from blood on coagulation.

Serum stain   A clear, yellowish stain with a shiny surface often appearing around a bloodstain after the blood has retracted due to clotting. The separation is affected by temperature, humidity, substrate, and air movement.

Sex chromosomes (X and Y chromosomes)   Chromosomes whose contents are different in the two sexes, usually labeled X and Y; the male species has the XY chromosomes and the female species has the XX chromosomes. In DNA profiles these chromosomes are referred to as *amelogenin* .

Sexual assault   Unlawful actions of a sexual nature committed against persons forcibly and usually against their will; criminal sexual conduct. Various degrees of sexual assault are established by state law and distinguished by the age of the perpetrator in relationship to the victim, the amount of force used, and the type of sexual contacts or conducts.

Sexual exploitation   Involvement of children and adolescents in sexual activities that they do not usually fully comprehend, that they are unable to give informed consent to, and that violate social taboos.

Sexual predator laws   Laws that allow the government to sentence certain sex offenders (those deemed likely to reoffend) to psychiatric hospitals after they have served their prison sentences.

Sexual ritualism   A series of acts committed by an offender that are unnecessary to the accomplishment of the crime. The offender repeats the acts over a series of crimes. The intent is to increase psychosexual gratification. Ritualism should not be confused with *modus operandi* .

FIGURE S.3 A partial latent shoe print impression.

Shading   A widening of the ink stroke due to added pressure on a flexible pen point or to the use of a stub pen.

Shank   Part of the sole of the shoe between the heel and the ball. Also a piece of steel, leather, or synthetic material placed between the insole and the sole from the heel forward, to support that area of the shoe. Also may refer to a weapon, fashioned in a prison, used to produce stab wounds.

Shock   A clinical syndrome in which the peripheral blood is inadequate to return sufficient blood to the heart for normal function, particularly transport of oxygen to all organs and tissues.

Shoe print   A two-dimensional impression of a shoe. A shoe mark (Figure S.3).

Shoot (shot) **(Photography)** A slang term for taking or having taken a photograph. **(Firearms)** A spherical pellet used in loading shotshells or cartridges (Figure S.4).

Shored exit wound   A bullet exit wound that has many characteristics of a distant entrance wound. It is caused by supporting or shoring the skin as the bullet exits.

Short tandem repeat (STR)   Repeating units of an identical (or similar) DNA sequence, where the repeat sequence unit is 2 to 5 base pairs (bp) in length. The repeat units are arranged in direct succession of each other, and the number of repeat units varies between individuals.

Shot sheet   A form for recording all pertinent photographic information on a particular roll of film.

Shot spread   The diameter of a shot pattern.

Shotgun   A smooth-bore shoulder firearm designed to fire shotshells containing numerous pellets or sometimes a single projectile.

Shotshell   A cartridge containing projectile designed to be fired in a shotgun. The cartridge body may be metal, plastic, or paper (Figure S.5A and B).

Shutter   Mechanical device that regulates the time light can act upon the film.

FIGURE S.4 Various sizes of lead shots.

Shutter preference   An automatic exposure system in which shutter speed may be selected and the aperture is adjusted automatically to give correct exposure.

Shutter speed   The action of the shutter that controls the duration of an exposure. The faster the speed, the shorter the exposure.

Sign of elongation   Referring to the elongation of a fiber in relation to refractive indices. If elongation is in the direction of the high refractive index, the fiber is said to be positive; if elongation is in the direction of the low refractive index, it is said to be negative.

Signatory   **(1)** A signer, with another or others. **(2)** A person whose name is being inscribed on a document who requires assistance in doing so.

Signature   (**Questioned documents**) The name of a person, or mark representing it, as written by himself or herself. (**Forensic psychology**) A killer's psychological calling card left at each crime scene across a spectrum of several murders. Characteristics that distinguish one murder from all others.

Signature analysis station (SAS)   A terminal paired with a server. Provides the tools to examine the images and correlation results stored in the server.

Signatures   Represent the location of each feature and mark on an image from the bullet or cartridge case. The acquired signatures can then be correlated with the IBIS correlation engine. These signatures, which are mathematical representations of the images, are sent along with compressed images and demographics to a server for correlation.

Significant figures   Number of figures that are consistent with the precision of the test.

Significant, statistically significant   Two values are significantly different if the probability of obtaining a difference as large as or larger than that found is less than $\forall$ when the true difference is zero. Conventionally, $\forall$ is taken as 0.05, although other values, such as 0.01, are also used. Said of a value

FIGURE S.5A Opening of a shotshell showing the inside.

or measure of a variable when it is larger or smaller than would be expected by chance alone. Statistical significance does not necessarily imply practical significance.

Significant writing habit   Any characteristic of handwriting that is sufficiently uncommon and well fixed to serve as a fundamental point in the identification.

Silencer   A tubular device attached to the muzzle of a firearm to reduce the sound of the report.

Silhouette   A photograph that shows only the mass of a subject in black against a white or colored background.

Single-action   A type of revolver that needs to be cocked before each shot by pulling back the hammer. Requires the firing mechanism (hammer or firing pin) to be cocked before pressure on the trigger will release the mechanism.

Single-element typewriter   Typewriters using either a type ball or type wheel printing device. The IBM Selectric machine was the first modern typewriter of the group.

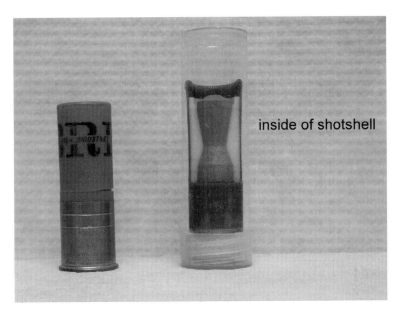

inside of shotshell

FIGURE S.5B Cut away section of a shotshell.

Single-lens reflex Camera system utilizing a hinged mirror between the lens and the film that swings out of the light path when the shutter is open, allowing the taking and viewing functions of a lens to be combined.

Single-locus probe A DNA probe that detects genetic variation at only one site in the genome; an autorad produced using one, single-locus probe usually displays one band in homozygotes and two bands in heterozygotes.

Sipe Small groove in a tire design element intended to provide better traction. Sipes vary in depth and are useful for documenting tire wear.

Siping The process of creating a pattern of parallel cuts across a rubber sole. Commonly found on deck or boat shoes.

Size marker DNA fragments of known molecular weight and base pair length, such as λ-phage digested with the restriction enzyme Hind III, run on electrophoresis gels for the determination of DNA sample fragment sizes.

Skeletonization Removal of soft parts of the body, leaving only the skeleton.

Skeletonized bloodstain A bloodstain that consists only of its outer periphery, the central area having been removed by wiping after liquid blood has partially dried. A skeletonized bloodstain is also produced by the flaking away of the central portion of a completely dried stain.

Skewness Said of measures or scores that are bunched on one side of a central tendency parameter (mean, median, mode) and trail out on the other. The more skewness in a distribution, the more variability in the scores. Also used to refer to asymmetry in, for example, a chromatographic peak shape ("tailing" and "fronting").

Skid marks (slippage marks) **(Firearms)** Rifling marks formed on the bearing surface of bullets as they enter the rifling of the barrel before rotation of the bullet starts. Skid marks are typically produced by revolvers and have the appearance of a widening of the land impression at their beginning point. **(Vehicle reconstruction)** Marks left on the road surface when the tire stops rotating, locks up, and skids.

Skill (handwriting) In any act there are relative degrees of ability or skill, and a specimen of handwriting usually contains evidence of the writer's proficiency.

Skylight filter A pale pink correction filter used on the camera when taking color slides to eliminate blue casts found in dull weather or when subjects are lit only by reflected blue sky light.

Slack space The hidden space on a disk where DOS attempts to write a file to clear its RAM memory.

Slant The angle or inclination of the axis of letters relative to the baseline.

SLICE Spectra library for identification and classification engine. A database for the archiving of x-ray spectra.

Slide A positive film mounted in a slide mount or a positive print on glass for projection upon a screen.

Slide film Direct reversal film; usually color film used in cameras for full-color projection positives. Sometimes called *color transparency film* .

Slippage Mark on the surface of a fired bullet made when the bullet slides along the tops of the lands of the rifling. Slippage marks appear when the rifling is worn or when a subcaliber bullet is fired.

Slit-width Size of the opening of the slit through which light emerges. Size depends on wavelength range, separation ability of wavelength selector, and desired isolation of specific wavelength.

Sloughing Process by which necrotic cells separate from the tissue to which they have been attached.

Slow Term indicating the relative speed of a lens, shutter, or film in capturing the photographic image.

Slow film Film having an emulsion with low sensitivity to light. Typically such films have an ASA rating of 32 or less.

Slow lens A lens with a relatively small maximum apertura, such as f-8.

Slug A term applied to a single projectile for shotshells.

Smear A relatively large volume of blood, usually 0.5 ml or more, that has been distorted to such a degree that further classification is not possible. A smear is similar to a smudge, but a smear is a stain produced by a large volume of blood.

Smeared-over writing An obliteration accomplished by covering the original writing with an opaque substance.

Smokeless powder Propellant composed of nitrocellulose (single-base powders) or nitrocellulose plus nitroglycerin (double-based powders). Smokeless powders contain additives that increase shelf life and enhance performance. They are made in a variety of shapes (rods, perforated rods, spheres, disks, perforated disks, and flakes).

Smooth bore   A firearm with unrifled bore.

Smudge   A bloodstain that has been distorted to a degree so that further classification is not possible.

Snapshot   A casual picture taken by amateurs, usually with simple equipment.

Snow Print Wax™   Registered name of an aerosol product used to assist in the photography and casting of footwear impressions in snow.

SNP   Single nucleotide polymorphism (pronounced *SNIP*). A one-nucleotide change or difference from one individual to another.

Sodium fluoride and potassium oxalate   Chemicals found inside a gray-top test tube; the sodium fluoride prevents bacterial growth and the potassium oxalate binds the calcium in the blood, which prevents blood from clotting. These chemicals are in gray-stopper vacutainer tubes used when testing for alcohol in the blood.

Solubility   Ability of one material to dissolve in or blend uniformly with another.

Solute   In thin-layer chromatography, a mixture of components to be separated. The substance dissolved in a solvent.

Solution   A single, homogeneous liquid, solid, or gas phase that is a mixture in which the components (liquid, gas, or solid) are uniformly distributed throughout the mixture.

Solvent   A substance capable of dissolving another substance (solute) to form a uniformly dispersed mixture (solution) at the molecular or ionic size level.

Solvent front   The final point reached by the mobile phase as it flows up or across the thin-layer chromatography plate during development of the chromatogram (Figure S.6).

Somatic cells   All cells of eukaryotes excluding gametes.

Souvenir   Personal item belonging to the victim of a violent crime that is taken by the offender, e.g., jewelry, clothing, a photograph, or driver's license. The item serves as a reminder of a pleasurable encounter and may be used for masturbatory fantasies. The offender who takes a souvenir is usually an inadequate person who is likely to keep it for a long time or give it to a significant other. Also known as a *trophy*.

Spatter   The dispersion of small blood droplets due to the forceful projection of blood.

Species   A group of individuals who are similar in structure and physiology, and are capable of interbreeding and producing fertile offspring.

Specific gravity   The ratio of the mass of a unit volume of a substance to the mass of the same volume of a standard substance (usually water) at a standard temperature.

Spectrometer   Photometric device for the measurement of spectral transmittance, spectral reflectance, or relative spectral emittance. An instrument used to measure the intensity of a specific wavelength of light entering and leaving a solution.

Spectrophotometer   An instrument used to measure the intensity of a specific wavelength of light entering and leaving a solution. A light-measuring device, which incorporates a monochrometer to isolate and project particular wavelengths of electromagnetic radiation through a sample, and a

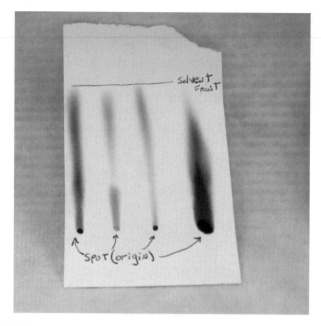

FIGURE S.6 Different types of markers spotted on filter paper, which is placed into a jar containing a solvent. Once the filter paper is removed from the jar the solvent front (where the chemical reagent solution stops) is noticed at the top of the filter paper.

      detector to measure the amount of radiation that has passed through the sample.

Spectroradiometer A form of spectrometer for determining the distribution of the intensity of any type of radiation, especially in the infrared region of the spectrum.

Spectroscopy Observation by means of an optical device (spectroscope) of the wavelength and intensity of electromagnetic radiation (light) absorbed or emitted by various materials.

Spectrum A colored band formed when white light is passed through a prism.

Speed The sensitivity of a photographic emulsion to light. ISO, ASA, or DIN numbers indicate their relative speed characteristics. The higher the number, the faster the film reacts to light.

Speed of writing Not everyone writes at the same rate, so that consideration of the speed of writing may be a significant identifying element. Writing speed cannot be measured precisely from the finished handwriting, but can be interpreted in broad terms as slow, moderate, or rapid.

Sperm (cell) fraction In a differential extraction, the portion of a sample containing DNA from the sperm cells.

Spermatozoa (sperm cell) A male reproductive cell. The male fertilizing element of an animal, usually in the form of a nucleated cell with a long flagellate process or tail by which it swims actively about (Figure S.7).

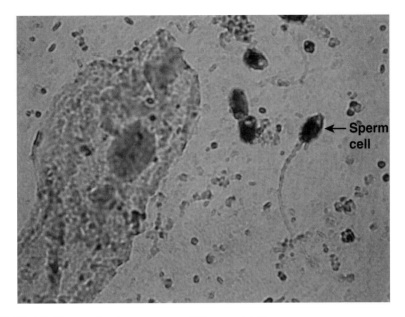

FIGURE S.7 Picture of an intact sperm cell (head and tail).

Spherulites Spheres composed of needles or rods, all oriented perpendicular to the outer surface, or a plane section through such a sphere. A common form of polymer crystallization from melts or concentrated solutions.

Spike A peak in an electropherogram caused by electrical fluctuations in the current (an artifact) (Figure S.8).

Spiked sample A test material containing a known addition of analyte.

Spine The pointed-edge characteristics that radiate away from the center of a blood-stain. Their formation depends upon impact velocity and surface texture.

Spinneret (1) One of the organs perforated by tubes connected with glands secreting liquid silk, as in spiders. (2) A metal plate pierced with holes through which filaments of plastic material are forced, as in the making of rayon fibers.

Spiracle A respiratory aperture, or tracheal opening in the exoskeleton of an insect. A breathing pore.

Spiral That portion of a letter executing a spiral formation, popular designs of commencement and termination in older styles of writing.

Spiral search Pattern in which a dog is worked in a circle pattern from a specific point.

Splash A stain pattern created by a low-velocity impact upon a quantity of blood approximately 0.10 ml or greater striking the surface.

Splicing A term used by document examiners to denote the slight overlapping of two strokes after an interruption in the writing. It may be a part of imitated, fraudulent signatures that are prepared one or two letters at a time.

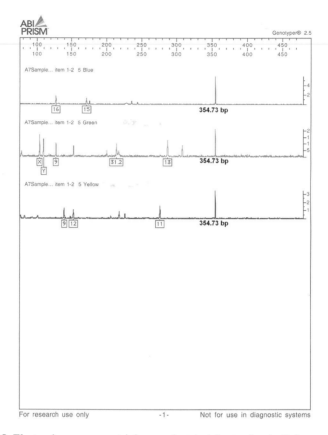

FIGURE S.8 Electropherogram containing an electrical fluctuation (spike).

Splitting   The division of an ink line into two or more, more-or-less equal, portions by a noninked area running generally parallel to the direction of the stroke; sometimes called *burring*.

Spontaneous heating   Also known as *spontaneous combustion*. Initially, a slow, exothermic reaction at ambient temperatures. Liberated heat, if undissipated (insulated), accumulates at an increasing rate and may lead to spontaneous ignition of any combustibles present. Spontaneous ignition sometimes occurs in haystacks, coal piles, warm moist cotton waste, and in stacks of rags coated with drying oils such as cottonseed or linseed oil.

Spot   A round zone of sample application at the origin; in a thin-layer chromatography plate, a round zone caused by migration of a component of the solute (Figure S.9).

Spot search   The handler chooses areas with a higher likelihood of evidence in an otherwise unfocused search; might include areas accessible by vehicles, footpaths, or refuse a reflector and lens that can either focus light into a small, concentrated circle or give a wider beam.

Spotlight   Lamp unit with a reflector and lens that can either focus light into a small, concentrated circle or give a wider beam.

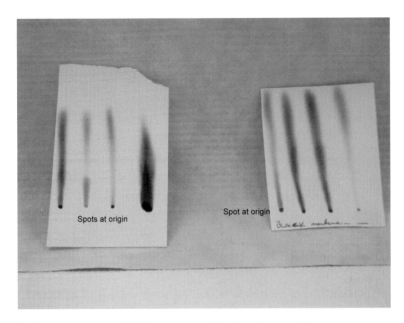

FIGURE S.9 The spotting of different types of black markers on filter paper.

Spotting Applying a solute sample at the origin of the thin-layer chromatography plate.

Sprawlers Aquatic insect representatives that inhabit the surface of floating leaves of emergent plants or fine sediments, usually with modification for staying on top of the substrate and maintaining the respiratory surfaces free of silt (e.g., Ephemeroptera, Caenidae, Odonata, Libellidae).

Spurious signature A fraudulent signature in which there was no apparent attempt at simulation or imitation. It is common form of forgery encountered in investigations of fraudulent checks where the person passing the check depends on the surrounding circumstances rather than upon the quality of the signature for his success.

Squid load A cartridge or shell that produces projectile velocity and sound substantially lower than normal. May result in projectile and/or wads remaining in the bore.

Stab wound Penetrating wound typically deeper than the external width that is produced by a sharp-edged object or instrument (Figure S.10).

Stability Resistance to decomposition or other chemical changes, or to physical disintegration.

Stabilizer Additive to smokeless powder that reacts with acidic breakdown products of nitrocellulose and nitroglycerin. Diphenylamine and ethyl centralite are common stabilizers.

Stage micrometer A microscope slide with a scale usually divided into 10-μm or 0.001-in. units. It is used to calibrate the eyepiece scale of a microscope used for measuring.

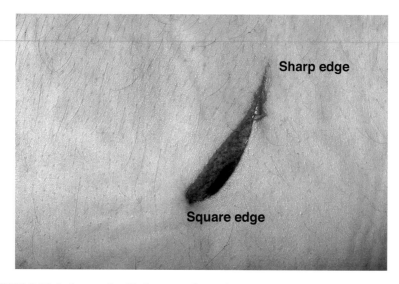

FIGURE S.10 Stab wound with features of squaring and a sharp edge consistent with a single-edged knife. (Courtesy of forensic medical examiner Michael Sikirica, M.D.)

Staged scene   A crime scene in which someone (usually the offender) arranges the scene or commits certain acts to have the scene convey a motivation different from the original motive or to mislead investigators.

Stakeout   A surveillance technique in which the surveillant remains essentially in one position or locale; the term is derived from the practice of tethering animals to a stake, allowing them a short radius in which to move (also called *plant, fixed surveillance*).

Stalker   An offender who, upon encountering a victim, follows them to attack at a later place and time.

Standard addition   The addition of a known amount of a pure component supposed to be present as a constituent of the specimen or sample in order to verify and quantitate this component. Operationally, a measurement is made on the specimen or sample, a known amount of the desired constituent is added, the modified specimen or sample is remeasured, and the amount of the constituent originally present is determined by proportionation.

Standard deviation (SD)   A statistic that shows the spread or dispersion of scores in a distribution of scores. It is calculated by taking the square root of the variance. It is applicable to all kinds of repeated measurements, e.g., between-batch, within-batch, repeatability, and reproducibility.

Standard lens   Lens whose focal length is approximately equal to the diagonal of the film format with which it is used. It is also referred to as the *prime* or *normal* lens.

Standard operating procedures (SOP)   Written procedures that describe how to perform certain laboratory activities.

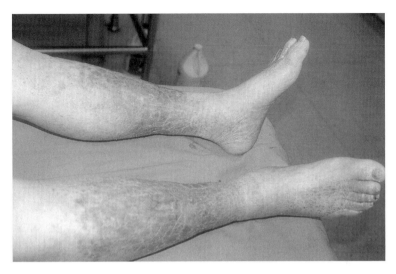

FIGURE S.11 Chronic stasis changes of the lower legs in an adult with atherosclerotic peripheral vascular disease. (Courtesy of forensic medical examiner Michael Sikirica, M.D.)

Standards A condensed and compact set of authentic specimens which, if adequate and proper, should contain a true cross section of the material from a known source.

Starch-gel electrophoresis A method that uses purified starch-gel as a support medium to hold proteins while they are separated in an electric field.

Stasis change Stoppage of the blood in its circulation, especially in the small vessels and capillaries; caused by abnormal resistance of the capillary walls, rather than by any lessening of the heart's action (Figure S.11).

Static streak Light streak that appears on photographic film, usually in cold weather when film is advanced too quickly. Static streaks can be harmful to development of clear photographic images.

Stationary phase The solid adsorbent coating layer on thin-layer chromatography plates. In a packed column, the stationary phase is a low vapor pressure liquid that coats a solid support. Compounds are selectively retained based on their solubility in this liquid. In a capillary column, the stationary phase is generally a modified or unmodified polysiloxane compound coating the walls of a fused silica column. Compounds are selectively retained based on their interaction with the coating's functional group.

Statistical control A procedure is in statistical control when results consistently fall within established control limits, i.e., when they have constant mean and variance. Statistical control should be monitored graphically with control charts.

Statistical correlation Extent to which two or more things are related to one another. This is usually expressed as a correlation coefficient.

FIGURE S.12 Steatosis of the liver (fatty liver in a chronic alcoholic). (Courtesy of forensic medical examiner Michael Sikirica, M.D.)

Statute of limitations The time within which a lawsuit must be brought or the time within which evidence must be analyzed. There are different statutes of limitations for different kinds of lawsuits and crimes.

Steatosis Accumulation of fatty compounds within the cells of organs, typically the liver. Often results in a yellow discoloration of the organ (Figure S.12).

Stellar pattern A bull's-eye-type fracture of the windshield when struck by a human or anthropomorphic head during a collision. Damage occurs in the form of a circular pattern, with cracks radiating from the center.

Stereo binocular microscope Two similar but separate optical microscopes for observation by both eyes simultaneously for low to medium magnification in the range of 4 to 40 times (Figure S.13A and B).

Stereoisomers Compounds with identical structural formulas; they differ in the way their molecules are arranged.

Stereomicroscope An instrument for blending into one image two pictures of an object from slightly different points of view so as to produce upon the eye the impression of relief and solidity. This type of microscope provides a three-dimensional image (Figure S.14).

Sterile technique A procedure that aids in the elimination of contamination with the use of gloves, sterile supplies, and a clean working area, as well as the frequent change of pipette tips for each reagent addition to each reaction tube.

Sternum Breastbone.

Steroid One of a group of polycyclic compounds closely related biochemically to terpenes.

Sticking Adherence of a drug formulation to the walls of a die used to produce tablets. Sticking causes unreproducible striations on the edges of the tablets.

Still A photograph lacking motion; a single frame.

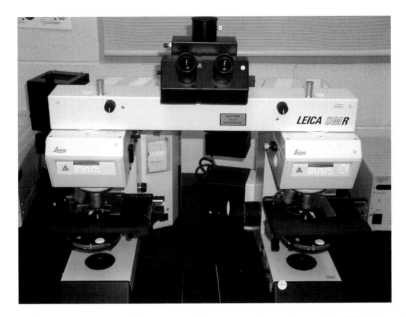

FIGURE S.13A Comparison microscope used to compare latent fingerprints lifted from crime scene to suspect's fingerprint cards.

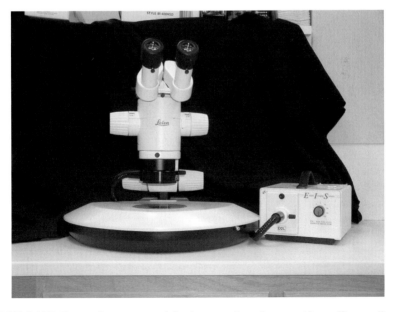

FIGURE S.13B Stereomicroscope used for the screening of trace evidence (fingernail scrapings, hairs, fibers, etc.).

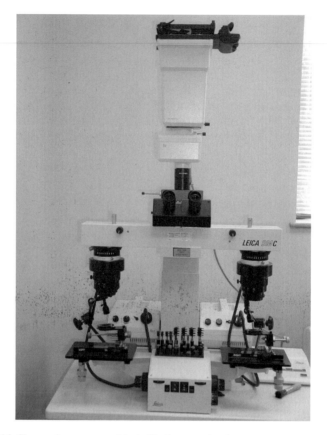

FIGURE S.14 Stereomicrocope used in ballistics examination.

Stimulants Drugs that increase the activity of the central nervous system, creating feelings of confidence and energy. A drug that produces a temporary increase of functional activity or efficiency. A drug that increases alertness and motor activity and, at the same time, reduces fatigue, allowing the individual to remain awake for an extended period of time. It can cause weight loss, increased respiration and heart rate, blurred vision, and anxiety when snorted, injected, smoked, or swallowed in capsule, tablet, or pill form.

Stippling Disposition of fragments of gunshot powder residue into the skin as the result of a gunshot wound of relatively close range; also called *powder tattooing* (Figure S.15).

Stipulation An agreement by attorneys on both sides of a case about some aspect of a lawsuit or criminal trial, i.e., to extend the time to answer, to adjourn the trail date, to admit certain facts at the trial, etc.

Stitching Characteristic marks left by a tool used when joining the various unvulcanized rubber parts of a shoe together prior to vulcanizing. It is associated primarily with shoes made utilizing unvulcanized rubber soles, foxing strips, and rubber upper components. Also, the application of thread

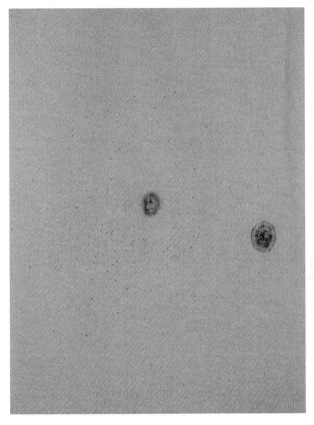

FIGURE S.15 Stippling or powder tattooing around a close-range gunshot wound. (Courtesy of forensic medical examiner Michael Sikirica, M.D.)

through the bottom (bottom stitched) or side (side stitched) of a shoe to help join the outsole to the upper.

Stock solution Concentrated standard solution used to prepare calibrators.

Stop A lens aperture or diaphragm opening, such as *f*-4 and *f*-5.6.

STR (short tandem repeat) Also referred to as *microsatellites*. An elementary form of repetitive DNA that occurs in mammalian genomes, determined by di-, tri-, and tetra-nucleotide repeats arranged in very short arrays.

Strand A single fiber, filament, or monofilament.

Stratification The actual observable sequential layering of soil, rocks, or surface debris.

Striae Noninked grooves left behind in an ink line by imperfections in the ball or ball housing of a pen. In firearms/toolmarks, these are lines or grooves in an object that are characteristics of the object that produced them and are the basis for an identification.

Striations Parallel surface contour variations on the surface of an object caused by a combination of force and motion where the motion is approximately

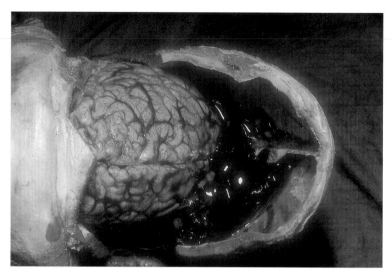

FIGURE S.16 Subdural hematoma due to blunt force injury. (Courtesy of forensic medical examiner Michael Sikirica, M.D.)

parallel to the plane being marked. These striations are accidental in nature and unique to a common origin (a particular firearm or tool).

Stridor   A harsh, high-pitched respiratory sound often heard in acute respiratory obstruction.

Strike   Highlighting, in the record of a case, evidence that has been improperly offered and will not be relied upon.

Stringency   **(1)** Specific conditions used in the hybridization of DNA. Also refers to a specific parameter used when searching a DNA database. **(2)** Variable condition, such as temperature or salt concentration, used in renaturation assays.

Strobe   Electronic flash unit. An electrical power supply charges the gas-filled flash tube emitting light between 1/1000 sec and 1/50,000 sec. A strobe can be manual or manual and automatic.

Structural isomers   Compounds that contain the same numbers and types of atoms but differ in the order of arrangement of the atoms. The types include chain, positional, and functional isomers.

Strychnine   An alkaloid found together with the less active brucine in the seed of *Strychnos nux-vomica* , a tree indigenous to India. It is a potent central nervous system stimulant and convulsant, acting by the selective blockage of postsynaptic neuronal inhibition.

Stutter   A minor band or peak appearing one repeat unit smaller than a primary STR allele. Occasionally, the repeat unit is larger than the primary allele.

Subdural hematoma   Bleeding that occurs between the arachnoid membrane and the surface of the brain, typically due to blunt force trauma (S.16).

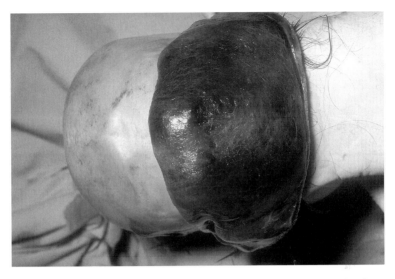

FIGURE S.17 Subgaleal hemorrhage due to blunt force injury to the head. (Courtesy of forensic medical examiner Michael Sikirica, M.D.)

Subgaleal hemorrhage Hemorrhage that occurs in the soft tissue of the scalp, typically due to blunt force trauma (S.17).

Submarining Action of the occupant sliding forward underneath the lap belt portion of the restraint system, with the lap belt webbing resting above the pelvic girdle.

Subpoena A written command summoning a specific individual to appear in court under penalty for failure to do so. Document issued by a court requiring a person to appear at a certain time to give testimony in a specified case. Failure to obey a subpoena may subject the person to contempt proceedings.

Subpoena *duces tecum* A court order commanding a witness to bring certain documents or records to court.

Subrogation Substituting one creditor for another as when an insurance company seeks to recover the costs paid to an insured by a manufacturer or service installer if the manufacturer's product can be shown to have inherent design flaws or the service provider engaged in negligent behavior.

Substance abuse Use of alcohol or drugs that results in adverse effects on the user. Substance abuse is a major health and social problem in the United States among adolescents.

Substrate control An unstained area of the evidence specimen adjacent to, or representative of the area upon which the biological stain is deposited.

Sulfur A nonmetallic yellow element. A constituent of black powder, sulfur burns readily when in powdered form.

Summary judgment (legal) Decision made by a trial court based on written documentation submitted before any trial occurs. Summary judgments can be granted only when there are no genuine issues of material fact.

Summary jury trial A brief presentation of both sides of the case, usually lasting only a day, in which a jury renders a verdict that is only advisory to a judge.

Summons (1) A notice to a defendant that he or she has been sued and is required to appear in court. (2) A jury summons requires the person receiving it to report for possible jury duty.

Superglue™ 2-Methyl and ethyl esters of cyanoacrylate; manufactured as an adhesive and incidentally found to be useful in latent fingerprint development.

Superglue fuming A technique for visualizing latent fingerprints on nonporous surfaces by using cyanoacrylate ester fumes.

Supernatant The liquid portion separated after a suspension is centrifuged.

Support zone The area beyond the decontamination zone that surrounds a chemical hazard incident in which medical care can be freely administered to stabilize a victim.

Suppression hearing A hearing before a judge, in which one of the attorneys argues that certain evidence should not be admitted at trial.

Surface dye A colorant bound to the surface of a fiber.

Surface texture The surface of any sheet of paper, which, when viewed under magnification, is not absolutely smooth and flat but irregular and rough. Surface texture describes this property.

Surfactant An agent that reduces surface tension (e.g., wetting agent, detergents, dispensing agents).

Surveillance The observation of a person, place, or thing — generally, but not necessarily, in an unobtrusive manner.

Surveillance photography A secretive, continuous, and sometimes periodic visual documentation of activities involving persons, places, or objects of importance to an investigation.

Surveillant The person conducting a surveillance.

Swab drying unit A hard, clear plastic rectangular box that has a fan that circulates air through the unit. The unit has a rack with holes so that wet cotton swabs can be placed into it and allowed to dry. A clear plastic front door with holes that slide down is in front of the drying unit (Figure S.18).

SWG Scientific working group; a representative group of practitioners in a forensic science specialty assembled to formulate and periodically review consensus standards for the specialty, including training, education, quality assurance, and interpretation of results.

SWGDAM Scientific Working Group on DNA Analysis and Methods, formerly called TWGDAM (Technical Working Group on DNA Analysis and Methods).

SWGFAST Scientific Working Group on Friction Ridge Analysis, Study, and Technology; formed in 1995 for fingerprint and other friction ridge skin comparison and identification.

Swipe, smear (bloodstain) The transfer of blood onto a surface not already contaminated with blood. One edge is usually feathered, which may indicate the direction the blood traveled.

FIGURE S.18 A container for storing wet swabs. Air is then circulated through the container, which will allow the swabs to air dry. The container prevents contamination of the swabs as they are drying.

Sync-cord An electrical power cord used to connect the flash unit to a power source.

Synchroflash A term applied to flash photography in which a flash bulb is ignited at the same instant that the shutter is opened.

Synthetic dye inks Any ink consisting simply of a dye dissolved in water together with the necessary preservatives. Various dyes are used in commercial ink manufacture today; the aniline dyes were the first of these, and some writers still refer to inks of this class as *aniline inks* .

Synthetic fibers A class of manufactured polymeric fibers that are synthesized from a chemical compound (e.g., nylon, polyester).

System (of writing) The combination of the basic design of letters and the writing movement as taught in school. Writing through use diverges from the system, but generally retains some influence of the basic training.

T

Tachycardia Rapid heartbeat (typically greater than 100 beats per minute).

Tachypnea Rapid breathing.

***Taq* Polymerase** A DNA polymerase isolated from the bacterium *Thermus aquaticus* that lives in hot springs. The enzyme is capable of withstanding high temperatures and is, therefore, very useful in the polymerase chain reaction (PCR).

Tandem repeats The end-to-end duplication of a series of identical or almost identical stretches of DNA. Repeating units of an identical (or similar) DNA sequence arranged in direct succession in a particular region of a chromosome.

Taphonomic agents Biological, chemical, and geological processes that influence postmortem change.

Target value Numerical value of a measurement result that has been designated as a goal for measurement quality.

Tattooing A characteristic pattern in the skin caused by particles of unburned and partially burned powder from a shotgun blast at very close range. Also may be called *stippling* (Figure T.1).

Technical fiber A bundle of natural fibers composed of individual elongated cells that can be physically or chemically separated and examined microscopically for identifying characteristics (e.g., hemp, jute, and sisal).

Technical review Review of bench notes, data, and other documents that form the basis for scientific conclusion. These technical reviews are completed by qualified and trained analysts who have the same knowledge and training as the analyst doing the initial analysis of the evidence.

Technical surveillance Surveillance conducted by means of scientific devices that enhance hearing or seeing the subject's activities — may involve electronic eavesdropping devices (wiretaps, pen registers), electronic tracking devices (beepers), or assorted visual and infrared optical devices.

Telogen A quiescent phase in the cycle of hair growth when the hair is retained in the hair follicle as a dead or "club" hair. The dormant or resting phase of hair growth. Hair in the telogen phase is shed naturally.

Template The single-stranded DNA blueprint for complementary strand assembly or the production of pre-mRNA.

Temporary restraining order A judge's order forbidding certain actions until a full hearing can be held. This order is usually for a short duration. Often referred to as a *TRO*.

Teratogenic Having the ability to cause congenital anomalies.

Terminal velocity The maximum speed to which a free-falling drop of blood can accelerate in air, approximately 25.1 ft/sec.

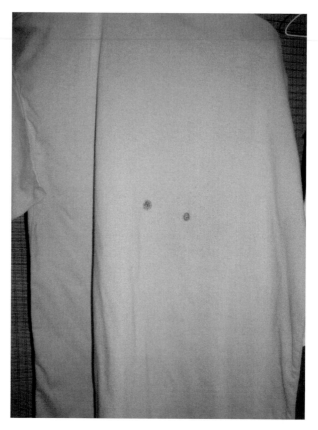

FIGURE T.1 Tattooing pattern on a shirt.

Terrorism   The use of threat of violence to achieve certain organizational goals.

Test   Technical operation to determine one or more characteristics of or to evaluate the performance of a given product, material, equipment, organism, physical phenomenon, process, or service according to a specified procedure.

Test bullet   A bullet fired into a bullet recovery system in a laboratory for comparison or analysis.

Test cartridge case   A cartridge case obtained while test-firing a firearm in a laboratory that is to be used for comparison or analysis.

Test-firing   The term used to designate the actual firing of a firearm in a laboratory to obtain representative bullet and cartridge cases for comparison or analysis. Also used to test for functionality of a firearm.

Test impression   An impression made utilizing a known shoe for the purpose of using it in a footwear impression examination (Figure T.2).

Test linearity   Ability within a given range to obtain test results directly proportional to the concentration (amount) of analyte in the specimen or sample.

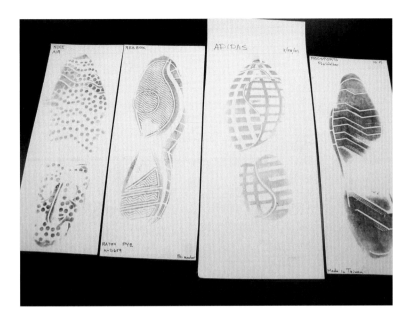

FIGURE T.2 Known test impressions of footwear.

Test mark A striated or impressed tool mark produced by the suspect tool, which is to be used in making a comparison with the evidence mark.

TESTED A mnemonic used by air accident investigators searching for the main parts of a crashed aircraft (**T**ips of the wings and tail surfaces, **E**ngines, control **S**urfaces, **T**ail assembly, **E**xternal devices like landing gear and **D**oors).

Testimony Evidence given by a witness under oath; does not include evidence from documents and other physical evidence.

Tetany Condition marked by involuntary muscle contractions or spasms.

Texture A rough surface of shallow design added to a mold through a stippling or a chemical etching process. Texture patterns vary in their position and features and are unique to a mold. The texture is reproduced in shoes made in that mold.

Texture maps A section of a two-dimensional (2-D) raster image of texture that is "mapped" onto a 2-D or 3-D surface automatically by the computer.

THC (tetrahydrocannabinol) The most active of the principal constituents of marijuana, contained in various parts of the plant.

Therapeutic jurisprudence A position that one aspect of the study of the law should be a consideration of the mental health impact of the legal system upon its participants and clients.

Thermal conductivity detector A type of gas chromatographic detector that is sensitive to the change in the ability of the gases emerging from the column to conduct heat. A thermal conductivity (TC) detector is not as sensitive as a flame ionization detector, but is capable of detecting some molecules, such as water, which give no signal on FID.

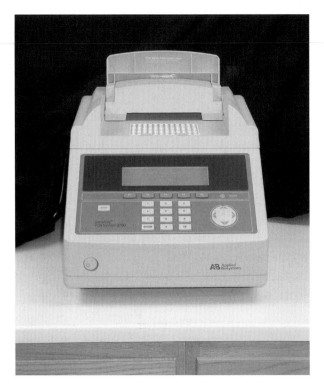

FIGURE T.3 Auto-Lid Single 96-well GeneAmp® PCR System 9700.

Thermocycler An instrument that is programmed to heat and cool automatically. This instrument is used to carry out the PCR steps in DNA amplification (Figure T.3).

Thermolabile Decomposed, destroyed, affected, or liable to be adversely affected by heat, as in some enzymes and toxins.

Thermoplastic fiber A synthetic fiber that will soften or melt at high temperatures and harden again when cooled.

Thickness (T) The optical path through the fiber used for the calculation of birefringence; typically measured in micrometers.

Thin-layer chromatography (TLC) A procedure for separating compounds by spotting them on a glass plate coated with a thin (about 0.01 in.) layer of silica or alumina and "developing" the plate by allowing a solvent to move upward by capillary action. TLC is especially useful for identifying and comparing materials that are highly colored or which fluoresce under ultraviolet light. TLC is used extensively in explosive analysis and in the comparison of gasoline dyes, inks, and various drugs (Figure T.4).

Threat assessment Analysis of written or verbal communication containing direct or implied threats to harm or injure individuals, industries, institutions, or government agencies. The communication is analyzed for content and stylistic characteristics. Analysis may include a profile of the unknown

FIGURE T.4 Drug chemistry spraying chamber on TLC plates.

perpetrator and evaluation of the unknown subject's potential to carry out
the threat.

Threshold (cut-off concentration)   A particular, significant amount, level, or
limit, at which something begins to happen or take effect.

Thromboembolism   An embolism; the blocking of a blood vessel by a thrombus
(blood clot) that has become detached from the site of formation.

Thymine (T)   One of the bases present in DNA; will only bond with adenine (A).

Tibia   The shinbone, often used as a guide for calculating a person's height.

Time exposure   The camera shutter is opened and closed manually, not
automatically.

Time-lapse   A timing device that can be set to take a photograph every few
seconds, minutes, hours, etc.

Tint   A color that has been made lighter by the addition of white.

Tire impression   When a tire contacts a surface, it results in the transfer of the
class characteristics of design and size and possibly of wear and individual
characteristics of the tire (Figure T.5A and 5B).

Tire patch   That portion of the tire that rests on the road surface. It is oval
shaped and has its longest axis along the normal direction of travel of the
vehicle. When a vehicle is sliding sideways, the tire marks left on the
road get almost twice as wide as the tire turns sideways and the short axis
is in the direction of travel that makes the tire marks.

Tire tread   Part of a tire that contacts the road surface and contains a design
(Figure T.6).

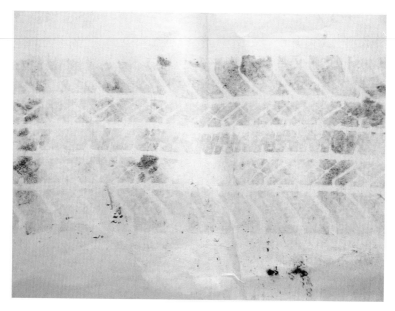

FIGURE T.5A Tire impression.

FIGURE T.5B Partial tire impression.

Titer   The concentration in a solution of a dissolved substance as shown in titration. The least amount or volume needed to give a desired result in titration.

Titrate   To make a series of dilutions.

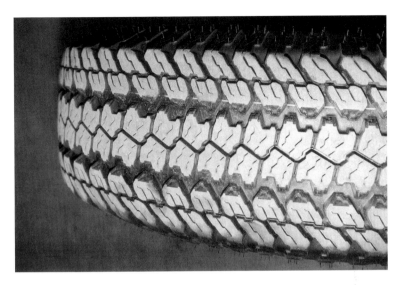

FIGURE T.6 Tire tread design.

Titration A method of analyzing the composition of a solution by adding known amounts of a standardized solution until a given reaction (color change, precipitation, or conductivity change) is produced.

TNT (trinitrotoluene) A high explosive used as a component of some priming mixtures.

Tolerance A state that develops after long-term exposure to a drug. *Metabolic tolerance* infers a faster removal and oxidation by the liver. *Functional tolerance* infers a change in sensitivity of the organ to the effects of the drug.

Toluene (methylbenzene) An aromatic compound having the formula $C_6H_5CH_3$. It is a major component of gasoline. Toluene has a flash point of 40°F and explosive limits of 1.2 to 7%.

Tongue A strip of material covering the instep of the foot, lying beneath the shoe laces.

Tool-mark identification A discipline of forensic science that has as its primary concern the determination if a tool mark was produced by a particular tool.

Topology A term referring to the physical connection method used to connect computers on a network.

Toxemia Any condition of blood poisoning, especially that caused by bacterial toxins transported through the bloodstream from a focus of infection.

Toxicity **(1)** The ability of a substance to cause injury to living tissue once it reaches a susceptible site in or on the body. **(2)** The quality of having a toxic effect on a person.

Toxicology The study of poisons, including the names, effects, detection, and methods of treatment.

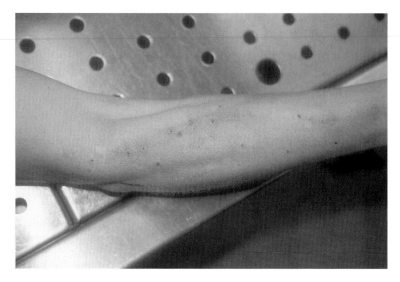

FIGURE T.7 Tract marks of the arm of a chronic intravenous heroin user. (Courtesy of forensic medical examiner Michael Sikirica, M.D.)

Trace evidence Physical evidence that results from the transfer of small quantities of materials (e.g., hair, textile fibers, paint chips, glass fragments, gunshot residue particles).

Trace forgery Any fraudulent signature executed by actually following the outline of a genuine signature with a writing instrument. Such a signature may be produced with the aid of carbon paper by first tracing a carbon outline and then covering this with a suitable ink stroke, or the forgery may be traced from an outline made visible by light coming through the model signature and the fraudulent document.

Tracer bullet A bullet that contains a pyrotechnic component ignited by the powder charge burn, leaving a visible trail of the flight path.

Tracking/trailing Canine behavior in which a dog continues to walk with nose held close to the ground and sniffing, or with obvious nasal air exchange.

Tract marks Scarring and fibrosis of blood vessels, typically veins, due to injection of foreign compounds with subsequent inflammatory response. Usually seen in intravenous nacrotism (Figure T.7).

Trailer Pattern of poured or solid material, e.g., a linear pour of a liquid accelerant or distribution of a twisted sheet of paper that will lead a fire from one location to another (Figure T.8A and B).

Trailing edge The edge of a land or groove impression in a fired bullet that is opposite to the driving edge of that same land or groove impression. Also called the *following edge* when used in conjunction with the term *leading edge*.

Trajectory The path described by an object or body moving in space. The path of a projectile after leaving the muzzle of a firearm.

FIGURE T.8A Paper and debris used as trailer, allowing the fire to follow a certain direction.

Transfer pattern A contact bloodstain created when a wet, bloody surface contacts a second surface. A recognizable mirror image or at least a recognizable portion of the original surface may be transferred to the second surface.

Transfer theory The theory attributed to Edmond Locard regarding the transfer of trace evidence between two objects.

Transient evidence Evidence that by its very nature or the conditions at the scene will lose its evidentiary value if not preserved and protected (e.g., blood in the rain).

Transitory defect An identifying typewriter characteristic that can be eliminated by cleaning the machine or replacing the ribbon. Clogged typefaces are the most common defects of this class.

Transmission The ratio of the light passed through an object to the light falling upon it.

FIGURE T.8B Arson using paper as a trailer and gasoline as the accelerant.

Transmittance (T)   The ratio of radiant power transmitted by the sample I to the radiant power incident on the sample, I T = I/I.

Transmitted light   Light that is passed through a transparent or translucent medium.

Transmitted-light examination   An examination in which the document is viewed with the source of illumination behind it and the light passing through the paper.

Transparency   A positive photographic image on film, viewed or projected by transmitted light (light shining through film).

Trash mark   Mark left on a finished copy during photocopying; results from imperfections or dirt on the cover glass, cover sheet, drum, or camera lens of a photocopy machine.

Trauma   An injury that is the result of any force such as blunt, sharp, or penetrating.

Tread design guide   Annual publication that shows thousands of tire designs.

Tread wear indicator (wear bar)   Raised rubber bar 1/16 in. above the bases of the tire grooves; it must appear at least six times on a tire.

Tremor   **(1)** A lack of smoothness due to lack of skill, consciousness of the writing act, deliberate control of the instrument in copying or tracing, or an involuntary, roughly rhythmic, and sinusoidal movement. **(2)** Wavy back-and-forth movement on a written line.

Triacetate fiber   Generic name for a manufactured fiber in which the fiber-forming substance is cellulose acetate, where not less than 92% of the hydroxyl groups are acetylated. The term *triacetate* may be used as a generic description of the fiber.

Trial   Judicial examination and determination of issues of law and fact disputed by parties to a lawsuit.

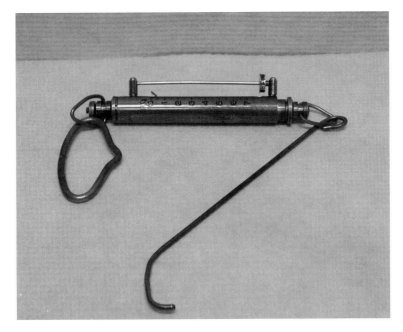

FIGURE T.9A Trigger pull gauge.

Trial consultants   Individuals who provide assistance to trial lawyers about effective ways to try cases.

Trial court   Local court that initially hears all cases in dispute. If an attorney or party believes that a trial court judge has exceeded judicial authority or inappropriately applied the law, an appeal can be made to the appeals court.

Triangulation   Method of measurement of a crime scene and physical evidence; every item of evidence is measured from two fixed points.

Trigger guard   A protective device consisting of a curved framework surrounding the trigger.

Trigger pull   Amount of force applied to the trigger of a firearm to cause it to discharge.

Trigger pull gauge   The mechanism used to release the firing pin of a firearm by applying pressure using a finger. Instrument used to measure the needed amount of force to be applied to the trigger of a firearm to cause it to fire (Figure T.9A and B).

Trilobate   Having three lobes.

Tripod   A three-legged stand used to support a camera or lens and camera (Figure T.10).

Truck   A specialized vehicle that can be used for commercial purposes, such as semitractor trailers, straight trucks, tankers, and stake trucks, or can be owned privately, such as pickups, sport utility vehicles (SUVs), vans, and minivans.

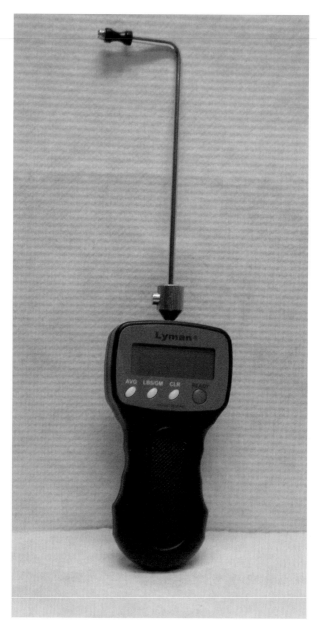

FIGURE T.9B A handheld trigger pull gauge wih a digital readout.

True value   Value that characterizes a quantity perfectly defined in the conditions that exits when that quantity is considered. The true value of a
quantity is an ideal concept and, in general, cannot be known exactly.

Trueness   Closeness of agreement between the average values obtained from a
large series of test results and an accepted reference or true value.

FIGURE T.10 Tripod.

Tumblehome The curvature of a vehicle body inward toward the roof. This gives the vehicle a rounder look from the front and decreases aerodynamic drag.

Tungsten Metallic element, atomic number 74, hard brittle, gray solid. Has high electrical conductivity. Used in high-speed tool steel, as filaments for electric light bulbs, and as heating elements in furnaces and vacuum-metallizing equipment.

Tungsten light Incandescent light, from a bulb having filaments usually of lower wattage, 15 to 500 W.

Tungsten light film Color film balanced to suit tungsten light sources, with a color temperature of 3200°K.

Turpentine (1) Gum form — the pitch obtained from living pine trees; a sticky viscous liquid. (2) Oil form — a volatile liquid obtained by steam distillation of gum turpentine, consisting mainly of pinene and diterpene. Turpentine is frequently identified in debris samples containing burned wood from arson cases.

Twine A string composed of two or more strands twisted together (Figure T.11).

Twin-lens reflex (TLR) Camera having two lenses of the same focal length; one is used for viewing and focusing, the other for exposing the film. The lenses are mounted above each other.

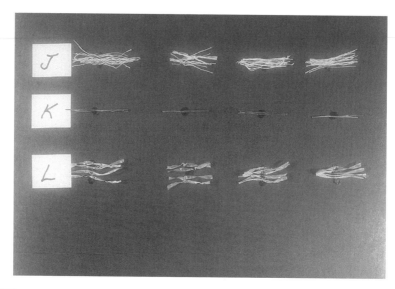

FIGURE T.11 Various types of twine.

Twist (lay) The direction of twist in yarns is indicated by the capital letters S and
  Z. Yarn has an *S-twist* if, when held vertically, the spirals around its central
  axis slope in the same direction as the middle portion of the letter S, and *Z-
  twist* if they slope in the same direction as the middle portion of the letter Z.

Twist of rifling Inclination of the spiral grooves (rifling) to the axis of the bore
  of a weapon; it is expressed as the number of calibers of length in which
  the rifling makes one complete turn.

Twisted letter Each character is designed to print at a certain fixed angle to the
  base line. Wear and damage to the type bar and the type block may cause
  some letters to become twisted so that they lean to the right or left of
  their correct slant.

Two-dimensional impression (1) An impression that for all practical purposes
  has the dimensions of length and width but not a significant depth. (2) A
  shoe mark.

Type ball A device containing a complete set of typeface of some single-
  element typewriters and which, by rotation and tilting, prints the type
  (Figure T.12).

Typeface The printing surface of the type block or type element. The name of
  a particular design of printed characters and symbols.

Typeface defect Any peculiarity in typewriting resulting from actual damage to
  the typeface metal. It may be an actual break in the outline of the letter where
  the metal is chipped away, sometimes referred to as *broken type*, or a distorted
  outline of the letter because of bent or smashed typeface metal. The defect
  can be corrected only by replacing the type block or element.

Typewriting system Typewriting device consisting of a machine, ribbon, and
  font (Figure T.13).

FIGURE T.12 An IBM type font ball.

FIGURE T.13 Manual Royal typewriter.

U

Ulnar A loop pattern on a fingerprint that has its open end toward the little finger.

Ultraviolet Radiation in the region of the electromagnetic spectrum including wavelengths from 100 to 380 nm.

Ultraviolet examination Ultraviolet radiation is invisible and occurs in the wavelengths just below the visible blue-violet end of the spectrum. The invisible rays react on some substances so that visible light is emitted, a phenomenon known as *ultraviolet fluorescence*. Thus, ultraviolet examination may be made visually or photographically by recording either the reflected ultraviolet or visible radiation.

Ultraviolet filter A filter that transmits ultraviolet light as used for photography by the reflected ultraviolet light method.

Ultraviolet light Light rays beyond the visible spectrum of light at its violet end with wavelengths longer than x-rays, but shorter than visible light.

Ultraviolet photograph Any photograph that records the document under ultraviolet illumination. With some of these the ultraviolet radiation strikes the film, but with others a filter is employed so that only the visual fluorescence caused by the ultraviolet is recorded.

Ultraviolet spectrometer A device that produces a spectrum of ultraviolet light and is provided with a calibrated scale for measurement of wavelength.

Unconscious transference An individual's mistaken recollection of an incident; in criminal investigation, a witness may have a mistaken recollection about a crime that implicates an individual who was not involved.

Undercover In secret; an undercover agent often gets to know or work alongside the subject under investigation. An undercover agent is said to be *planted*; a form of surveillance.

Underexposure Results of insufficient light exposing the film. A condition in which too little light reaches the film producing a thin negative, a dark slide, or a muddy-looking print.

Undetermined cause Destruction accompanying some fires may be too extensive to allow determination of the origin and cause with a high degree of confidence.

Uniaxial With one axis, movement only in one plane, as that of hinge-joint.

Uninterruptible power supply A surge protector with a built-in battery. This unit clamps excessive power from the outlet and runs the computer for a short time on its battery in case of power loss, which enables computer users to save their work and "power down" (turn off) the computer if the power fails.

Unipod A one-legged support for a camera.

Unix   A time-sharing operating system allowing powerful processors to share their power with many users. Xenix and AIX are versions of Unix produced by other companies.

Unload tire   Trailing tires that have less weight as a result of a weight transfer to the leading tires of a rotating vehicle. In this situation some weight is shifted to those tires but not enough to leave a gap between the tire surface and the ground and not enough to allow downward force to produce a yaw mark.

Upper   All of the components of the shoe above the midsole and outsole.

Up-wind   A term used to describe the position of the searching dog team relative to the odor source where the wind is blowing from the team toward the source.

Urea   A protein denaturant, urea is qualified for use as the denaturing component in polyacrylamide gels.

Urine   Liquid produced in the kidneys; contains biological waste products.

Urobilinogen   Intermediate product in the metabolism of bilirubin. When combined with zinc acetate, it forms a compound that fluoresces in ultraviolet light; used for the identification of feces.

V

V-shape pattern   Fire pattern seen when a flame impinges on a vertical surface.

Validated method   Method whose performance characteristics meet the specifications required by the intended use of the analytical results. Some of the performance characteristics to be evaluated are limit to detection, limit of quantitation, linearity, precision, range, ruggedness, selectivity and specificity, and trueness.

Validation   Confirmation by examination and provision of objective evidence that the particular requirements for a specific intended use are fulfilled.

Value   The expression of a quantity in terms of a number and an appropriate unit of measurement.

van der Waal's forces   Weak attractive forces acting between molecules. They are involved in the van der Waals equation of state for gases that compensates for the actual volume of the molecules and the forces acting between them.

Vanillin   The methyl ether of protocatechute aldehyde, occurring in vanilla bean extract and in many balsams and resins.

Vapor   The gaseous form of a substance that is normally a solid or a liquid at room temperature and pressure.

Vapor density   The weight of a given volume of a vapor or a gas compared to the weight of an equal volume of dry air, both measured at the same temperature and pressure.

Vapor pressure   A measure of the tendency of a liquid to become a gas at a given temperature.

Vaporization   The physical change of going from a solid or a liquid into a gaseous status.

Variability   Spread or dispersion of scores in a group of scores; the tendency of each score to be unlike the others.

Variable   Generally, any quantity that varies. More precisely, a quantity that may take any one of a specified set of values.

Variable number of tandem repeats (VNTR)   The variable number of repeat core base pair sequences at specific loci in the genome. The variation in length of the alleles formed from the repeats provides the basis for unique individual identification.

Variance   Statistic that shows the spread or dispersion of scores in a distribution of scores. It is calculated as the sum of the squares of the differences between the individual values of a set and the arithmetic mean of the set, divided by one less than the number of values.

Variate In contradistinction to a *variable*, a variate is a quantity that may take any of the values of a specified set with a specified relative frequency or probability. It is often known as a *random variable*.

Vasodilation Increased diameter of the blood vessels.

Vector graphics Computer-generated images are represented as points in space with line segments between.

Velocity The speed of a projectile at a given point along its trajectory.

Velvet A fabric with a short, thick-set pile of silk, cotton, or other fiber on a back that is closely woven and of the same or different fibers.

Venire Facias A writ summoning persons to court to act as jurors. More popularly, the term is used to refer to the people summoned for jury duty.

Ventricular fibrillation Rapid, tremulous movement of the ventricle that replaces normal contractions of the heart muscle; results in little or no blood being pumped from the heart. Uncoordinated nonpropulsive quivering of the heart often produced by myocardial infarction or heart attack; also produced by low-voltage electrocution.

Venue A neighborhood, and synonymous with "place of trial." It refers to the possible place or places for the trial of a suit. Among several places where jurisdiction could be established.

Verdict Conclusion, as to fact or law, that forms the basis for the court's judgment. A general verdict is a jury's finding for or against a plaintiff after determining the facts and weighing them according to the judge's instructions regarding the law.

Verification Confirmation by examination and provision of objective evidence that specified requirements have been fulfilled.

Vermiculite A micaceous hydrated silicate mineral used as a planting medium and as insulation.

Vernier caliper A measuring instrument having a fixed jaw and a sliding jaw with an attached vernier (short scale) (Figure V.1).

Versal letters Those that mark important parts of the text, used for headings and words written at the beginning of books or chapters; often distinguished by size, color, and ornamentation, which tends towards curves and flourishes.

Vertebrate Any animal with a backbone or vertebral column.

Vertigo Sensation of spinning or revolving.

Vestibule Circular space formed at the junction of the cheeks and jaw.

Vestigial Small remnants or rudimentary structures of a previously functional body part.

Victim impact evidence Evidence offered at sentencing to show the impact on the victim of the crime for which the defendant has been convicted; the victims' testimony in the Oklahoma City bombing case is a good example of victim impact evidence.

Victimology The study of the process and consequences of victim's experiences, including recovery. Victim's history (personality characteristics, strengths and weaknesses, occupation, hobbies, lifestyle, and sexual history) that

FIGURE V.1 Vernier caliper with a digital display. Used by firearm examiners to measure the gauge of a firearm.

impacts the analysis of a crime; a behavioral study of the victim of a violent crime (usually homicide). The analyst examines reputation, lifestyle, habits, associates, and pastimes to form an opinion about the individual's risk of becoming the victim of a violent crime.

Video   Visual; when applied to a television system, the picture portion of a signal.

Video dubbing   Replacing portions of existing video recording with new video material.

Video image capture   The securing of an image from a videotape source, storing it in a computer as a still image to be retrieved later in photographic format.

Video spectral comparison   Comparison and differentiation of inks by analyzing the infrared reflecting and luminescing qualities inherent to the ink; most often accomplished using a device made by Foster & Freeman, Ltd. (Figure V.2).

Videocassette   A plastic container used to hold videotape.

Videography   The recording of visual images electronically on magnetic tape. Usually accompanied by a recorded soundtrack.

Viewfinder   A viewing instrument attached to a camera that is used to obtain proper composition.

VIN   Vehicle identification number; the serial number that car manufacturers stamp on several motor vehicle parts (many of which are inaccessible) for the purposes of tracing and identifying car ownership.

Virus   A computer program introduced into a computer from the outside, either by copying files by modem from another computer or by placing a floppy disk in the computer. The virus automatically copies itself into the computer and begins overwriting files and the system, replicating itself and otherwise damaging the usability of the system.

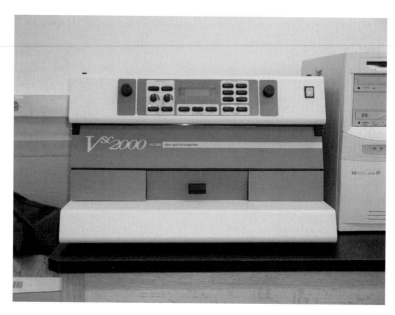

FIGURE V.2 Video spectral comparator.

Viscosity   The internal resistance to flow exhibited by a fluid.

Visible print   Made by fingers stained with colored materials, such as blood, ink, paint, grease, or dirt. Ordinarily, a visible print does not require further treatment to be fully visualized (sometimes referred to as a patent print).

Vitreous humor   The fluid that fills the eyeball and shows changes after death that can be used as an accurate way of identifying the time of death. Ocular fluid that is often utilized as a sample for testing in postmortem toxicology.

VNTR locus   Chromosomal locus at which a particular repetitive sequence is present in different numbers in different individuals of a population; a simple sequence tandem repeat polymorphism in which the core repeat unit is usually 250 bases long.

Void or shadow   Absence of bloodstain in an otherwise continuous bloodstain pattern. Often the geometry of the void will suggest an outline of the object that has intercepted the blood, such as a shoe, furniture, person, etc.

Voir dire   Process of questioning potential jurors so that each side may decide whether to accept or oppose individuals for jury service.

Volatile   Prone to rapid evaporation. Both combustible and noncombustible materials may be volatile.

Volumetric flask   A laboratory flask primarily intended for the preparation of definite, fixed volumes of solutions (Figure V.3).

FIGURE V.3 Different sizes and shapes of volumetric flasks.

Vulcanization An irreversible process in which a rubber compound is heated under pressure, resulting in a chemical change in its structure. The process to which shoes with raw rubber components are subjected in order to permanently bond the components together.

W

Wad, base A cylindrical component that is assembled into the head end of a shotshell.

Wad, shot protector Various designs of shot cups made of plastic and designed to reduce pellet deformation during barrel travel (Figure W.1).

Wagner's reagent An aqueous solution of iodine and potassium iodide; used for microchemical analysis of alkaloids. Also known as *Wagner's solution.*

Waiver of immunity A means authorized by statute by which a witness, before testifying or producing evidence, may relinquish the right to refuse to testify against himself, thereby making it possible for his testimony to be used against him in future proceedings.

Wale A column of loops lying lengthwise in a knit fabric.

Walk-through An initial assessment conducted by carefully walking through the scene to evaluate the situation, recognize potential evidence, and determine resources required. Also, a final survey conducted to ensure the scene has been effectively and completely processed.

FIGURE W.1 Gunshot cartridges showing the wading material inside.

Walker test The original chemical test for the detection of the spatial distribution of nitrites in gunpowder residue.

Wanton (legal) Characterized by reckless disregard of consequences and the safety and welfare of others; malicious or immoral; undisciplined, unruly, or unjustified.

Warm match A warm match occurs when CODIS matches DNA profiles based on prior knowledge. As with a cold match, a warm match is verified by a qualified DNA analyst after CODIS makes the match. A typical example of a warm match is when an investigating officer develops a suspect in a rape case, obtains a blood sample, and has the qualified DNA analyst search it against similar cases from the same jurisdiction. In this example, the investigator believes several crimes are related and uses CODIS-generated matches as an investigative tool.

Warp The set of yarn in all woven fabrics that runs lengthwise and parallel to the selvage and is interwoven with the filling.

Warping Mapping the texture onto the object in perspective.

Warrant Most commonly, a court order authorizing law enforcement officers to make an arrest or conduct a search; an affidavit seeking a warrant must establish probable cause by detailing the facts upon which the request is based. The judge must be given probable cause to believe that a crime has occurred and that the warrant is necessary for the apprehension of a criminal or to obtain evidence of a crime.

Washed out A negative or print lacking detail and contrast.

Watermark A translucent design impressed in certain papers during the course of their manufacture. This is accomplished by passing a wet mat of fibers across a dandy roll, which is a metal cylinder containing patches of specific pattern designs. The design patches are generally of two types, wire or screen.

Watson and Crick model Refers to the DNA molecule that forms a double-helix ladder with the complementary strands held by hydrogen bonds between specific base pairs.

Wave, castoff A small blood droplet that originates from a parent drop of blood due to the wavelike action of the liquid in conjunction with striking a surface at an angle less than 90°.

Wavelength The distance, measured along the line of propagation, between two points that are in phase on adjacent waves. A property of radiant energy, such as IR, visible, or UV.

Weapon of mass destruction (WMD) Title 18, U.S.C. 2332a, defines a weapon of mass destruction as (**1**) any destructive device as defined in section 921 of the title, [which reads] any explosive, incendiary, or poison gas, bomb, grenade, rocket having a propellant charge of more than four ounces, missile having an explosive or incendiary charge of more than one-quarter ounce, mine or device similar to the above; (**2**) poison gas; (**3**) any weapon involving a disease organism; or (**4**) any weapon that is designed to release radiation or radioactivity at a level dangerous to human life.

Wear The erosion of the outsole due to frictional and abrasive forces that occur between the outsole and the ground. Effect of frictional forces on a tire or shoe; wear eventually changes the design.

Wear bars Marks on the tires where no tread appears. Manufacturers build these into the tires.

Weft (filling) In a woven fabric, the yarn running from selvage to selvage at right angles to the wrap.

Wernicke's syndrome Consists of defective memory, loss of sense of location, and confabulation. Seen in chronic alcoholics.

Wet origin impression Footwear impression containing significant moisture from the shoe sole or substrate.

Wheelbase Measurement between the centers of the hubs of the front wheels to the centers of the hubs of the rear wheels; it is very difficult to measure from the tracks made by a vehicle.

Wheezing Breathing noisily and with difficulty; usually a sign of spasm or narrowing of the airways.

Whirl The curving upstroke, usually of letters that have long loops, but also on some styles of the capital "W."

White balance A procedure used to tune a video camera's color by setting it to perfectly reproduce a white object.

Whorl A form composed of spiraling strokes, produced by a loose, circling writing movement.

Whorls Fingerprint patterns where the ridges turn through at least one complete circuit.

Wipe A bloodstain pattern created when an object moves through an existing bloodstain, removing blood from the original stain and altering its appearance.

Witness One who testifies to what he or she has seen, heard, or otherwise experienced. Person whose declaration under oath is received as evidence for any purpose.

Wood's lamp Light source used by physicians to detect various substances, including semen stains. It may be used in cases of suspected child sexual maltreatment.

Word processing unit Any typewriter or other printing unit that is combined with a memory system and is thus capable of automatic typewriting or repetitive typewriting of certain matter. Material can be stored on disks, tapes, or memory chips.

Work product Work done by an attorney while representing a client, such as writings, statements, or testimony on regard to legal impressions, tactics, strategies, and opinions, that are ordinarily not subject to discovery. Discovery may be obtained only when the party seeking it has a substantial need for the material to prepare the case and is unable to obtain the substantial equivalent of the material by other means without undue hardship.

Working standard solution Standard solutions prepared by diluting the stock solution containing the concentrations used to establish the calibration curve.

Wound An injury resulting from a blunt force or sharp instrument.

Woven fabric Generally used to refer to fabric composed of two sets of yarns, wrap and weft (filling), formed by weaving, which is the interlacing of these sets of yarns.

Writ A mandatory precept issued by an authority in the name of the sovereign or the state for the purpose of compelling a person to do something.

Writing condition Both the circumstances under which the writing was prepared and the factors influencing the writer's ability to write at the time of execution. Circumstances pertaining to preparation involving the writer's position (sitting, standing, bedridden, etc.), the paper support and backing, and the writing instrument; writing ability may be modified by the condition of the writer's health, nervous state, or degree of intoxication.

Writing impression The small writing indentation completely or virtually devoid of any pigment. It may be made on the sheet of tablet paper that was immediately below the one on which writing was done or remain after the pencil or typewriting has been thoroughly erased.

Writing ink Solution of colorant in water, usually containing a low percentage of tannic or gallic acid. Fountain pen inks retain the fluidity of water; for ball-point pens the mixture is of a pastelike consistency.

Writing offset The results of a paper coming in contact with fresh ink writing. It may be the mirror image of entire words or sentences as are sometimes found on a blotter, or merely a fragment of words or letters.

Wrong-handed writing Any writing executed with the opposite hand from that normally used; often referred to as writing "with the awkward hand." This is a means of disguising the handwriting of an individual. Thus, the writing of a right-handed person written with his left hand accounts for the common terminology for this class of disguise as "left-handed writing."

X

X-chromosome A chromosome responsible for sex determination. Two copies are present in the genome of the homogametic sex and one copy in the heterogametic sex. The human female has two X-chromosomes and the male has one X-chromosome.

Xerox™ A positive photocopy made directly on plain paper. Although Xerox is a trade name, its success, like Photostat's before it, has resulted in many people referring incorrectly to all present-day photocopies as Xeroxes.

X-ray diffraction An analytical technique used to identify crystalline solids by measuring the characteristic spaces between layers of atoms or molecules in a crystal. X-ray diffraction can be very useful in the identification of explosive residue.

X-ray fluorescence emission spectrometer An x-ray crystal spectrometer used to measure wavelengths of x-ray fluorescence in order to concentrate beams of low intensity. It has bent reflecting or transmitting crystals arranged so that the theoretical curvature required can be varied with the diffraction angle of a spectrum line.

X-rays Electromagnetic radiation of high energy and very high frequency that can penetrate most materials to different extents and reveal their underlying structures.

Xylotomist An expert in the study of wood.